*CRAZY
MOUNTAINS*

SUNY Series in Environmental Public Policy
David W. Orr and Harlan Wilson, editors

CRAZY MOUNTAINS

Learning from Wilderness
to Weigh Technology

David Strong

State University of New York Press

Cover art: Pine Creek Canyon, oil on canvas, 1991, 66″ x 54″, by Russell Chatham.

Excerpts from "Little Gidding" in *Four Quartets*, copyright 1943 by T. S. Eliot and renewed 1971 by Esme Valerie Eliot, reprinted for the U.S.A. by permission of Harcourt Brace & Company, and for other parts of the world by permission of Faber and Faber Ltd.

Excerpts from "Horses" in *Collected Poems* 1957–1982 by Wendell Berry. Copyright © 1980, 1984 by Wendell Berry. Reprinted by permission of North Point Press, a division of Farrar, Straus & Giroux, Inc.

Excerpt from "Wild Geese" in *Dream Work* by Mary Oliver, by permission of Grove/Atlantic, Inc. Copyright 1986 by Mary Oliver.

Excerpt from "A New Language" in *A New Language* by The Cantrells, by permission of Turquoise Records. Copyright 1991 by Emily Cantrell.

The lines from "Sonnet 24, Part I" are reprinted from *Sonnets to Orpheus* by Rainer Maria Rilke, translated by M. D. Herter Norton, by permission of W. W. Norton & Company, Inc. Copyright 1942 by W. W. Norton & Company, Inc. Copyright renewed 1970 by M. D. Herter Norton.

Published by
State University of New York Press, Albany

© 1995 State University of New York

For information, address State University of New York Press, State University Plaza, Albany, N.Y., 12246

Production by Diane Ganeles
Marketing by Bernadette LaManna

Library of Congress Cataloging-in-Publication Data

Strong, David, 1955–
    Crazy Mountains : learning from wilderness to weigh technology / David Strong.
        p.   cm. — (SUNY series in environmental public policy)
    Includes index.
    ISBN 0-7914-2652-1 — ISBN 0-7914-2651-3
    1. Technology—Social aspects.   2. Technology—Philosophy.
    3. Environmental degradation.   I. Title.   II. Series.
    T14.5.S8   1995
    179′.1—dc20   94-23807
                                                                  CIP

10 9 8 7 6 5 4 3 2 1

*To my friends and former teachers
Albert Borgmann and Henry Bugbee*

The Crazy Mountains with Sheep Mountain and Yellowstone Valley. Photo by Paul Dix.

CONTENTS

ACKNOWLEDGMENTS

Many people, too numerous to thank individually here, contributed in one way or another to the process of completing this book. Special thanks go to Edward S. Casey, Robert Cummings Neville, and Marshall Spector, all of whom spent much time helping me to formulate the basic ideas. Other friends and philosophers, Albert Borgmann, Walter Gulick, and Drew Leder, made valuable suggestions and assisted with honing arguments and arranging chapters. My colleague in English, Ken Egan, provided support and encouragement. Louisa Willcox of the Greater Yellowstone Coalition kept me informed and updated about environmental issues in this region. Russell Chatham generously donated the use of the artwork for the cover. Literary parts of this book, especially chapter 6 "Granting the Thing its Eloquence," benefited from comments by several readers: Kevin Bezner, Randall Gloege, Tami Haaland, Maureen Theisen; Jack Hicks and Gary Snyder of "The Art of the Wild" writing workshop in Squaw Valley; and also, the participants of that workshop along with those of a Writer's Voice workshop in Billings. I'm especially grateful to poet Wilbur Wood for his detailed editing of the entire manuscript.

Portions of this work first appeared in more technical versions in the following journals and have been reprinted here with permission from the publishers: "Challenging Technology," *Research in Philosophy and Technology*, Vol. 14, George Allan, ed. (London: Jai Press, 1994): 69–72. Disclosive Discourse, Ecology and Technology," *Environmental Ethics* (Spring 1994): 89–102. "The Implications of Albert Borgmann's Theory of Technology for Nature and Natural Beings," *Research in Philosophy and Technology*, Vol. 13. Frederick Ferré, ed., (London: Jai Press, 1993): 223–52. "The Technological Subversion of Environmental Ethics," *Research in Philosophy and Technology*, Vol. 12. Frederick Ferré, ed., (London: Jai Press, 1992): 33–66. "The Significance of the Loss of Things: Walden Pond As Thing," *Soundings: An Interdisciplinary Journal* Vol. LXXV (Spring 1992): 147–174. "Wilderness' Call for Openness," *The Trumpeter: Journal of Eco-*

sophy Vol. 9 (Winter 1992): 10–14. "The Possibility of a Homecoming for Us: A Reflection on The Odyssey," *Philosophy Today* Vol. 35 (Winter 1991): 325–338. "The Promise of Technology and God's Promise to Job," *Theology Today* Vol. XLVIII (July 1991): 170–181.

PART I

THE SPELL
OF TECHNOLOGY

CHAPTER 1

THE CRAZY MOUNTAINS

Much Madness is divinest Sense—
To a discerning Eye—
Much Sense—the starkest Madness-

—Emily Dickinson, #435

We shall not cease from exploration
And the end of all our exploring
Will be to arrive where we started
And know the place for the first time

—T.S. Eliot, *"Little Gidding"*[1]

The vast expanses of central Montana have an edge and a suddenness. Along the Yellowstone River, sandstone rimrocks line the horizon. Beyond these rims, the flats, benches and swells of the high plains, arid and mostly treeless, yet gold in autumn with prairie grasses, define a precise division between a yellow earth and a youthful sky. As a boy I was told that 'Montana' meant land of the shining mountains. Mountains, especially the Crazy Mountains, seem to explode here into the blue as a child might draw them.

The Crazy Mountains tower isolated and crown-like out of the surrounding plains, reaching heights of some seven thousand feet above the Yellowstone. This tall island range is located in south central Montana between the Great Divide of the Rockies to the west and the Great Plains to the east, between the Missouri River to the north and the Yellowstone to the south. The sharp wedge of Crazy Peak, the highest in the range, reaches 11,214 feet above sea level. To the east, across the Great Plains, one will not find a higher peak on this continent. South, across the Yellowstone, it is true, the nearby Bighorn, Beartooth, and Hilgard ranges have taller peaks, but due west, beyond the Rockies, only a few of the famous volcano peaks of the Pacific Cascades attain greater heights, Mt. Hood being only twenty-five feet higher. To the north, one must travel far into the Canadian Rockies to find higher ground.

Geologically, the Crazies probably formed about twenty-five to fifty million years ago when the much older Elkhorn Mountains eroded and built up a vast plain to the east.[2] One hypothesis has it that as the depositions grew, pressing downward on the Earth's magma, an upward intrusion eventually broke through the lower layers of sedimentary rock, melting and cutting across these layers, finally forging an intrusive mass, called a 'stock,' with radiating dikes flung outward from this core. Although on the flanks of the peaks there are remnants of slightly baked metamorphic rock, the upper layers of sedimentary rock above the intrusive mass have long since disappeared and glaciers from the previous ice age have carved the ridges of the Crazies sharp until these mountains look anything but mound-like. On a map, however, the vestigial oval outline of the original intrusion remains.

Once home to grizzlies, wolves, bison, and, a step farther back, woolly mammoths, giant sloths, and saber-tooth tigers, the Crazies now support elk, black bears, goats, mountain lions, wolverines, deer, antelope, Yellowstone cutthroat trout, golden eagles, great grey owls, a passing loon, and possibly an occasional grizzly roaming between the Yellowstone and Glacier ecosystems. Standing isolated between the ecosystems of the Great Plains and the great mountain chain of the Rockies, the Crazies could tell a unique ecological story. Some rare plants are found there such as Pink Agoseris, *Agoseris Lachshewitzii*. Maybe they sport unknown plant species. Maybe they shelter rare animals and insects. Who knows? Life on Mars has been studied by scientists far more than life in the Crazies.[3]

The first Native Americans in this region used the Rocky Mountain Front to guide them along a route from Alaska to the south. Archaeological evidence suggests some of these earliest people from the Clovis tradition eleven thousand years ago were drawn east to the foothills of the Crazies whose tall peaks provide a similar signpost of guidance.[4] Perhaps this is the most original meaning of travel by highway.

Sometime during the sixteenth century, the Absarokee or Apsaalooke people, literally, Children of the Large-Beaked Bird, migrated from the area of northern Minnesota or Wisconsin, "The Land of Forests and Many Lakes," to North Dakota, where they remained until the late 1600s or early 1700s when Chief No Vitals had a vision at Devil's Lake. In it he was said to have received tobacco seeds and told to plant them in the mountains. Under the guidance of this vision, the Crow people, so-named by the whites because of their description in sign language—the flapping of bent arms— migrated to south-central Montana and north-central Wyoming where they were near many mountain ranges, the Wolf, Bighorn, Pryor, Heart, Beartooth, and Absaroka mountains. The Crazy Mountains lie in the western portion of the Crow heartland.

Arapooish or Sore Belly, a great war chief, spoke of this place in 1833:[5]

> The Crow Country is a good country. The Great Spirit has put it exactly in the right place; while you are in it you fare well; whenever you go out of it, whichever way you travel, you fare worse. If you go to the south, you have to wander over great barren plains; the water is warm and bad, and you meet the fever and ague. To the north it is cold; the winters are long and bitter, with no grass; you cannot keep horses there, but must travel with dogs. What is a country without horses? On the Columbia, they are poor and dirty, paddle about in canoes, and eat fish. Their teeth are worn out; they are always taking fish-bones out of their mouths. Fish is poor food. To the east, they dwell in villages; they live well, but they drink the muddy water of the Missouri—that is bad. A Crow's dog would not drink such water. About the forks of the Missouri is a fine country, good water, good grass, and plenty of buffalo. In summer, it's almost as good as the Crow Country, but in the winter it is cold, the grass is gone and there is no salt weed for the horses. The Crow Country is exactly in the right place; it has snowy mountains and sunny plains; all kinds of climates, and good things for every season. When the summer heat scorches the prairies, you can draw up under the mountains, where the air is sweet and cool, the grass fresh, and the bright streams come tumbling out of the snow banks. There you can hunt the elk, the deer, and the antelope, when their skins are fit for dressing; there you will find plenty of white [grizzly] bears and mountain sheep. In the autumn, when your horses are fat and strong from the mountain pastures, you can go down into the plains and hunt the buffalo, or trap beaver on the streams. And when winter comes, you can take shelter in the woody bottoms along the rivers; there you will find buffalo meat for yourselves, and cottonwood bark for your horses; or you may winter in the Wind River Valley, where there is salt weed in abundance. The Crow Country is exactly in the right place. Everything good is to be found there. There is no place like the Crow Country.[6]

Sore Belly's eloquent testimony showed the Crow community good reasons for staying put, for caring for and dwelling in this place, a particular place with a proper name.

Naturally, as a result of No Vitals' vision, the Crow people had great spiritual regard for mountainous areas in general. According to Crow traditionalists, they quickly came to view the Crazies as "the holiest of holy places," "the mountain of mountains."[7] The Crows thought of the Crazies, generally, as their "Helper"; they often fled into them for special protection from their enemies.[8] As with other mountains, sacred power resided there and sometimes radiated outward. So young men undertook vision quests there.[9] High and rugged, the Crazies presented a challenging ordeal. However, according to the Crow culture, the greatest challenge promises the most help, so these Mountains were ambivalently named both Awahawapiia, "Mean" or "Rugged Mountains,"[10] and "Bird Home Mountains."[11] Crazy Peak was called "Bad Mountain"; Granite Peak, "Snow Mountain." The dreams from fasting without food and water varied in significance. The greatest dreams, called visions, were used to interpret the nature of existence and foretell the future both for the individual and the tribe. Great visions received in the Crazies bestowed charisma and political power upon those who were visited by them.[12]

About 1858, Plenty Coups, between the age of ten and twenty, received his famous great prophetic vision on Crazy Peak after fasting for four days without food or water and cutting the end of his index finger off.[13] In his vision, as interpreted a few days later by wise elders, he foresaw the displacement of the bison by cattle, the inevitable domination by whites, the displacement of nomadic tribal ways by white culture, and himself as childless and living in old age in a log house, not a lodge. The sacred helper animal in his vision, the chickadee, survives by being wily and attentive, and the Crow people needed to learn from this bird in order to survive. Pressed in on all sides by enemy tribes and believing what was forecast, the Crow allied themselves with whites, never making war against them. Partly because of this vision, Crow scouts aided Custer when he fought at the Little Big Horn.[14] On the basis of his visions, his achievements in battle and skill in diplomacy with whites, Plenty Coups became the last of renowned Crow chiefs.

Among the various legends of how the Crazies got their name, the most common is that a woman left a wagon train near the town of Big Timber, got lost, went insane, and lived in the foothills of the mountains. However, I find it hard to believe that these mountains, these first definitive mountains of the Rockies, did not have a settled white name long before the wagon trains. The story that makes the most sense to me is the following: When the first white people came to the region, they asked the natives what they called these mountains. Not understanding each other's language, they had to communicate in sign language. The natives tried to tell them that they were a place of visions. The whites interpreted the signs to mean that these mountains were a place where people went crazy.[15] Such a misunderstanding may persist even to this day.

After the trappers disappeared, but before my ancestors—homesteaders and railroad workers—arrived, ranches sprang up in the west. The Van Cleve family has run cattle and horses in the Big Timber and

Sweet Grass drainages of the Crazies for the past century. In the 1920s they began dude ranching as well. A third generation account, Spike Van Cleve's *40 Years Gatherin's,* is a lively portrayal of a region that "was never easy on people or horses, and it was tough to get by, but it marked its own with a wry humor, a streak of nonconformity, and an innate decency."[16] The stories attest to a man who is sure of who he is. "I am a horse man," he says,[17] and from the unexpected turns his writing takes, one can see that indeed he is. He also shows a deep love for the place and pride in western ranching life, and he enjoys sharing and showing-off the western experience with his visiting dudes.

> I am a lucky man. I was born, grew up, and have lived all my life in what I figure is the prettiest country God ever made—under the Crazy Mountains at the western edge of the high plains . . . It's good country. Where a man can sit in his saddle and see, southwest to south across the Yellowstone Valley, the dark flanks and the white peaks of the Absarokas. . . . All across the west stretch the Crazies, and, swinging in the stirrups, a man has to throw back his head to follow their abrupt shoulders up to the white crests of the peaks. A pretty, clean country where a man can see a long way—and have something to see . . . Even the names sing. Creeks like Otter, Whitetail, Big Elk, Big Timber, Little Timber, Horse, Cayuse, and especially, Sweet Grass.[18]

The names sing, he suggests, because the country itself first sings to humans.

However, most of the stories he tells are from a by-gone era when the timber cut was comparatively of little account and went into making fine shingles, when the miners explored by foot and dug by hand, and the ranch hands rode a grub-line. He has a feel for the beauty of the landscape but one senses that for him people can affirm beauty only after paying their dues through a tough and risky struggle with nature. Speaking of the times he escaped avalanches, he writes:

> Even so, though mountains can be damn dangerous, to me, who grew up at their feet, they can be friendly and strangely protective; but only if a man respects them. They demand respect. Get careless and they are unforgiving.[19]

In Van Cleve's writing and his life, the quick, easy, comfortable, safe, and convenient are to be avoided. They make one soft, lazy, impatient, and cowardly. Here is a person, representative of a people still flourishing in the West, who is confident about what he has built and does not quite see what is coming. He is, it seems, too close to the pulse of what he affirms.

Somehow the hereafter is the least of my worries . . . What could be finer than a bright spring day in the lovely country under the Crazies, at a long lope on a good horse, with the wind in my face, the smell of lupine and sage in the air, and a string of slick, spooky colts to be gathered. Hell, I've already had heaven![20]

Such a person is apt to resist the cheapening of this way of life that announces itself as wilderness 'protection.' Such protection would seem to lock him out of what nourishes the western way of life and keeps it healthy and thriving.[21] I can imagine him saying that the Crazies are too rugged to harm. Indeed these words would seem to issue from his family's three generations of experience with the Crazies. Until the day he died, Spike fought wilderness designation of all lands, especially the Crazies.

Having grown up among people not unlike the Van Cleves, I, too, felt that the Crazies were too rugged to suffer much harm, until I discovered a newly bulldozed road in Cottonwood Canyon. Just the year before I had hiked the trail into what I was coming to recognize as a special place—a secluded, unnamed lake, nestled in a cirque with the peak's two thousand feet high cliffs embracing it on three sides. While in high school a friend and I had discovered this lake by mistake when we wandered off the trail. Goats were there that time, as they have been many times since, astoundingly high in the impossible cliffs, like little white mustard seeds, barely recognizable but for their seemingly unconcerned, playful movements. That time, too, lower down in Cottonwood Canyon, the trail wound and looped through meadows such as I'd never seen before nor have I seen since, completely blue with the blue of bluebells. Remembering the dark earth of the trail in those meadows, the moist, fragrant air, and the soft, warm sunlight, I can see now it was an eventful day, one that slides easily into mind and visits me often when I think about the Crazies, or other mountains, or Monet or Debussy, or what it means to have a good day. It was a day when the mountains relaxed, warmed and came near.

Now I came to make a return pilgrimage only to discover that the lyrical presence of the place was shattered. The trail that once teased me along had become a road, an ugly scar laid out straight. The groaning sounds of the bulldozer engine and the clink-clink screeching of the tracks and blade, actually gone, even now seemed to echo in the canyon: Earth twisted unnaturally over, showing crushed plants, exposed roots, and the gravel of gravel pits. Unwashed, scarred boulders caught, jammed, fixed out of time wearing expressions of horror. Trees knocked flat and bull-dozed aside; the ones left standing gashed by the absent-minded pull of a lever. Though in mileage the road was built about halfway into the lake, I felt that the whole had been ruined. Mountains so rugged I thought them invulnerable had been changed almost overnight.

This was the beginning. It is not the case that all the de facto wilderness in the United States receives the protection of legally designated wilderness. Much federal and state land, some nine million acres in Montana alone, remains in its original wild state but is not protected. Motorcycles and jeeps sometimes disturb its silence. Timbering, mining, oil drilling, irrigation and other resource development projects threaten to transform this land, destroying its wild character. The Crazy Mountains are among these de facto wilderness lands that have not been designated legal wilderness. For a number of years now, many of us in Montana have tried without success to get the Crazies included in a national wilderness bill. I hope that someday the Crazies will receive adequate protection.[22] Beyond that, I hope that the Crazy Mountains and other wild places will challenge us to rethink, to weigh, our vision of technological culture. Is mining, logging, or other development of the Crazy Mountains really going to make them better or are they already as good as they can be, just as they are? In this book we will plunge into a philosophical examination of the various and far-ranging facets of this question.

Make no mistake: Although I am sympathetic toward cultural practices other than my own and at times adopt what seem like good ideas, I never have gone and never will go on a vision quest in the manner of the Crows. I would not know what to do with my dream if I received one. In a way that I cannot reject without rejecting myself, my training in the discipline of philosophy has taught me to use my waking hours in order to understand my world and the things around me. Yet we in the western philosophical tradition also have our visions. Vision, in fact, is the dominant metaphor in ancient Greek philosophy for which a philosopher ought to strive. According to no less a philosopher than the sober and ever practical Aristotle, the highest excellence attainable by humans is theoria, a resourceful and comprehensive vision of the world. Such a vision we will attempt here.

The Western tradition also has its *guiding* visions. From the seventeenth century on, the visionaries of the modern period foresaw that the age of technology would put reason or science to practical use. The culture of technology would use science to dominate nature.[23] The survey instruments used to plot the road up Cottonwood Canyon put mathematics to use. The engineers who designed the bulldozer put physics and chemistry to use. More to the point, the general idea of 'development', from developing lands such as the Crazies to imaging the planet as spaceship Earth, is to get something under control and make it produce for human purposes.

Using reason to dominate nature is a vision we now hear everyday, everywhere.

At its best, this guiding vision does not merely urge us to dominate nature for domination's sake, but for the sake of liberating us from toil and misery, relieving us of our burdens. And it is true that many of us in the middle-classes of industrialized countries—those blessed by modern technology—can thank modern medicine for making it possible for us to live and enjoy things such as the Crazies. We can thank the car that takes us to the trailhead, freeing us from having to walk or ride a horse for days before we finally arrive there. Back home, we can appreciate indoor plumbing that relieves us from having to fetch water from the creek or spring. When we think of the familiar objects of technological culture, such as washing machines, refrigerators, microwave ovens, automatic doors of supermarkets, we may say, "Of course, what more could there be to this vision than domination of nature for the sake of liberation?" Yet in the following chapters, we will wonder whether relief from all effort and every burden is good.

This relief is a negative freedom, freedom from, but, more importantly from the standpoint of this book, our culture also views technology as giving us positive freedom, freedom for. Technology will enrich our lives with the various goods of the Earth and beyond. A highway splitting the Crazies would yield its peaks and lakes as scenery without the toil of hiking or backpacking. Meanwhile, proponents of virtual reality promise to install cross-country ski trips in our basement. We as a culture believe that our domination of nature will yield, say, more leisure, and further we assume that technology will also fill up our leisure time with goods that will make us happy. But does the technological domination of nature really make our lives better? Does it make for the good life? We will examine these questions in the pages ahead.

One crucial problem with technological affluence is its lack of balance. Some twenty percent of Earth's present population of 5.6 billion people use eighty percent of the resources.[24] Moreover, to bring everyone up to the standard of living of those in the middle-class of western industrialized countries would require an estimated two additional planet Earths.[25] For reasons of social justice we ought to "live simply so that others may simply live." And these 'others' include animals, plants, species, ecosystems, and landforms. Thinking of others solely as humans is anthropocentric "just us" justice. Hence, we ought to live more simply for reasons of environmental as well as social altruism. However, technology too often subverts these two good moral concerns. So we will have to meet this problem by pursuing another alternative. It is a twofold alternative and is the central theme of this book. The unsimple life, the life of affluence measured by a high and rising standard of living, while glamorous, is nonetheless misleading and ironic. Many of us feel this in our gut. Why is affluence so attractive and yet so disappointing? Examining this will weaken the hold that technological prosperity has on us. But we can do better than this by showing, secondly, that there are things other than affluence that are both simpler and genuine improvements, even and especially from the standpoint of those with too much. Under the currently prevailing vision, however, our understanding of the quality of our lives, the equality of people everywhere, and the quality of the environment— the good, the equal, and the wild—could not be more out of balance.

Of course, one could return from a hike up Cottonwood Canyon in the Crazy Mountains and conclude, "You can't stop progress." Most of us may have accepted that without even thinking about it. The Crazy Mountains, to the contrary, challenge us to rethink what seems inevitable about technology. They provide us with other measures of progress. They show us another way *to be*.

Etymologically, "crazy" comes from crazen, to crush. Originally it was related to breaking and shattering. The Crazy Mountains challenge the technological society in a way that may break and shatter the older vision of domination and materialism. In its place may arise a new vision of respect for things.

Such a new vision and story will surely seem crazed to many people aligned with the dominant culture of our time. The technological vision currently guiding our culture makes it seem reasonable to want to cut the trees, now seen as timber, in Cottonwood Canyon; makes it seem reasonable to want a higher income and larger gross domestic product; makes it seem reasonable to want to win the lottery. "Who wouldn't?" When such a vision is reigning, all other visions and ways of life become marginalized. Anything counter to the prevailing culture seems silly, irrational, nonsensical, crazy. So, these mountains will teach us of a crazy vision and what I have to say here may seem unreasonable. But take heart, I am a friend of a truer, disciplined reason, as I said earlier. Crazy sanity is a virtue.

Part I: *The Spell of Technology* pinpoints the pivotal issue. The Crazy Mountains stand at the crossroads for our culture. We will either view them as a resource to get under our control, and thereby change them from their wild state forever, or we will protect them as they exist in their own right. We may well make this decision, as we have so many times in the past—having bought into the basic framework of technology—without due consideration. We may make this decision as if the matter were already decided, as if any alternative to the development of our resources were merely an academic question.

To make a reasonable case for what at first glance may seem crazy, we must understand the reasonableness of the case for development. We will begin on that ground by considering the rationale for the Cottonwood Ibex Timber sale, one of three timber sales proposed for the Crazies. We will also consider potential damage to the mountains from a perspective within the framework of technology. Then we will build a quite different account of damage and danger to the Crazy Mountains from a standpoint that acknowledges this wild range in its own right. By focusing on a particular thing, the Crazy Mountains, we will see how the technological order is incompatible with "things." If it were not incompatible with such "things," we would have fewer reasons to care about reforming technology.

Once we find the Crazy Mountains and things similar to them threatened, where do we turn for help? To examine and challenge the basic assumptions of our culture calls for a variety of tactics. We can and should use empirical information, cogent arguments, and comprehensive theories, but this is not enough. So we will also summon narrative and poetry to show the significance and powers of things that more abstract discourses miss. Chapter 6, "Granting the Thing its Eloquence," relies on my personal narrative to point out how the Crazy Mountains are able to claim us, and it points us toward another way to be.

Before undertaking this narrative account, we need to address the philosophical task. It is not all that unusual in philosophy, especially in the European Continental and the American Pragmatic traditions of contemporary philosophy, to begin with the concrete, raise the issues of the concrete to a reflective and philosophical level, and then return to the concrete, interpreting and approaching the concrete and everyday in a new and fresh light. So chapters 1 and 2 will begin with the Crazy Mountains, then chapters 3, 4, and 5 reflect philosophically upon environmental ethics and technological culture, and finally, chapter 6 returns to an evocative account of the Crazies. Finding a theory to help us comprehend the problem of technology and speaking of things in their own right are two nearly opposite tasks, yet all parts are essential to the greater whole. We will, indeed, arrive where we started and know the place for the first time.

Whereas Part I focuses the problem of technological culture and the Crazy Mountains, Part II: *Learning from Wilderness*, articulates the broader implications. Thus, Part II draws out the general lessons we can learn from Part I and develops what we need to learn if we are going to counter the culture of technology effectively. To go on does not mean to go back; nor does it mean getting to where we are presently headed. We need to learn to build again. Currently we are building a culture ordered by the consumption of commodities; our challenge is to find a way to build a culture which is both set in a context of technology yet ordered by things as opposed to commodities. We need to learn to listen to our traditions again, to consider and experience things on their own terms again, and to speak of them in appropriate ways. Wilderness is our guide. The thing shows us where to put our shoulder or rather our mountain goat horns— our thoughts, words, practices, and collective actions—to the task of turning technology.

CHAPTER 2

THE DANGER TO THE CRAZY MOUNTAINS

Everything flows and nothing abides; everything gives way and nothing stays fixed.

—Heraclitus

Remaining always the same and in the same place by itself, it stays fixed where it is.

—Parmenides

That forest which seemed so vast to us was only a small thing after all, as bulldozers, earth movers and dragline shovels have proved.

—Edward Abbey[1]

. . . the very perishing of what we love might be an essential moment in the clarification of the worthiness of love of that which perishes. . . . As never before, perhaps, we understand their reality. . . . But for their perishing we might not have become clear with respect to their importance.

—Henry Bugbee[2]

I

What does it mean for the Crazies to be endangered? How can they be damaged? The bulldozed road led me on through the doors of the Forest Service and to environmental groups and back to my own discipline, philosophy. There was no ready language for what I sensed was at stake for ourselves and the Crazy Mountains. We need a vision and a language to comprehend the conflict between technology and wilderness. To begin to develop this vision and language, we will consider the danger to the Crazy Mountains from radically different perspectives: from within the framework of technology, the seemingly rational view, and then from a position counter to that framework, a philosophical view.

The Need for Resources

In the early 1980s, the Forest Service, an agency in thorough agreement with the framework of technology, undertook a "Resource Area Analysis" of Cottonwood Canyon in the Crazies. Why? "The *need* for timber management decisions in the Cottonwood-Ibex Area stimulated this analysis."[3] The trees in the canyon are infested with the insects, spruce budworm and mountain pine beetle, and with diseases associated with the old age of the trees.[4] The forest in the canyon is mostly old growth. Faced with the possibility of losing raw wood fiber material, the Forest Service then proposed a timber sale and planned to act quickly to cut these stands of trees.

Still we can ask, "Why?" For what purpose do we need to convert trees into boardfeet? Boardfeet *for what?* Only by following the raw material to what it is finally reshaped into can we analyze 'need'—and also make apparent the world within which trees are seen as raw material.

First it is necessary to note that production is often carried out for production's sake and has no end outside itself. It appears that this is the case, at least, with some projects undertaken by government agencies and private individuals. Farmers sometimes pay enormous amounts of money to fertilize their fields even when the expected monetary return from increased production will not come close to paying for the fertilizer. Similarly, when deciding whether or not to go ahead with a dam project, engineers' egos can become so involved that they push the project ahead even though, considered even from the standards of rationality assumed by the technological society, it would be irrational.[5] And so, too, a District Ranger may have a vision of the forest as a wood products producer even though such a vision may be irrational from the standpoint of the national economy.

In fact, as it turns out, the timber sale planned for the Cottonwood-Ibex area will probably cost the federal government over $300,000 to implement even after the receipts from the timber are included.[6] However, it makes some economic sense from the Ranger's point of view because no matter how much the federal government loses on the sale, a quarter of the receipts from the timber sale return directly to the district and not to the general budget of the Forest Service. The Ranger's actions are also consistent with a pattern already established on National Forest lands in Montana east of the continental divide, a drier region than the Pacific side of the Rockies. These lands lose $25 million annually on below-cost timber sales.[7] On the Gallatin National Forest (within which the bulk of the Crazy Mountain Range is located), for instance, the agency spends about $2.5 million annually on its timber program. Its receipts from timber sales average $500,000 annually. Thus, the federal government is losing $2 million a year on its below-cost timber program there.[8] Thoreau thinks that self-magnification, an effort to play God, is the best explanation of this need to dominate and deform the landscape. Surely, self-magnification is a good explanation for some pretentious projects, but the Cottonwood-Ibex timber sale does not stand out as unusual for the Gallatin Forest.

Production for production's sake may seem to have a long history in America. The pioneers often did not care whether a project was cost-effective—such a term would seem very foreign to them. But, more sympathetically, their efforts were not all that irrational since the struggle itself to tame the wild land was perceived as good for one's life and sufficient to make one sturdy, as we shall later see. Some of this vision is surely at the bottom of the Forest Service's concern to harvest timber—not to cut the timber strikes at the very core of the American West's way of life. But such a desire to tame the wild ignores dramatic changes and subversions wrought by technology. Conquest is no longer a human struggle. Loggers have been replaced by machines that clip the lodgepole pines and bunch them. Log truck drivers would not find it difficult to do other truck-driving jobs and vice versa. Much of millwork is now mindless and assemblyline-like. Some of it is effortless. The volume of timber from the Cottonwood-Ibex sale, although directly affecting eight square miles of forest land with scattered clear-cut areas and roads, will last a local highly-efficient mill less than six weeks.[9] Obviously, choices are being made here for something other than the pioneer's rugged way of life.

Making the land produce for human purposes has been the technological project from the beginning of the seventeenth century, yet often those in the early modern period did not reap the benefits of this initial vision. They were willing to persist and make sacrifices because the vision itself seemed promising. In light of this established pattern, it makes some sense for the Forest Service to sacrifice now, economically, to achieve renewed production at some future date. Assuming that Forest Service in the next century has in this area several more sales that finally harvest all the remaining old-growth trees, and assuming the trees in the Crazies will grow back in one hundred years, then all the costly roads should be more or less in place. After that point, it is supposed that truly cost-effective production can begin.[10] Seen in these terms, satisfaction from this project comes not simply from egocentric wielders of technology lording it over the Earth but more from long term participation in building the technological society. Bumper stickers in the logging communities read: "America Builds

With Lumber" and "Wilderness: Land of No Use," (partly a parody of the Forest Service's slogan, "Land of Many Uses"). Thus, it may seem that to log Cottonwood Canyon is to produce for production's sake, yet, viewed in light of the larger historical context and the general pattern of technology, a long-term goal of continual future production stands out.

Why is increased production important to the citizens of the technological society? For some, this may be like asking an entirely idle question. Who could really reasonably challenge the idea that production is good so more production is better? More production means more consumable items for the technological society. Second homes, television sets with wooden cabinets, recreation rooms, hot tubs, extra bathrooms, disposable cardboard boxes are all among the items increased production cashes out into. The more of these commodities people have, the better off they are, or so we commonly think. As long as we warm to this vision of the good life, then certain steps fall out as necessary in order to achieve it. Hence, the forest of Cottonwood Canyon is interpreted as so much volume of raw material needed for the production of commodities for the technological society. Letting raw material be lost when it could be used to build America is seen, then, as negligent. The spruce budworm and pine bark beetle infestation, without 'treatment', seems to threaten our gross domestic product. To neglect treatment of logging may seem, from this perspective, to be significant forest mismanagement. To fail to log is seemingly to choose weakness, poverty, and backwardness over national security, wealth, and greatness. Of course, it can still be questioned whether logging Cottonwood Canyon will have this effect on either the gross domestic product or the local economy or whether there are more cost-effective means of achieving these goals. We will address this when we take up the standard counter of environmentalists in the next chapter. For now we will continue to plumb the meaning of need at a more fundamental level.

How Needful is Need?

Even if stopping the Cottonwood-Ibex Timber Sale were to deprive America of some of its raw material, to lower its total volume of lumber, how much of a real difference would that make? Is choosing not to log the canyon really to choose poverty, weakness and backwardness? Honest responses to these questions demand that we become critical of technology's standards and refuse to call a project successful merely by these standards. Let us look closely at the choices being made here on the local and national levels.

Brand-S, the local Livingston, Montana, mill claims "to process" forty-three million boardfeet of timber a year. At just over five million boardfeet, the Cottonwood-Ibex Sale would not last the mill even six weeks. Had the mill not often overproduced—with workers putting in five to ten hours overtime each week during much of the 1980s—this five million boardfeet of timber and much more besides would not be "needed" by the mill now. Had the workers not striven for the bonus pay awarded for high weekly production volumes, we all would have been able to save more wild land. Had workers chosen to unionize and thus gain more control of their working conditions and hours, they might have been able to save the amount of the Sale and much more. Most loggers and millworkers profess a love for Montana, its beauty, its high environmental quality.[11] Most hunt, fish, and enjoy the outdoors. Many hike and backpack. They recognize the importance of (though on private land the company employing them is often hostile to) sound forestry practices, yet they are proud of their comparatively high-paying jobs, bonuses and production rates. Not much different from the majority of citizens of the technological society, many like to buy fancy four-wheel drives, snowmobiles, motorcycles, video-cassette recorders and to frequent the bars and restaurants in town. So, all along, at various points, they have chosen higher incomes and the access to more commodities higher income gives one; they have chosen to increase productivity by complying with technology; they have made these choices in opposition to preserving the wild land and maintaining the pristine character of the surroundings. Given these choices, "Brand-S says it can't afford to lose any more timber to wilderness or study areas. Even small sales like Crazy Woman [three million boardfeet] are vital to keep the sawmill running, its manager says."[12]

Considered from the standpoint now not of the local but of the national economy, "need" turns out to have the same conditional character. In the 1980s, the mill claimed to ship ninety-five percent of the studs it specializes in out of state, primarily to the East Coast.[13] The only requirement one must possess to purchase the lumber is having the money for it. Most of these studs will be used in construction. Some will be hammered together making forms for concrete to be poured into; then they will be discarded, thus generating additional problems, e.g., the landfill problem on Long Island. Others will be used to build houses quickly by people merely concerned to get the job done and who have no intention of building something to last. A significant portion of the total volume will go toward building second homes.

Focusing on this latter, we see at last how this raw material is required by and fulfills the vision of the technological good life. Erica Abeel, in "Magnificent Obsession: A House in the Country," presents us with this picture of a typically successful life within an advanced technological society. Here are what the trees of Cottonwood Canyon, interpreted as so much raw material to be made over, are finally reshaped into:

> Stanley Gulkin, a trim, fiercely energetic man in his late 40s, is a tax and corporate lawyer who has, he says, 'worked very hard and done very well.' At his office in Livingston, New Jersey, he gets fifty phone calls a day. 'You get pulled in every direction—this is success! It makes me feel important.' But a couple years back, he felt he was 'on a merry-go-round. My daughters were growing up, I started noticing my gray hair, started worrying about mortality. You ask yourself, What's it all for? So instead of having a mid-life crisis, I bought a house in the country.'[14]

In Gulkin's response we see technology's promise to liberate people by disburdening them of problems. In fact, Abeel notes, "The leitmotif sounded in virtually all my interviews was escape."[15] Escape from work and urban living. A house in the country is a place for "gaining sanity before I return to New York to battle out the next five days."[16]

More than this, owning a house in the country is "experienced as the standard package necessary to the good life," according to one researcher.[17] What is the picture of this good life? At his second home in East Hampton, Gulkin is "at peace. I lie on the lounge in the water, look up at the trees, listen to mellow music."[18] Unlike in New Jersey, Gulkin spends time with his wife and kids in East Hampton, "We go out together, cook together, go to the movies together."[19] And so it seems to the same researcher, "the house is a retreat from the way of life they've created for themselves. The country house is where they can live as they should be living all week— that is, as human beings."[20]

A fundamental split between means and ends is at the heart of modern technology and technological culture. It shows up as the split between what people do in the city and what they do in the country, between work and leisure, between activity and passivity. For instance, most people's exertion is put to productive activity and, so exertion has less of a place in leisure, thus often making leisure as passive and uninvolving as watching television. Indeed, a second home is, according to one commentator, "a form of conspicuous leisure to go with conspicuous busyness."[21] This means and ends split appears again as a split, a discontinuity, between surfaces and depths. Hence, building designs for these new homes are, to put it as an oxymoron, "authentic imitations." As a realtor tells Abeel, "People have cleaned up reality into a romantic fantasy."[22] A 1740s Colonial will have a jacuzzi and a microwave oven. One homeowner called an exterminator for a troublesome covey of quail.

The ironies are many. People often find the burdens of the second home outweigh the reliefs. Typically, newcomers bring to their second homes an unneighborly attitude foreign to the place. Natives such as farmers and their interests are often in conflict with the new homeowners. A final irony is they kill the thing they love.

> Emblematic of it all is a sign on Route 25 in Hunter, NY. You're driving along a beautiful, twisting, tree canopied road when suddenly you come upon a swath of bulldozed land. Next to the brown swath stands the sign, in Day Glo turquoise and black: ESCAPE TO THE WILDERNESS.[23]

It is a small step to connect the above brown swaths with similar scars in the wild canyons of Montana's Crazy Mountains.

This affluent second-home lifestyle is typically regarded as successful by our culture. But do the second home and the typical diversions and distractions entailed in consumption allow people to live genuinely free and good lives? *If* we were to renounce that affluent vision and not build second homes, the Crazy Mountains and other undamaged places could easily be protected in their wild character.

To summarize, we examined carefully the particular goods that this raw material would serve. It was found that on the local and national level people are making choices *for* a life of consumption and *against* the wild land. More formally, once we as a culture grant the goal of technology, the steps taken to achieve that goal fall out as hypothetical imperatives. If our culture agrees to the goal symbolized by "owning a second home is the latest fashion imperative," and continues to believe that the raw material from the Crazy Mountains forwards that goal, then raw material from the Crazies becomes *needed*. However, if this goal is not granted, the steps toward it lose their imperative character. Renounce our allegiance to technology and what happens to the raw material of the Crazies? As raw material it no longer matters. We are freed to consider the life, growth, old age and death of forests in a new light. But to do so is to get ahead of our analysis.

II

Thinking Like the Forest Service: The Utilitarian Calculus of Damage to the Resources

Damage to the "wood fiber resource" from the insects and disease is only one way to understand damage in Cottonwood Canyon. Wood fiber is not the only feature of Cottonwood Canyon that counts, even for the Forest Service. In this section, we will begin to examine this other kind of damage (and what the Forest Service calls other benefits) that would be wrought by logging Cottonwood Canyon. We begin by turning to the Forest Service's own assessment, its attempt to balance benefits and losses. We do this because, first, Forest Service decisions and appeal of those decisions regarding our public land are worked out entirely within this loss-benefit framework, making it necessary to address it. I know from experience that the Forest Service and other public agencies are mostly deaf to other, more important appeals. Second, a utilitarian principle such as net public benefit may seem reasonable as long as it remains at a high level of abstraction. In its details, however, this net utility principle must reduce everything to commensurables that can be added or subtracted. Every gain and loss must be assigned a quantity—at least that is the ideal. This attempt to quantify quality makes us suspect that the method itself is incapable of registering real damage to things. Third, the Forest Service's assessment of environmental impacts contrasts sharply with assessments carried out later from the standpoints of ecology and, especially, philosophy. We will see that the philosophical approach is the only one capable of assessing the full damage that will be done to this thing if the planned timber sale is implemented.

Although insect and disease damage to the wood fiber resource moved the Forest Service to perform the initial *Resource Area Analysis,* saving wood fiber alone cannot serve as the only overt reason to harvest the timber. Even from a narrow timber-management viewpoint, the Forest Service must follow guidelines and requirements established by the National Environmental Policy Act, the National Forest Management Act, the Endangered Species Act, the Clean Water Act and other federal laws. And beyond this fixation with timber, the Forest Service is mandated by a policy of multiple-use to meet objectives of other forest uses, including wildlife, hunting opportunity, fisheries, visual quality, livestock grazing, and various forms of recreation. Specifically, a Forest Plan is drawn up which allocates different areas of the Forest to various dominant management concerns. The Cottonwood-Ibex Sale area is divided into two management areas: timber and livestock, and timber and big game. Such dominant management objectives generally do not mean that other objectives such as recreation can be ignored, but only that these other objectives play minor roles compared to the dominant objectives.

Given these and other constraints, an *Environmental Assessment* (EA) must be undertaken before a final decision can be made to offer a timber sale.[24] Through this assessment, the Forest Service considers various "alternative actions," including no action, for an area it proposes for a timber sale. The EA studies the benefits and costs or losses for each objective of concern for each action, and, in the case of this particular EA, especially the selected action. An EA is supposed to assure the Forest Service that all the viable alternatives have been weighed and that "no significant impact" to an area will occur because of the proposed action, the Cottonwood-Ibex Timber Sale.[25] So on the basis of the findings of the EA, the proposed action may go forward as initially planned, it may become modified, an alternative action may be selected or the proposed sale may halted. A "decision" is made by the Forest Supervisor who selects from among these actions one which has a net public benefit and which fits the overall plans of the Gallatin Forest.

Again, for any timber sale to go forward it must show a net public benefit and it also must benefit other areas than timber alone. The Cottonwood-Ibex EA found "no significant impact." So we learn, not surprisingly, that the selected action entailing the timber sale will benefit other forest "users" besides the wood products industry. It will also damage some things of concern but it will or should not damage these below set standards, and so, overall, the selected action, logging, has a net public benefit. It seems that nearly everyone wins or at least is appeased by the final plan.

What about logging's effect on recreation, visual quality, and one of recreation's counterparts, wildlife? Logging is claimed to enhance the area for recreation by encouraging a "moderate variety" of recreation opportunities.[26] It is asserted that the resource area is sufficiently large and diverse "to allow separation of conflicting recreational uses while providing the opportunity for a variety of recreation activities." Hiking, backpacking, horseback riding, skiing, fishing, hunting, camping, picnicking, motorcycling, snowmobiling, bicycling, off-road vehicle and four-wheel drive use, and firewood gathering can all make use of the area, it is implied. Forest-wide there seems to be an increased demand for these opportunities. Cottonwood Canyon can serve this demand if it is made more available. Because the pre-logging access road is rough (spring thaw makes the road nearly impassable for any vehicle and deep ruts makes it practically impossible for ordinary cars and Winnebagos), the EA claims an improved road from the timber sale as well as a picnic area and parking lot will make the canyon more available in terms of safety, ease, comfort, speed of access, and make it accessible in more seasons and to a larger class of users. It will be more available, too, because its primitive character can be enjoyed without the constraints of wilderness restrictions. Finally, it will help reduce pressure on other "wilderness portals." Thus, though the assessment admits much less logging would provide for the most variety of recreation, still the roads that come with logging will favor this objective for recreation to a great degree, or so it is claimed.

Visual quality is closely associated with recreation. Cottonwood Canyon is established in the analysis to have high scenic beauty, so objectives were set out to take this scenery into account. Yet, the selected alternative without modification was least likely to meet the visual quality objectives. Here technical resourcefulness came to the rescue. In upper Cottonwood Canyon, for instance,

> a "natural appearing" setting is being managed for. In this ROS (Recreational Opportunity Spectrum) setting, the management (and other human) activities do not dominate the foreground, and although they may be apparent, the overall effect to most users is one of a natural setting.[27]

Thus, the clearcuts high on the steep sides of the canyon are designed to look like avalanche chutes.

How does "big game" fair? Rising abruptly from the treeless plains, the Crazies stand with gray, bare peaks against the sky. This means that the comparatively narrow band of timberlands girding them and winding up the canyon floors is ecologically the most important wildlife habitat. More specifically, considered in terms of big game, logging will harm elk and deer habitat. Superficially considered, it seems that cutting the trees will open the canopy, thereby allowing more sunlight to reach the ground plants and increase forage. Indeed, the animals are seen in clearcuts more often than the forest. But studies show that forage is not a factor that limits the size of big game populations east of the continental divide because most of this canopy opening of forest by clearcut logging will be done in summer range areas where the animals already use only a small percentage of the forage naturally occurring in these places.[28] Hence, increased forage is a commodity for which there will be no demand. Moreover, clearcutting reduces the amount of cover and security for animals, and these are limiting factors for population "numbers." Thermal cover is important against summer's heat and winter's cold winds, and forests provide security against predation and hunting. Hunter "success" increases enormously because deer and elk are easier to kill in clearcuts; and roads also allow for easier access than trails. Thus clearcutting and roads actually will decrease the big game population.[29]

Yet, big game is a dominant management goal for this area and some fairly high standards must be maintained. Following what we will come to understand as the pattern of technology, managers resourcefully vary the means to maintain the same end. Big game populations can be given some protection through placement, size, and shape of clearcuts. Road density can be reduced by closing all but the arterial roads of the sale area. But even closed roads still make these areas easier to access with off-road vehicles, mountain bicycles, and foot and horse traffic.

Big game populations also could be maintained by reducing the length of the hunting season.[30] But shortening the hunting season impinges upon another standard, Hunter Opportunity. Most of Montana still has a five-week hunting season while some nearby states have shortened their seasons to five days with most elk and deer taken the first two days. Moreover, where clearcutting has occurred, the character of the elk and deer herds changes. For instance, trophy bull elk, unable to find security, tend to be wiped out. So the population of bulls comes to consist almost entirely of spiked, not antlered, bulls. These young elk, not having to compete with older and stronger bulls, do not provide the healthiest gene pool for the herd. Managers call these "trade-offs."[31]

In the Cottonwood-Ibex EA, the proposed action fails to meet the adopted standards. A seventy-five percent big game habitat effectiveness is adopted while the timber harvest will result in a habitat effectiveness of sixty-five percent, reducing "the probability of elk use in the area by ten percent."[32] A .60 hunting opportunity index was adopted but the action will actually decrease it to an expected .55, resulting "in eight percent fewer hunter days" from the adopted objective.[33] For these and other reasons, the Montana Fish, Wildlife, and Parks Department, a separate agency, came out against this proposed timber sale. The damage apparent in the Forest Service's own figures may allow conservationists to appeal this sale successfully.[34] Many of us would feel relief if the sale were successfully appealed on such grounds; timber sales like this one seem otherwise unstoppable. Such is the usual framework within which damages and benefits are assessed by the Forest Service and other "resource managers."

Quality, Quantity, and the Assessment of Damage

In this *Resource Area Analysis* and *Environmental Assessment*, the Forest Service, attempting to weigh benefits against costs and damages, has attempted to quantify quality wherever possible, as shown above, with big game statistics. Quantifying quality is pretending to be scientific, objective, and fair. However, the more profound reason that quality is harnessed in quantity is not to answer the concerns of the public but to get everything under technological control. We saw this occur with the visual quality and hunting objectives. From the standpoint of control, such a move is useful, i.e., flexible, but the things become shadows of themselves in the process. Viewed as essentially resources, things become only so much raw material needing to be reshaped. To the wood products industry, a forest really is only so many boardfeet of timber and nothing more. Viewed essentially as commodities for final consumption, hunting, fishing and other forms of recreation are viewed in a similarly shallow fashion. Their meanings become calculable in advance, fixed and capturable.

Quantity talk, commodity talk, has become the poetry of our age. It is poetic because its shorthand is taken by people to invoke and sum up the thing's entire meaning. Quantity talk is our language for expressing the powers that move us. Technocrats seek the poetic number, the one that grabs people; on the other hand, they condemn genuine poetry and narrative as merely emoting.[35] But, once seen through, poetic numbers rest on a crude and superficial understanding of the way things hang together, accounting for a few features but not things in their depth.

Things of uncapturable meanings reveal just how thin and artificial commodities and poetic numbers are. The practice of fishing, for example, cannot be caught in numbers of fish, weight and size. Hunting is more than the number of hunter successes. The wild beauty of Cottonwood Canyon is more than superficially viewed scenery. Recreation is more than the number of recreational visitor days. We have a sense that these practices and things never really get a hearing from these figures.

Things in their wholeness make us understand that the selection of what is essential about a thing is far from scientific, objective, fair and calculable and, is rather, quite the opposite—arbitrary, forced, blind, unfeeling and stale. And so, the Environmental Assessment finding of no significant impact for Cottonwood Canyon is a Pyrrhic victory. *No significant impact was found because things were forced into predetermined categories eliminating their significance in advance.* Their eloquence was reduced to a number which was taken to be their everything. Numbers held up but meaning dropped out. "Everyone wins" turns out to be "everyone loses." As one conservationist put it, "We realize you can raise elk in a parking lot but we want wildlife in wild places."[36]

Poetry and narrative present things in their fullness. As a step toward articulating (however negatively) the fullness of things, we will consider more thoughtfully the damage that will occur in Cottonwood Canyon from the proposed action of the Forest Service, first ecologically and then philosophically.

III

Damage Considered Ecologically

An ecosystem can be likened to a waterbed in the sense that, when pressure is applied to one area, other areas have to give way and move in the "opposite" direction.[37] As the Forest Service presses an area to produce more boardfeet, to produce more forage for increased numbers of livestock, and to maximize big game numbers, other species must give way and diminish in numbers and kind. For instance, old growth forest is not viewed as maximally productive of boardfeet, and it would be more productive of wood fiber to have a sustained-yield forest without any old-growth trees eventually. However, many species of wildlife and plants are indigenous to old-growth forest and appear nowhere else. For instance, some woodpeckers need dead trees the size of old-growth trees. Fallen trees provide security for animals and their decay provides food for plants and microorganisms. So, even if big game population numbers could be maintained with hunting conditions remaining tough, still, this would enhance only a few species of forest life. A respectful concern for *all* living creatures would direct us to consider the damage from logging to other forms of forest life and injury to the soils that sustain all life.

The Crazies are an island-like range isolated by wide, treeless valleys from other mountain ranges, and now they are isolated as well by technology. As such, the range can be looked at in terms of island ecology. Its rocky core offers little habitat for its larger animals aside from goats and golden eagles. Even most of the canyons offer only limited summer range for deer, elk, moose and bear. Preserving the comparatively narrow band of forested land surrounding the Crazies, where rocky peaks dovetail with grassy foothills, is crucially important. Island ecology may indicate more extreme measures; e.g., securing conservation easements for wildlife on the grasslands, protecting corridors between differing habitats, making sure genetically different wildlife populations can mix, ensuring that the Crazies themselves serve as corridor between the Glacier Park ecosystem and the Yellowstone ecosystem for grizzly and wolf recovery, and beyond this to seeing that steps are taken to ban pesticides, prevent acid rain, halt ozone depletion, and ameliorate the greenhouse effect. Even preservation of tropical forest is of fairly direct concern since clearcutting tropical forest has ruined the winter habitat for warblers that feed on the spruce bud worm moth "infesting" this northern forest.[38]

However, problems arise if we look to ecology *alone* for finding our bearings. If we want to preserve the present day biological diversity of the Crazies, ecology can tell us what steps to take. But no matter how many steps we take, the island ecology of the Crazies will eventually stabilize at something different from the present. Nor is the present-day biological diversity of the Crazies the range's former wild diversity. At one time not so long ago, the Crazies were home to grizzly bears, wolves, and bison. If these were to reside in the Crazy ecosystem now using their past natural patterns of migration, immense and impractical changes would have to occur. In fact, preserving an ecosystem strictly untouched by humans would be impossible. In even earlier times the Crazy Mountains were likely inhabited not only by jaguars but also by species, giant sloths and woolly mammoths, which have long since become extinct. Admittedly, the presence of these species would make the Crazies a wilder place, but their absence does not make us refrain from calling its land wild. The Crazies seem to be caught in Heraclitean flux.

Going to the opposite Parmenidian extreme, the Forest Service at present has no plans to develop most of the land mass of the Crazies, especially the glaciated core. Neither sufficient mineralization nor sufficient reserves of oil and gas have made exploration and development of these worthwhile to the agency. Road expense and avalanche danger make subdivision developments impractical. Exploiting the lakes and streams for irrigation and hydroelectric power has not yet become economical or fashionable. No ski areas, Disneyland roller coasters, nor giant water slides have been proposed. With more roads and reconstructed roads, the lakes and peaks will be more available and greater numbers of people may frequent them. But, even so, the high peaks will remain much the same. Yet, somewhere between this flux and sameness, between the Crazies with woolly mammoths and letting their ruggedness fend for itself, the wild character of the Crazies will be lost. (And ultimately, why should it matter whether the Crazies are damaged or protected?) We need to get our bearings for what is worthy of protection from somewhere outside the science of ecology.

IV

Damage Considered Philosophically

How will the proposed sale damage the mountain range considered as a thing in its own right? What difference does the proposed timber sale make for the quality of human life and experience? The answer to this latter question depends on the way they matter for people. In turn, the way the mountains matter for them depends largely upon their mode of contact with them. Whose experience is telling?

In his book *Zen And The Art Of Motorcycle Maintenance*, Robert Pirsig finds that much of today's technology blocks out and insulates people from their surroundings. Of the most common mode of travel, an automobile, he writes,

> You see things vacationing on a motorcycle in a way that is completely different from any other. In a car you're always in a compartment, and because you're used to it you don't realize that through a car window everything you see is just more TV. You're a passive observer and it is all moving by you boringly in a frame.[39]

We can think of many other ways in which devices detach us from the environment. If cars do this to some extent, jets remove us even more. An exercise machine that imitates movements of cross-country skiing detaches one from the trail and trees. One senses a general pattern of separation here which will be exposed with our theory of technology. For now it is important just to see the various ways technological devices come between people and the environment.

When devices block out the environment they reduce the number of ways it can affect us.[40] For most people who experience the Crazies they are mountains to be enjoyed. That is, they are a final good and are looked to in some sense to enrich life. Yet, even so devices have come between them and the mountains, impoverishing their experience of them and insulating them from the possibility of encountering the depths of the place. For many of these people, the full depth of the thing will not be crucial. The timber sale may not matter so much to them.

Most people are acquainted with the Crazies by driving Interstate 90 (whether by car or motorcycle). Coming from the east one is apt to experience and remember the Crazies as the first real mountains of the Rockies one meets on ones way west. Near the town of Reedpoint, they confront drivers head-on with their towering peaks and massive presence spread across the horizon. Occupants of the vehicles do not pass them unnoticed. Recognizing this, the highway department developed a rest stop and put up a sign noting one story of how the Crazies received their name.

What impact will the changes brought about by the three proposed timber sales have upon these visitors? Attempting to avoid eyesores, the Forest Service in some areas does take into account visibility from the highway. If a clearcut would be noticeable from the highway, steps are supposed to be taken to minimize its visual effects, e.g., varying shape and placement. If all the difference the Crazies make to human experience is this view from the road, then the desire for timber and pleasing scenery need not conflict. The Forest Service managers will say that people can have both.

How will the timber sale in Cottonwood Canyon affect car campers? The Forest Service is betting that car campers will not stray too far from their cars, and so may well accept the veneer of forest left between the road and the clearcuts as sufficient for their taste. With many of the logging roads closed in order to favor wildlife and with the picnic facility located in the middle of the sale area, the agency seems more concerned about motorists being upset with the closed roads. Vandalism is expected; some may even consider their defiance of a locked gate an act of civil disobedience. My hunch is that this thinking on the part of the Forest Service is too stereotyped. Many campers, especially those wanting to hike with small children, will resent the forest veneer and the timber sale. Others will demand to get to the end of the road. Eventually wildlife concerns will probably be overridden and the picnic area relocated at the end of the road at the far boundary of the timber sale area, farther up Cottonwood Canyon and closer to the lakes. Since much of what is really good and beautiful about this place will have been destroyed in this process, I find it hard to believe that many of these motorists will count it as a bonus that the lakes are more available to them. However, some no doubt will say just that. They may also say that there are always other wild places to go, and besides, it's all part of progress.

Understandably, since legal wilderness precludes logging and motorized use, motorcyclists and snowmobilers as interest groups have aligned themselves with the timber industry against wilderness; what ought to be taken as cause for wonder is the harmoniousness of the relationship between these recreationists and industry, for under current Forest Service policy, if an area is open to motorized off-road vehicles, such as trailbikes and snowmobiles, it is, with few exceptions, also open to timber harvest if suitable timber exists in the area. If logging made a significant difference to these motorized recreationists, one would expect conflict between them and industry. Special forest areas would be set aside for them apart from the timber base. How should we read this harmoniousness existing between them? One reason may be that they are literally riding what they see as the need for development. Traditionally, development promises affluence and everyone can always use more money which translates into the means to procure more commodities. In this light, development pays off for everyone. Hence, wilderness advocates are accused of being selfish, unlike motorcyclists and snowmobilers.

Second, the conquest of nature is incorporated into the very design of these machines and the way that they make sense for their riders. From knobby tires, to advanced hydraulic suspension systems, to high clearance, to plenty of horsepower, to low and variable gearing, to lightweight aluminum alloy, such machines are designed to take one wherever, whenever, regardless. Not to submit the land to domination, then, is unmanly.

Third, though motorcyclists and snowmobilers certainly register different qualities and claims of the landscape, e.g., steep grades, windblown snows, smooth trails, bogs, rock slides, downfall, and loose gravel, less of the landscape matters to them than it does to those without the devices detaching them from the landscape. One focuses on the trail ahead with a quick glance now and then to the surroundings. Oil and gas odors preclude inhaling the symphony of forest fragrances. Engine noise and helmets preclude hearing a nearby stream or of being startled by a flapping grouse. The noise keeps wildlife not only unheard but out of sight. When cyclists stop to contemplate a view, the sound of other cyclists is not disturbing to them, whereas for those without these devices the noise is commonly experienced as incongruent with and shattering of the serene calmness of the forest. Unlike the body, the machine limits where its riders can and want to go; they mostly stick to the trails and roads. The size of the place is not measured by hiking steps since much more ground can often be covered. Cyclists do not feel a steady sweat in keeping with one's pace, but they sweat mostly at heavily cussed bog holes, downfall, and steep, loosely-graveled trails. Causing trail erosion may even be fun for them.

What do the proposed changes to Cottonwood Canyon mean to motorcyclists and snowmobilers? They seem to mean more affluence and availability. Roads are places to speed up and speed through. If clearcuts are not experienced as pleasing, running the logging roads probably is, or, at least, a motorcycle allows one to pass by clearcuts quickly. Closed roads are not closed to these vehicles, and, since off trail and road is not where one can normally take a cycle, a set of collector roads radiating through a logging sale may take one to places and heights not possible before.

On the whole, the full depth of the wild landscape is blocked from motorcyclists and snowmobilers. Less of the genuinely wild matters to them. Many may not like the changes proposed—aside from the ugliness of roads and clearcuts, trails are perhaps more difficult and fun to bike than roads, but nearly all will find the changes tolerable, especially considering the other sweets derived from development. They will speak to one another of the benefits—the improved road for their pick-up trucks and the new roads to explore. On the other hand, wilderness designation will bring about a halt to what little trailbiking and snowmobiling is done in Cottonwood Canyon presently.

Hikers and backpackers constitute the largest share, the vast majority, of recreationists who use the Cottonwood Creek trailhead. It is the most popular trailhead on the west side of the Crazies. Of these people, most people will have come from less than 100 miles away. Many will have come to Cottonwood Creek for the first or second time wanting to get to know different trails and mountain ranges of the region. However, many others will have returned to this trailhead time and again as one of their favorite haunts and mountain ranges. It's been my experience that most, if not all, of these people who have walked these trails up Cottonwood and Trespass creeks from this trailhead care about what happens to the wild character of this place. These people who walk the place tend to care about it and are open to it in the fullness of their body and attention, and, on a bodily-sized scale. *They let the land be on its own terms.*[41]

The planned timber sale for Cottonwood Canyon calls for building roads where there are now trails, clearcutting forested areas up to forty acres in extent, shaping some of these "cutting units" to imitate avalanche chutes and leaving a veneer of trees between the roadways and clearcuts. We have already seen how the Forest Service assesses the benefits and damages that result from this planned sale. Here we will determine the difference this change will make for practitioners of hiking: those who are most open to the wild character of the land. What difference would this timber sale make to hikers? As hikers, what is being suggested to us by what these changes make us feel and think? What does our intelligence uncover as damaging about these changes? What it is our reactions are corresponding to, what are they telling us?

The Natural Wild Order and Our Experience of It

Damages obtrude from the wild order. This wild order is, of course, *biological:* spider webs, woodpeckers, tree trunks, insects dancing in forest filtered sunlight, the creaking and groaning of trees under the force of a storm's wind, thick mosses on rotting logs, delicate flowers in need of shade. The wild forest is the skin of the mountains. Below it course the living inhabitants, graceful as deer and cool as trout in a stream. The actual wild order is a geological order as well: glaciers carved its valleys and distributed the boulders, streams wind through its meadows, winds sweep its peaks. Above all, this wild order is not planned or constructed by humans. Not built, it is given. My backpack is made by humans for human use; wilderness is neither made by humans nor made for human use. Its order is not *for* any person. Normally the scientific questions it raises in people are not answered by the human sciences but by the natural sciences. In place of the absence of human ordering is the fact that this place is the consequence of natural forces entirely. Hence, each of its beings reflects the other beings and the wild order itself as a whole. Its rhythm is its rhythm; its music, its own composition.[42]

The biological wild order stands out in the *experience* of hikers as well. Even calloused but experienced people will acknowledge, for instance, that there is "just nothing like" the presence of old growth forest. Beneath the crowns of the trees whose deep-barked trunks stand timeless, it is cool, enclosed and very still. Fragrances of growing trees and rotting logs drift freely about in the resonant silence of the place. Here, time, like a river flowing into the ocean, slows, expands, and pervades the silence. In genuinely wild places, none of the beings suggest human making. Rather, each of the beings reflects the other wild beings and the wild order itself. The order as a whole generates the mood of the place and gives one a frame of mind for taking up with it. Questioning how a wild place could be better is out of place here; wanting to improve wild places is the impulse only of a newcomer, one not yet fully immersed. The place and beings themselves are pristine, not because there is not mud, dirt and hair here, but because they are like the deep pools of Idaho's Clearwater river, seeming so transparent that only depth prevents one from seeing all the way to the bottom. Its own otherness and sufficiency, transparency, mirroring simplicity, integrity, and depth pervade the order of the wild place.

The fisherman and writer Roderick Haig-Brown in *Fisherman's Summer* relates a definitive experience of this natural wild order. He remembers the supremely enjoyable times he had catching Arctic Grayling in Canada's Coppermine region. After catching grayling in other places, he began to think he would never catch such fish of grace, shape and color again, but he had the opportunity in northern Saskatchewan. The few inhabitants of the region cared nothing for the grayling, only for other fish, so he contemplates why he cared.

> What did I want of them? Not to kill them, certainly, nor to eat them, though I would probably do both of these things. Not even to match my skills against their instincts, because I cheerfully assumed they would be arising freely, as Arctic Grayling so frequently are, and present me no problems. Not for the excitement of setting light tackle against their strength and watermanship, for I had long ago learned to handle faster and stronger fish on lighter gear than they would make me use. Really, it was only to see them and know them, and through them somehow to become more intimate with the land about the streams their presence graced.[43]

Here we see as clearly as possible the otherness and sufficiency, the reality, of the wild being; it needs no care or tampering, only to be cared for in this relation. The mirroring simplicity, transparency and depth pervading the place announces itself through the eloquent wild thing. Such announcement is possible because of integrity: the unblemished grayling is of one piece with the wild place and the place is unblemished, whole, and wholesome.

This wild order does not have to be in the old-growth stage as we usually think of it in order to be experienced as wild in its entirety. Consider the difference between an area burned over by a forest fire and one which has been clearcut in accordance with the guidelines of a forest management policy. It is sometimes pointed out that the trees will grow back in the clearcuts. In fact, the National Environmental Policy Act requires that regeneration of seedlings in clearcut areas must be expected within five years or no harvesting in the area is allowed. On the other hand, a cycle of bug-kill, forest fires, and regeneration occurs about every 300 years in the Yellowstone bioregion. Moreover, many of the fires were started by Indians flushing out game. The trees came back. So, what is the difference between naturally forested places and places where forestry management is practiced? A clearcut and a burn?

Ecologically, suppressing naturally-caused fires in wild places creates unnatural conditions, such as fuel build-up, whereas forest fires, so long as they remain less than extreme, create places where "a greater diversity of plant species will grow, and that translates into more kinds of animals."[44] But in this section our concern is to reflect on what a burn reveals to fully embodied human experience, and some people think that, from the point of view of human experience, a "well-managed" forest which does not burn is better than a burned wild forest.[45] If they are concerned about merely the scenic view from the distance of a highway, there may be reason to believe this is correct. But hikers are open to the wild character of the land in its full dimensions. For them, there is a world of difference between a managed forest and a burned wild forest.

Sometime ago in Yellowstone Park following day-old grizzly tracks in a burn of the year before, I was overcome with an eerie sense of wildness in that place. There was not a sign of life present as I recall. Though it was twilight, no birds or crickets interrupted the complete silence of the place. There were no plants—only ash and charred logs—yet it was unforgettable. Why? It was not beautiful nor was it simple. The blackened absence of life did not yet impress me, except cerebrally, as holding out a promise of life to come. Yet the place was streaked with tension. Dead, still, silent and foreign—a graveyard so obviously made by the event of raging fire, now gone, too. It was the long-clawed prints in the dusty trail, I think, that set the place into motion—the bear having passed here, too. Two capriciously powerful and wild beings, the fire and the bear, having passed leaving signs brought to mind strangely destructive powers and moods as quickly shifting as flame and as dark as charred still-standing trees at nightfall. I would not separate them. Each announced itself in the wake of the other. Clearcuts, on the other hand, shatter and obliterate this natural wild order.

From this human experience of the wild order a series of paradoxes result. Wilderness is a place we understand as ruled by chance and necessity simultaneously. Like tossed dice, a tree may seem to fall where it falls by chance, and yet, we understand it could not have been otherwise, given the determining conditions of its fall. Whatever happens here seems to "just happen" but happens decisively. The natural order is so heavily laden with unknowns and what is unknowable, that we often experience its events as chance occurrences, as emergent from mystery. Yet, simultaneously, whatever happens happens with matter-of-fact force, especially when heard out of its profound silences. So we experience this same event as ruled by necessity.

Even though wilderness is self-sufficient and does not need us, for, unlike forms of algae lower on the food chain, humans do not play an important positive role in the Earth's ecosystems, and even though wilderness cares nothing for us, for a tree may well blow over on my tent, still it is a place, as we saw with Haig-Brown's account, that humans can care for deeply. We are awed by it and we can become intimate with its presence. Its beauty is a beauty humans respond to. It is a place that has been good to us and beckons to continue to be good. So, paradoxically, even in its uncaringness wilderness can be good to us.

Even more paradoxical, for wilderness to be definitive wilderness it must have the capacity to be good for human life. Mars, for instance, is not wilderness except by metaphorical extension of the term. Wilderness does not need their actual presence in order to be wilderness, but, for the natural order to be wilderness, it must have the capacity to correspond to humans were they present. It must be able to move those who have the capacity to be moved by it. This happy coincidence signifies that wilderness has a distinctive character: To be worthy of the name, wilderness must distinguish itself for those who name it. That ability is the specific difference which sets it apart from all other places where human ordering is absent.[46] Without this capacity it would not merely be changed, it would be lacking, deficient. Importantly for our concerns here, if it had *lost* this ability, we would say that it had been killed or ruined. What has died is not only its ecological web, although this is a precondition of its life; what has died is its ability to animate human life. It is substantially different; it no longer speaks to our humanity in the way of wilderness. So, paradoxically, we do not need to protect the pointless order of the uncaring wilderness for reasons of environmental altruism alone, although these would be justifiable reasons to protect it. Good reasons for the protection of the Crazy Mountains have to do with how they are already as good as they can be— even for humans.

It is possible for people to be in wilderness agreeably and unobtrusively from the standpoint of experiencing the wild order. However, it is easy to make intrusions which damage it. For instance, had the grayling Haig-Brown caught been a hatchery fish planted in the stream, it would have made a difference to his experience of what these fish radiate. Had a dam upstream controlled the flow of the water, it would have been a less wild stream in his experience. Had the bright colors of the fish been caused by toxins from the tailings of a mine upstream, the appearance of the fish may have caused in him revulsion instead. Had he caught these fish out of a "catch out pond," there would be no story worth printing. At this point, having outlined key features of the wild order, we can make headway toward understanding what changes damage the wild order and in what way they do it. What makes obtrusion stare out in the wild?

Garbage in the Wilderness

Far from any road and accessible only by way of a steep, rugged trail, Rock Lake lies hidden high in a cirque beneath Iddings peak, the second tallest peak in the Crazies. I was angered by finding a large rusting barrel in the creek. Upstream there were others, and where the stream tumbled in a cascade from the lake was a dump where some crew had obviously spent the season. These oil drums were too big even for horses to carry. I had forgotten that Rock Lake was privately owned and that it had been tapped, tunneled into, for irrigation water. Agribusiness, Texas oil money, and helicopters had ordered it to make the creek supply a constant flow of water throughout the summer to the ditches of the ranch far below.

Garbage is not just another object, not just another x beside other x's. Hikers notice garbage. It obtrusively stares out in the wild. Its features do not radiantly mirror the simplicity of the other surrounding wild things and the wildness of the place. It does not cause one to pause and peer through its transparency into the depths of the wild. One does not get a feel for the entire integrity of the place through it. However, garbage is something more positive and active than the minimal sense of not wild. It actively points, first, to the incident which led to its being where it is. That incident is not a natural event such as bear scat, or a meteor fallen from the sky. These natural things, if they rouse wonder in us, take the mind back to events not of human ordering, and therefore, without moral implication. The absurdity of thinking that the bear should have done otherwise, should have buried its scat, makes us laugh. Garbage forces upon us the fact that this is a place where humans have been before, taking one back to an event of human ordering. Finding it in the wilderness takes ones mind into an inquiry that is moral in nature, for we are not first and foremost curious about what this person ate, rather, we think, "Why? How could one do this?"

We need to probe further the conditions for the possibility of a moral reaction to littering in the wilderness. Litter actively disagrees with its surroundings and the one littering is not in agreement with the wild order either. It wars with the wild because the world this commodity packaging vibrates with is in conflict with the world of the wild. The act of discarding, "trashing," too, is merely a manifestation of the style of consumption, of what it is to consume. Since litter wars with this wild world, every blotch of litter intrudes as sign of the defeat wilderness and its replacement by technology.

Such tension provokes feelings ranging from annoyance to anger to disgust to sadness and disappointment. Quite likely it rouses thought to take account of the incident of littering, the person, the motive, the world, the culture. When impressive, it becomes a memorable event which bids one to think further. What did one see in this trash anyway? Finally, and importantly, such an experience issues into prescriptive directives. One wants it out of there. One may try to get it out of there by excusing it. The best immediate action may be to put it out of mind, look away. Or one can put it in ones pack, imagine how it could be cleaned up, or think of preventive measures, e.g., laws, social practices, education. The garbage *should* be packed out of Rock Lake.

Roads and Wilderness

Ecologically, no study has ever shown that roads benefit wildlife.[47] Likewise, turning to the human hiking experience of finding a road in what was taken to be a wild area, we can apprehend even more clearly the tension, conflict, and defeat garbage discloses. Unlike litter, however, roads seem useful. Like what most technology *seems* to be, they are a convenient means of getting you where you want to go. As such they disburden us. And if the end, the destination to which the road leads, is some place attractive and exciting, it holds out the promise of making the day. To be sure, the road at the trailhead is usually eyed with some relief by one burdened with a backpack for the past few days. Now one can lift the pack from ones shoulders for the last time, take off the hot and heavy boots, clean up at the stream, fetch an apple and chocolate bar stashed in the car, and slip into comfortable shoes. However, the reaction backpackers have to a road in wild areas is not a feeling of relief. Nor is their reaction excitement in anticipation of the scenic view it might offer to the motorist. Roads, like money, are of no use to those who have no use for them.

Roads are not wild. In fact, the Forest Service has defined its de facto but not legal wilderness lands as "roadless areas," known only by their negation. So, like garbage, roads do not pull together the wild character of the land, but neither are they merely negative in the minimal sense of not wild, for roads obtrusively stare out and point to human ordering. Like litter, the tension which exists between the road and the surroundings directs thoughts to the moral realm, the conflict one sees is between the technological universe and the wild world, and the defeat one sees is on the side of the wild. One feels more distressed and angry about what has happened here because, unlike litter, a road damages and destroys beyond mending. Bulldozing could be merely rearranging one gravel pile into another. Such rearranging hardly evokes ones concern. To feel sadness, something about which one is concerned must be harmed. But harm as such is not a sufficient condition for this feeling of loss, for harm itself might rouse one to action provided one is in a position to do something. When something valuable one cares about is harmed in a way one can do nothing about, that is, harmed irrevocably, one feels distressed. I felt that Cottonwood Canyon had been irrevocably changed by the road I found there.

Why is this road here? At first anger is focused on the builder, the most immediate destroyer. The landowners wanted to build a cabin in a secluded spot all to themselves.[48] Before one condemns this action unqualifiably, one should remember how patterned this individualism is. Nearly every day people are told to do likewise. A bank advertisement shows a picture of a flimsy two-person tent entitled "Vacation $130" and an A-frame house among pines entitled "Vacation House $49,500." Underneath these is written:

> So you've decided your family deserves a vacation home. A nice little getaway in the country. Together we'll find a way to stake your claim to the more leisurely side of life.[49]

Thus, anger, if allowed to lead inquiry, sooner or later becomes directed at deeper sources of destruction, the guiding vision of technology itself.

Part of my sense that the whole had been damaged was intensified by my knowing how deceptively small the range actually is. On a map, the Crazy Mountains have an oval shape around a core of high peaks. Cottonwood Canyon is located midway up the oval and extends to the very center. A mining claim road penetrates far in from the east, the opposite side. Together these two roads nearly pinch the Crazies in half so that even now—with the mining road closed, the Cottonwood Canyon road in a low-grade condition and, at present, no further development—one has to wonder if its wild character has been compromised to the point where the thread it was hanging by has been cut. Part of my sense of loss came later as I followed out the motives and learned the political ramifications. The person who built the road owned a parcel of land in the canyon and had recently acquired the legal right to some form of access through an amendment to the Alaskan Lands Bill.[50] Though the Forest Service is supposed to carry out policy and not make political decisions, it has been claimed by some administrative personnel that the supervisor and, in general, the Forest Service, actually desired the private inholder's road, rather than any alternative form of access, because they did not want wilderness in the Crazies and the road would allow the Cottonwood-Ibex Timber Sale to move forward unimpeded. Politically such a road seemed to preclude the range from consideration for legal wilderness designation from another angle as well. It was characteristic of Montana's then Senator John Melcher to exclude from consideration for wilderness any area that had even a fenceline, much less a road. From the standpoint of forest management, privatization, and politics such a road seemed like a victory for the culture many of people worked so hard to build and the defeat of another mighty mountain range.

I was forced to acknowledge the imbalance between our overwhelmingly powerful technology and even the ruggedness of these mountains. This is not the Old West any longer. The tension between the road and the wild mountains also prescribes action. It generates in the hiker—and the philosopher—an idea of what ought to be. One sees that the road should not be there or in other similar places. Such prescription may lead to advocating for wilderness designation to stop such senseless destruction. The tension prescribes that either one turns away from this place as hopelessly destroyed, as Hetch Hetchy Valley was for John Muir, or, given that it is not beyond hope, one attempts to ameliorate the effects. It directs one to work with the landowner to find solutions to the problem. It calls for reclaiming the road to as natural a condition as possible and possibly building a new trail on the other side of the creek. Such tension may even prescribe the formation of a new political party, one which does not allow this kind of destruction to wild land except for the most weighty of reasons. These are the kinds of effects roads have on hikers and hiking. These are what the changes mean, what they make hikers feel, think, and do.

The Experienced Damage of Logging

What would be the effect of these clearcuts in Cottonwood Canyon on the experience of hikers and backpackers? To understand the devastation of logging, one must be witness to both sides of the land's story, the before and after. Places visit their blessings on us and become special to us, even perhaps unnoticeably so. When changes occur to these special—what other traditions would call sacred—places, we feel it. It touches us. The significance of the change is unmistakably brought home to us.

Every year or so my father visited the place where his mother had grown up—a homestead in the foothills of the nearby Absaroka mountains. Last time, though, he, who had seen nothing at bottom really wrong with logging our renewable resources, was shocked to find the shack entirely gone, the woods clearcut, and not even a clue to how things were before. "I'll never go up there again. You couldn't even recognize the place." That was a response wrung out of him, and it has made all the difference in his attitude toward logging.

The loss of the old shack of his mother's intensified for my father the sense of loss clearcutting results in, but this did not make it qualitatively different from other people's experiences of a clearcut. The place itself is unrecognizable after logging has taken place. The trail is gone. The rock at the bend of the trail where one sat once watching a grouse is nowhere to be seen. Sunlight no longer filters through the high crowns of old growth trees. It lights no dancing insects in the air nor spider's web. This place was once good and just how it was can no longer be found.[51]

The experience of a clearcut is not only the experience, negatively, of a missing tree—the stump left with so many rings to suggest its years and height, the droughts, hard winters, and fires it weathered. Once you've seen one stump of a clearcut you've seen them all. Nor is it the absence of the forest as if the clearcut were a meadow. A recent clearcut, such as the one I am now thinking of in Sunlight Creek in the Crazies, wrenches the hiker with its contrast to the wild forest. Everything that was seems obliterated. It is a wasteland and a war zone. Having no sign but a map, a hiker must guess where the trail leaves the clearcut. Springs are dozed over; no water flows. A flowing stream looks like a ditch. Grass does not grow in new clearcuts. Temperatures soar. Nothing is left untouched. Everything yields the presence of inhuman human disordering ordering. Violent, heedless, overpowering, wasteful—the undisturbed presence of five thousand years is rent in less than a month. In the presence of this gap one sees the missing forest but finds it impossible to imagine how it once went. What is absent is irretrievably absent like a life that has slipped away. More than this irretrievable loss, what was once something that called for singing and a mood as cheerful as one is ever likely to have, now stares back blank, a skull of what was.

I hear in these places the trivialization of what was once admired, of what kept me well, of that which there is none better. It was a place worthy of being loved, and it went unrecognized, unappreciated, unheard, unsought and unadmired. It was not seen as a privileged place a privilege to behold by a privileged being walking the planet. Ones thoughts travel to the question, "What for?" This small-sized timber yields a small volume of raw material. "What for?" With such a public outcry for the limited wild land, can anyone feel good about its loss? Many loggers do not. What for? Muscles and human dignity? Rather, levers and diesel engines. What for? Not food, not clothing, not housing but motorcycles, four-wheel drives and snowmobiles. What for? Not homes but houses built poorly. Not homes to be dwelt in but places to escape to. What for? For a life no more engaging than watching television?

Hiking has a beginning, middle, and end. Having entered the wild for a few days and returned, one has had an experience which cumulatively grows and comes to a closure. It is like mixing flour, kneading dough, and finally baking loaves of bread. One must be careful with the glutinous strands or else the bread will not turn out good. Likewise, a hiker made whole and simple must leave carefully and come back gently, protecting the risen loaf in ones chest. One needs boundary space—a bath, hot meal, simple sleep. Tomorrow the loaf will stand by itself. Tomorrow one can rise early, drink coffee, read the newspaper, and confront the political and management decisions to log the valley just hiked, but today one needs to protect the experience just as one would protect the forest. If the planned timber sale for Cottonwood Canyon is implemented, the trailhead will be established in the middle of the sale area with locked gates (for wildlife's sake) which allows hikers and motorbikes but no cars. Having to walk along the roads through clearcuts will matter enough to make the sensitive hiker not want to return. Losing Cottonwood Canyon is like losing the first movement of a string quartet piece. Or maybe it's like losing the first violinist. Or perhaps it's nearer to the truth to say it's like replacing the first violin with a chainsaw.

How will clearcuts designed to look like snowchutes affect someone who has a practice of hiking in the Crazies? The other danger in this damage is that of forgetting. Above Cottonwood Lake looms a massive pile of huge boulders. It reminds me, on a grand scale, of the piles of rock road construction equipment sometimes moves to build an on-ramp for a freeway. A friend is reminded of mine tailings. But the mountain of loose rock above the lake is not of human construction. That is not even a possibility to be considered except for a chuckle. This is wild land. The rock piling was the work of a glacier. To think that the avalanche chute I am viewing may be human-made, may be artificial, an intentional illusion, intensifies my anger because of its insidiousness. Not only is the wild order removed and made to serve as raw material for the production of commodities, but here the wild order is replaced by the very ersatz found at the center of the consumptive style of life.

In the presence of a clearcut, or, even more so, in the presence of a well-managed forest, what is present is the absence of absence. To those unacquainted with the genuinely wild, the oblivion of the wild is even rubbed out. To them, this seems wild. To them, this seems natural. They feel no pain because they know no loss. This oblivion is an oblivion of depth and its replacement by shallowness. Viewed in this way, a tree is no more than boardfeet and decoration, and a forest is no more than a boardfeet production factory and pleasant scenery. This well-managed forest was harnessed for maximizing sawed lumber production while not affecting visual quality. The surface quality of the forest is left intact while the background is obliterated, transformed and the surface secured by other means: artificial avalanche chutes. The transparency, simplicity, wholeness, depth and integrity of the wild order is cut off and replaced by an artificial order, by human technological ordering. It is as though the canyon walls become wall-papered; a home for dwelling was transformed into a motel deluxe. This is the gift our society leaves to the human community—the oblivion of oblivion. To one who cares about this valley, these mountains and about what is coming to pass for the human community, clearcutting Cottonwood Canyon is a double loss. From this potential experience of loss and the understanding it leads us to, we receive prescriptions to protect these mountains and to initiate steps to reform technological culture. Where can we turn for help?

CHAPTER 3

THE ENVIRONMENTALIST'S REPLY

The 'key-log' which must be moved to release the evolutionary process for an ethic is simply this: quit thinking about decent land-use as solely an economic problem. Examine each question in terms of what is ethically and esthetically right, as well as what is economically expedient.

—Aldo Leopold[1]

The cure preserves the disease.

—Wendell Berry[2]

When I attend wilderness hearings or join organized hikes, I am impressed by the serious attention given to scientific accounts of wild places. For both speakers and listeners these accounts exhibit an air of authority that makes a difference politically, it seems, if anything does. By comparison, other, more testimonial accounts are easily dismissed by listeners who characterize them as subjective, as sentimental and as lacking, it seems, a solid basis in facts. These testimonial speakers often seem shy, hesitant and a bit defensive—their speeches filled with mere hints, understatements, and abstract characterizations of their responses to these places.

In the 1990s, which may well become viewed as the decade of the environment, the science of ecology and ecologists themselves claim the central focus of the movement in the popular mind. Increasingly, the world citizen of nature is expected to present us with an ecological account of the places, plants and animals encountered by her or him. Anything different is something less and a little naive; or, at most, it is a watered-down, popularized version of the rigorous and precise scientific accounts. Here ecology is thought to be the subversive science, subverting the attitudes and ways of life which are getting us into so much trouble with the environment. "Ecological consciousness" is heralded as just what

43

our time calls for. But will the environmentalist's reply to the danger to the Crazy Mountains be sufficient? We need to understand their arguments before we test them against the Crazies.

A Map

Many writers in environmental ethics have looked to ecology as a way of disclosing value in nature. If an ecological understanding of nature does reveal values inherent in nature, how much does it reveal? I present three views. Aldo Leopold in his theory of the *land ethic* and land aesthetic sees ecology as revealing new levels of depth and breadth to perception as well as showing us humans that we play a more humble role within a community whose members include the rest of nature. He believes that this last insight triggers moral respect for nature. Holmes Rolston III argues that ecology discloses facets of the natural world that, coinciding with their discovery, we see as valuable. From this discovery of value he develops an ethic of *environmental altruism*. Alternatively, one might think that ecology shows us what to do from a merely prudential point of view, while Mark Sagoff shows that this is too often not the case. Moreover, Sagoff finds that the science of ecology can go either way—toward further domination of nature or toward enhancing respect for nature. He argues that *ecologists as practitioners* play a decisive role for the direction ecology takes.

I am sympathetic to these approaches. Nevertheless, I find that these ecological approaches need to be supplemented by other ways of disclosing the importance of things. The testimony of ordinary citizens as well as works of literature, art and music—in a more basic way than ecology— show the ways nature and natural things engage us and orient us in the world. These two approaches, the scientific and the testimonial, can be integrated to achieve a more profound understanding.

Yet one may still wonder whether even these combined approaches will be sufficient to constrain our urge to transform the Earth in the first place. The answer developed here is no. No, not unless and until we understand technology, see its consequences for both the environment and our personal lives, and become emancipated from its framework as a way of life. Showing that this is the deeper problem and then constructing a theory to comprehend it will occupy us in the next two chapters.

That's the map. In chapters 3, 4, and 5, we will work with theory and argumentation to attain a rigor more characteristic of conventional philosophy.

The Land Ethic and Aesthetic

Philosophers in the early nineteenth century noticed in western history a progressive sequence of extending ethics to wider and wider communities. The story begins by humans having ethical regard solely for members of their own class or tribe. In the next phases, respect is extended to the entire human community and even beyond to any rational being. Following this trajectory, Aldo Leopold believes, in his essay "The Land Ethic," that the time has arrived in western civilization for an extension of ethics to natural things and nature itself or what he calls 'the land.' Holmes Rolston, currently the most comprehensive and sensible philosopher in this field, begins his *Environmental Ethics* by aligning himself with Leopold on this point: "The outcry for a life ethic, a land ethic has only begun."[3] Leopold and Rolston are optimistic about the development of a new respect for nature because they believe that the recent biological sciences enable us to find values in nature.

In the foreword to *A Sand County Almanac,* Leopold writes, "These wild things, I admit, had little human value . . . until science disclosed where they come from and how they live."[4] Later he tells us that we have no yardstick to measure this change in the mental eye, but that even experienced and proficient pioneers, such as Daniel Boone, saw only the surface of natural things compared to a contemporary ecologist. How then does science, for Leopold, disclose wild things as having more than a little human value?

According to J. Baird Callicott, Leopold sees that background conceptual knowledge builds depths into what would otherwise be merely shallowly perceived.[5] Biology, history, paleontology, and geology supply this background knowledge and inform what is perceived in the here and now. For example, in his sketch "Marshland Elegy," Leopold tells us that the first settlers in Wisconsin disparagingly called the sandhill cranes "red shikepokes" because of the rusty hue that often stains the crane's gray color. These same farmers saw the marshlands either as undevelopable wastelands or obstacles to be overcome for the development of a more productive agricultural industry. Neither cranes nor their habitat, the marshlands, had much human value in the eyes of those settlers. On the other hand, knowledge of evolution can deepen perception:

> Our appreciation of the crane grows with the slow unraveling of earthly history. His tribe, as we know, stems out of the remote Eocene. The other members of the fauna in which he originated are long since entombed within the hills. When we hear his call we hear no mere bird. We hear the trumpet in the orchestra of evolution. He is the symbol of our untamable

past, of that incredible sweep of millennia which underlies the daily affairs of birds and men.[6]

Similarly, just as evolution yields depth, *ecology* gives breadth to our perception of wild things. Wild things do not exist in isolation from one another. They are gathering points in a network of a myriad of processes. Thus, even if our appreciation of sandhill cranes grows out of our knowledge of their evolutionary history, still, having an understanding of ecology in addition to evolution, we cannot love cranes and hate marshes. We perceive the crane in its connection to the marsh.

An understanding of ecology supplies a host of independent reasons for loving marshes, for perceiving beauty in textures that were only God-forsaken wastes to the settlers. Plains, bogs, swamps, fallow fields, river bottoms and ponds all can be appreciated visually and in depth by one whose perception has been enriched by the sciences. By ennobling the commonplace, scientific knowledge enables us to find value in those wild things that may be entirely unattractive to the tourist.

In addition to this land aesthetic, Leopold provides support for a land ethic. Mere prudence is not enough. People must be moved to respect, admire and love the land. How does science disclose the land as worthy of such ethical regard? First, as we saw, Leopold puts this new disclosure of the value of wild things in the larger context of the story of western civilization. The key to humankind's expanding ethical regard requires the *perception* that people worldwide are united into one society, one community. "The land ethic simply enlarged the boundary of the community to include soils, waters, plants, and animals or collectively: the land."[7] The community concept was the central teaching of ecology in his time. So, ecological literacy, which enables us to read nature as a larger community of which we are plain members, will trigger this love, respect and admiration for the ecological community—a new environmental ethic.

It is clear, then, how new developments in science play a pivotal role in disclosing value. Aesthetically, the new sciences provides depth and breadth to our perception of wild things, and ethically, they show that we are all members of one biotic community. Both the members and the community itself warrant respect. Leopold is optimistic, therefore, about genuine progress being made toward better human attitudes and behavior in relation to the land.

Rolston's Environmental Ethics

In his comprehensive environmental ethic, Rolston follows-up Leopold's idea that ecology discloses the value of natural beings, but he does so in a more philosophically sophisticated and elaborate manner. For him, ecology and biology yield knowledge of what *is* and from that we come to acknowledge what *ought* to be.

> What is ethically puzzling, and exciting, in the marriage and mutual transformation of ecological description and evaluation is that here an *ought* is not so much *derived* from an *is* as discovered simultaneously with it. As we progress from descriptions of fauna and flora, of cycles and pyramids, of autotrophs coordinated with heterotrophs, of stability and dynamism, and move on to intricacy, to planetary opulence and interdependence, to unity and harmony with oppositions in counterpoint and synthesis, to organisms evolved within and satisfactorily fitting their communities, arriving at length with beauty and goodness, it is difficult to say when natural facts leave off and where natural values appear.[8]

Science, here especially biology and ecology, plays the important role of uncovering for us what is the case with regard to natural things and nature. In discovering for the first time what is the case, we come into contact with its importance. The importance of what is generates claims upon us which guide our understanding of what ought to be the case concerning our proper respect and conduct toward these things and processes.

With much rigor, Rolston develops altruistic duties toward all living organisms, endangered species, ecosystems and land forms. For instance, respecting ecosystems for the unique kinds of communities they are requires a scientific approach and disclosure which he spells out at length.

> Ecology discovers simultaneously (1) what is taking place in ecosystems and (2) what *biotic community* means as an organizational mode enveloping organisms. Crossing over from science to ethics, we can discover (3) the values in such a community system and (4) our duties toward it.[9]

We find we cannot love lions and hate jungles. We also discover integrity, projective creativity, life support, community and other values. And this discovery of values imposes a prima facie obligation upon us: "Humans ought to preserve so far as they can the richness of the biological community."[10] Without this scientific insight, none or at least not much of this value would be seen by us. Hence, Rolston and Leopold have good grounds for believing that a new form of respect, unavailable in the past, is opened to us and generated for us by a scientific disclosure of nature.

Disclosing the Importance of Things

Does a biological disclosure of the value of wild things, however new and different from traditional accounts, fully reveal the importance of these things? Perhaps the most telling shortcoming in this regard shows up when Rolston discusses beauty. Taking his cue from Leopold's principle that we ought to preserve the integrity, stability and beauty of the biotic community, Rolston tries to establish that the beauty of nature which ought to command our respect is biological beauty. The ecosystem regularly produces in us a sense of beauty (or sublimity) because of the regular occurrence of objective, biological properties within it.

> The experience of beauty that we seek is not a recreational finding of something one can frame in a snapshot (that might be only a projection from the eye of the beholder) but a locating of oneself in and reconciling with the forces of creation that are objectively there. One ought not to look at nature expecting pictures; one should thrill over projective nature, where Earthen nature is regularly splendid.[11]

In these biological properties, then, reside nature's aesthetic powers.

No doubt the beauty experienced in nature has much to do with its general, regular biological features. No doubt everyone can agree that ecological features are manifest everywhere in wilderness. By going there, anyone in any kind of receptive state can observe these properties. No doubt these properties are least likely to come from us. But notice the cost of making these patterns the standard for natural beauty. Biological harmony, diversity and unity can be found anywhere on our public lands. Mark an X on a map. Go there. Applying biology and ecology you will derive these insights from what you observe there. Anywhere and everywhere display this biological arrangement. Is this all that nature itself projects—something anyone, anywhere, anytime can realize so long as the person is capable of ecological insights? Isn't the aesthetic power of some places more powerful than others? If the aesthetic power is everywhere equal, what would ever cause us to focus, turn our heads, and linger or what would ever orient us in the wilderness?

By trying to sort out what comes from nature and what comes from humans in the experience of beauty in order to uncover what is valuable, "able to produce value," in nature, Rolston throws out the baby with the bathwater. That all too common beauty he finds is no longer *orienting beauty*, that kind of beauty which makes a place stand out.[12] Only that beauty which is orienting beauty is sufficient to animate us and keep us coming back. The beauty of wilderness comes home to us in particular places at particular times. It follows that beauty escapes or withstands trivialization when it comes to the fore in its particular and proper disclosive language, the language of engagement.

An especially vivid experience relevant to this point occurred when I was working on a trail crew in the Cascades a few years ago. The day came for us to finish a trail we had been building for a month. I'd grown fond of the place—it had a spectacular waterfall and I often ate my lunch beside it listening to its roar and enjoying the cool air. Each day we walked in three miles, crossing the creek along the way where we usually stopped for a break and filled our canteens. This last day as I stood on a rock in midstream watching the water swirl into my canteen I suddenly felt myself drawn into it, and it felt very right to be in this place watching the glistening water swirl, my hands holding the canteen, and my feet firmly fixed on the rock. When the canteen filled and I looked up, it seemed as if everything had been filled, including me. The waters in the creek seemed to be alive, to be laughing and dancing as they poured over the rocks. Banks, shrubs, green mosses and boulders emerged distinct and pure. The giant trees stood quietly and majestically.

The Ambiguity of Ecology

Does ecology teach us to respect nature and natural things? The ecological disclosure of the significance of natural things has a deeper problem than its inability, seen above, to reach a richer significance of things. One may have thought that we have overlooked here the true value of ecology. According to Mark Sagoff, one reason ecology has been called the subversive science is that it seems to tell us what to do and what not to do with the environment.[13] It seems to put such restrictive constraints on our exploitation of nature so as to call for fundamental changes. For instance, the hypothesis that salt marshes function as sources or sinks for nutrients essential to coastal fisheries served as a cornerstone for legislation protecting these salt marshes from further destruction. Thus, economic, prudential, and ecological reasons seemed to harmonize with one another to the end that we now conduct ourselves more respectfully toward these salt marshes. However, Sagoff goes on to show that such arguments—that prudence demands preservation—often do not work. In particular, the hypothesis concerning the relationship between the fisheries and salt marshes is now considered to be dubious.[14] Moreover, Sagoff shows that ecology can actually be used to help understand how ecosystems can be manipulated to serve human purposes. Ecology may help us to understand, for example, how to produce more commercial fish in Chesapeake Bay, which now may be seen as an aquaculture reserve.[15] Thus, Sagoff finds that ecology as a science is highly ambiguous. He thinks he finds two sciences of ecology.

The first provides a scientific framework in which we may manage ecosystems to maximize the goods and services we may derive from them. The second provides a scientific framework in which society can appreciate the qualities of those systems and evaluate policies concerning them.[16]

The first gives us power over nature; the second enhances our respect for nature.

Unlike the path we will pursue later, Sagoff's perspective *looks to* and *not outside of* the science of ecology for reasons why it presents these two understandings of nature. He concludes that the differences in goals—whether utilitarian or preservationist—makes us prefer one framework to the other. Nevertheless, science and scientists themselves have much to do with those goals. For example, he finds the scientists and writers, John and Mildred Teal, in *Life and Death of the Salt Marsh*, "beautifully describe and explain the life cycle of salt marshes and the species that inhabit them; they make it clear that a self-respecting political community should go out of its way to protect such environments."[17] In this way ecology and ecologist can both generate concern and respect for these marshes and show us what it takes to protect them.

No doubt Sagoff is correct on a certain level, but from a philosophical standpoint this matter requires more thought. Sagoff's first insight into ecology, that it fails to direct us toward preservation for prudent reasons, is sound. Ecology is not likely to show that it is more prudent to protect the Crazy Mountains than to have a few timber sales, mines and oil wells. However, he is mistaken in thinking there are two sciences of ecology. It is correct to think that the goals of the so-called different sciences of ecology are different; it is mistaken to think that the different goals are given to us by the science of ecology itself.

Sagoff's confusion here arises from his failure to clarify the ambiguities of the meaning of science generally. Science can be used in three different senses: (1) science as a human activity, (2) science as a body of well-established theories and laws, (3) science as application.[18] The second sense—the only division that can claim to be pure science—is shared by both of Sagoff's sciences of ecology. With regard to the other two senses, the human activity of the scientists may either be in the field or in front of a computer screen, and their respective interests and applications of the laws of ecology, the second sense, may be very different.[19] Moreover, these two senses, science as a human activity and science as application, are very value-laden activities. The directives which issue from and into them are not given by the theories and laws alone, that is, science in the second and central sense. The laws alone do not tell us where to apply them, for instance. Because Sagoff mixes up these three senses, he is misled to think there are two sciences and a scientist is a kind of supercitizen who is able speak for us about the importance of things.

A better way to think about this is that the one science of ecology can be applied in very different ways, depending on what directives it receives from outside itself. As we have seen in a preliminary way, the guiding vision of technology directs our culture to dominate nature; this vision or framework of technology explains why we expect to use the science of ecology to turn Chesapeake Bay into an aquacultural reserve. Scientific insight as foreseen by early scientists and others would be used by technology in order to dominate, not respect, nature. Here ecology is not subversive to the technological vision of nature. To the contrary, it fits neatly within it. What people feel admiration and wonder for today, the delicate blue-green globe image of Earth from outer space, may give way tomorrow to a higher tide of wanting to control the system for their own ends, a spaceship for their purposes. So, too, ecology can be and is used to rearrange a wildlife refuge for duck production.

In terms of the vision of technology, nearly everything today is seen as a resource. These resources challenge us to set upon them and exploit them. Natural beings, ecosystems, and even species are mined in this way. It follows that the science of ecology is no exception, and so our prevailing culture asks: How can we exploit the insights of ecology? For the most part, the culture of technology knows no respect for things in their own right. This technological approach and vision must be countered in a deeper way by learning what it means, both in significance and manner, to respect things and to take up with them in another way.

So, scientific insight *alone* is not sufficient to generate the kind of respect Leopold and Rolston ultimately want for the preservation of nonhuman beings and natural systems. Granted that people want to respect nature in the first place, then science can provide insight into what form respectful concern should take. It may teach them what to do if they want to respect nature. However, the desire to respect nature is just what is in question. Where, then, does this other outside directive come from which uses ecology to enhance our respect for nature? To answer this question requires a closer look at the work of the Teals on salt marshes.

The Hidden Supplement of Respectful Ecology

No doubt field ecologists do generate respect for life forms and their interconnections. What we study long enough has a way of getting under our skin. When sharing their information and stories, they are sharing something of interest. Given the universe in its entire extent, comparatively little of it engages us lastingly, if at all. Science as a human activity is involving, engaging.

In Teals' account of the salt marsh, science is used to help explain salt marshes, but an appeal to science alone explains neither the importance of the salt marsh nor Teals' use of science.[20] Given the emphasis on laws of science that are universal, the Teals could have randomly selected an X and attempted to explain it. They could have explained salt marshes in general and no marsh in particular. Had they done so, however, the significance of salt marshes would have constrained the application of the general ecological laws; we are not just talking about any X in the universe, since ecology and specifically salt marsh ecology tell us in what direction to look. The Teals, however, went beyond this general level. They selected a particular salt marsh. The laws of ecology did not tell them which to select; nor did they randomly select it. They selected one they were familiar with and which exemplified not just the neutral formation and transformation of an area, but the "birth," "growth," and the human caused "decline and death" of a salt marsh in New England.[21]

Again, the context within which the Teals elected to speak about salt marshes makes a difference. In their book, they do not merely discuss the marsh ecology at its height and then show the decline and death in the past 350 years. Nor do they go back to the formation of the universe. Rather their discussion begins with the last glacial period, showing how little by little the marshes grew and how comparatively vast a time was necessary for their full establishment. They then show how the changes that occurred in the fifteen years after WWII, changes which brought about its drastic decline and finally death, occurred within the blink of an eye from this perspective. None of this discussion is guided by science itself.

In addition to the geological context, which makes changes in our time seem comparatively rapid, the revelation of the ecological context of the marshes' life shows a complexity and delicate integration of life forms to a depth not penetrable by eyes uninformed by science. Here is Leopold's scientifically disclosed drama which lets us in on the value of wild things. Against these geological and ecological contexts which the Teals uncover for us, the changes that humans have caused from seemingly minor actions are sufficient to make one pause and become hesitant about making any kind of changes. That is, against this account of fragile and irreplaceable network of life forms, human action, especially recently, seems rapid, myopic, overpowering, crude, and devastating. In the end, the salt marsh served as a landfill for garbage upon which an industrial park was latter built.[22]

In ecological terms, the changes in the marsh occur in many species and in many relationships, not all of which are equally noteworthy. In fact, many of these changes are too complex even to understand. The natural but not science-guided response to this problem is to let powerfully disclosive things be highlighted and bear the torch for the others. These are the most noticeable and significant creatures as well. Not many like to think of the grizzly bears of Yellowstone dying out. The account of the Teals focuses on the disappearance of the last bald eagle from the salt marsh.

The Teals also use physics and chemistry to explain certain things, but the laws themselves do not tell us where to apply them. One example: when differing concentrations of salt and water solutions are brought together, water moves from the less to the more concentrated solution. This law becomes significant when plants are exposed to salt water: water moves out of the cell walls by osmosis to seawater with its higher concentrations of salt. This loss of water dehydrates and kills the cell. In this context, the Teals account of how the tall salt grass "Spartina survives in this hostile atmosphere of the salt marsh . . . is a success story of the most complicated nature."[23] Here the laws of physics, chemistry, and biology are employed selectively to tell the story of these tall, unique, and particularly heroic plants which beckon the attention of those visiting a marsh.

Although the application of the sciences of geology, ecology, botany, chemistry, and physics has much to do with the success of Teals' account, the account is not dominated by them. To the contrary, sight, the most basic mode of scientific observation, is almost absent in the way they present the salt marsh to us in the introduction.

> The undisturbed salt marshes offer the inland visitors a series of unusual perceptions. At low tide, the wind blowing across Spartina grass sounds like wind on the prairie. When the tide is in, the gentle music of moving water is added to the prairie rustle. There are sounds of birds living in marshes . . . These are clean, fresh smells, smells that are pleasing to one who lives by the sea but strange and not altogether pleasant to one who has always lived inland . . . As sound and smell of the salt marsh are its own so is its feel. Some of the marsh can be walked on . . . At low tide the salt marsh is a vast field of grasses with slightly higher grasses sticking up along the creeks and uniformly tall grasses everywhere. The effect is like that of a great flat meadow.[24]

This passage is disclosive discourse. Through it we are asked to attend to different modes of encountering the marsh. We are made to do so, not by instructions, but by the different things that stand out to the senses and call for fitting modes of encounter. The place in its many dimensions is invoked and, in turn, evokes the fullness of the observer's body. A language of *engagement* invites us to be fully present in the place. The simile of the prairie grass reminds those not familiar with salt marshes of similar experiences; e.g., a farmer watching sparkling irrigating water flood a field can grasp the setting. Simultaneously, we realize its uniqueness.

An experienced eye will notice that Teals' writing does not, for the most part, *impose* science and a scientific context on the marsh to make it look attractive.[25] Theirs is a sensitive and concerned writing which is prompted by the various powers of marshes that stirred and awakened them. The Teals are always and already in a world oriented by things. These things dawn in an earlier, more primordial light than scientific insight yields. Disclosive discourse shows wild things and nature in this primordial light.[26] What supplements and guides ecology in making Teals' account attractive, then, is the language of engagement and the engaging salt marsh which reach us through that medium.

Pluralistic Accounts of Nature

Ecology is never pure but always constrained and applied physics, chemistry, geology, botany and so on. However, it is never, as such, constrained *enough* until and unless engagement orients and focuses it. So, having distinguished and liberated the language of engagement from science in the central and cogent sense of a body of laws and theories (the ambiguous science of ecology), we are now free to think of these respectful scientists, not as supercitizens, but as individuals who are involved with things, e.g., the Teals with salt marshes or Leopold with a farm in Sand County. Analogous to an explanation of how a building hangs together, the Teals' account is best characterized as the language of engagement, informed by science, which explains the importance of salt marshes and threats to them. This discourse leaves us free, then, to consider, in addition to scientists, other people who are also engaged with things and who have articulated the importance of things much more forcefully. These nonscientists employ unique forms of discourse that do not rely as often on a scientific understanding of natural things.

Thoreau's *Walden* provides a model for writing that discloses the manifold ways a natural thing, Walden Pond, can be realized by us. *Walden* contains biological, ecological, and other scientific elements. Yet these aspects, it seems to me, play a comparatively minor role in the work as a whole. Thoreau spends much more time showing how the natural elements of Walden can be realized in human experience. There are many ways to take in Walden's color, for instance, just as there are an indefinite number of ways to interact with its water. These, in turn, may not hold our attention if we did not also see that the materiality of Walden is constantly far more suggestive than merely, flat-footedly looking at it. To the contrary, simple living with simple things sponsors high thinking. Walden Pond is rich enough, in fact, to evoke from Thoreau an epic of world culture. It is, indeed, a deep capacious spring!

Moving further from a directly scientific account, William Faulkner in "The Old People" shows us, through the teachings of the Chickasaw chief Sam Fathers, what an event such as Isaac McCaslin's shooting of his first deer can amount to in the life of a boy about to become a man. In their modern, hurried, restless, ravaging, consumptive ways people miss the importance of things and events which should bring them to a pause and mean something to their existence. Native peoples were and are sensitive to these ways of realizing natural things and events, and so is Faulkner.

In his essay "On Top," Leopold writes, "if anyone had ever been here before, he must of necessity have sung a song or written a poem."[27] Though Leopold himself does not present us with these songs and poems, others do compose them. Wild places sponsor songs and poetry. These ways of realizing a wild place are as dependent on the material arrangement of the natural conditions as wild life and wild plants are. Mining and clearcutting destroy this capacity of these places to sponsor songs just as much as they destroy habitat.

In other words, there are many ways of realizing the importance of natural things. A scientific account brought to bear on the way things engage us, as the Teals' account does, is unique to our age and certainly significant. Much can be learned from Leopold, John Muir and Gary Snyder all of whom use disclosive discourse involving ecology. Many other ways for natural things to engage us exist as well. Thoreau, Gretel Ehrlich, Linda Hogan and Leslie Marmon Silko at times make minimal use of ecology. Being enthusiastic, or at least sympathetic and tolerant, about these possibilities will generate a pluralistic approach to uncovering the importance of natural things. A cellist's place-songs are telling us something as important about the special character of a place as a biologist's discovery of a rare plant species in that place. The cellist shows what is there, what it has to do with us and what we have to do with it.

The Inconsequential Character of Environmental Ethics

In addition to the story of a maturing human consciousness and conscience, Holmes Rolston notices another factor which makes developing an environmental ethic even more urgent. Our increasing technical competence has given our culture enormous and overwhelming power. "Power without ethics is profane and destructive in any community . . . Few as yet have seen how the escalating human use of the world, unchecked by any ethics, prevents us from appreciating values on Earth where we reside."[28] Thus, Rolston in his book attempts to provide an ethic for this Earth to constrain the heedless exercise of this unprecedented power. Since Rolston and Leopold see that what is needed by our time is the development of new and different ethical constraints, both understand the conflict between humans and the environment to be fundamentally an ethical problem. Is it chiefly so? We have seen that a plurality of approaches and disclosures of the natural world and natural things can bring people into contact with the importance of these natural things once again and in fresh ways. Most of us in our culture have lost touch or, at least, are not in touch with these things. Yet this loss of contact with the importance of natural things is only half of the problem.

What exactly is the problem that these disclosive accounts of nature are trying to resolve? Is the problem that people look upon nature as a mere value-neutral stuff to be manipulated? *If* that were the entire problem and not just half the problem, then accounts which disclose how valuable nature is should be able to meet this problem. In fact, sometimes they do. However, I believe it strikes the ear of most people as insensitive when a developer regards undeveloped natural places in his project area as "sterile zones," that is, as mere resources that are of no use. Granted that they commonly do not see nature as valuable as it is (and disclosing that importance is certainly the task of nature writing), still another issue needs to be brought into focus. Many of the same people who would find the developer's remarks insensitive still *side* with the development of land, saying, "It's sad, but that's progress." They think, in other words, that they are choosing something more valuable than undeveloped nature, even if they regard that nature to some degree important. To counter this perception, not only does the importance of these natural things require disclosure, but also, alongside these accounts, the alternative they are choosing needs to be brought into relief and examined.

Rolston, for example, shows that humans and other life forms sometimes must cause pain in order to live, but he argues that giving pain should never be pointless.[29] "Instrumental pain has contributory reference to further goods; intrinsic pain has no such reference. Intrinsic pain is a bad thing, absolutely."[30] What does pointless mean here? It can mean pointless destruction in a traditional sense as with killing for mere sport. Quoting from Joseph Wood Krutch,

> Killing 'for sport' is the perfect type of that pure evil for which metaphysicians sometimes have sought. Most wicked deeds are done because the doer proposes some good to himself. The liar lies to gain some end. . . .

The killer for sport has no such comprehensible motive. He prefers death to life, darkness to light.[31]

Moral constraints against this kind of purely destructive pointlessness are common in many cultures. The kind of pointlessness that Rolston has most in mind, however, is of a different sort.

> As these uses of animals pass from essential through the serious into the merely desirable and finally to the trivial, the ecological pattern rapidly fades, and the justification collapses. The use of fur for survival—a jacket on a frontiersman—is much closer to the natural, and the suffering is justified thereby. The use of fur for status—a jaguar coat on an actress— is highly artificial. Status is a cultural artifact, as is the status symbol. The suffering traded for it is not justified by any naturalistic principle . . . Shoes for bare feet are one thing; anaconda cowboy boots worn to a pro football game in Texas are another.[32]

For Rolston, vanities are a far cry from basic necessities. This, it seems, is how he measures them as pointless.

Many of us in our more considered moments may agree with him, but what gets covered over in this way of putting it is the attractive hold that those commodities and the conspicuous consumption of them as a way of life have upon us as a culture. In their unreflective pursuit of these commodities, most people do not see them as genuinely pointless, especially to the degree Rolston rightly does. Rather, most see them as promising not just living, but living well. This means that the *point* most people see to consumption is prosperity. The status procured by these symbols is a measure of affluence—of who can possess and consume the most, of who has the best life. What Rolston calls vain many call the good life.

Rendering the pointlessness of this pursuit intelligible requires far more examination than Rolston gives it. If nearly everyone really saw conspicuous consumption as vain, then they would not pursue it in the first place regardless of what it does to the animals, although an altruistic regard for anacondas does give an additional reason not to pursue consumption. That is to say, what people are choosing positively is a more basic problem than the vision of nature that results from that choice. If people did not regard technological progress as better, then the transformation of nature would lose its grounding. What is the payoff of the industrial park, for instance, that destroyed the salt marsh? In one way or another, it had to do with commodity production. For a similar reason, the Earth has been transformed nearly everywhere in an unprecedented way in the last century and a half. Nor is the problem caused only by scale, the fact that our culture can exercise so much more muscle in our dealings with nature, although that is doubtlessly correct. The radical transformation of the Earth in the technological age has taken place in one way and not others only because people could generally agree with what they are building, with the overall project and its goal. If we do not examine philosophically the standards that define technological progress as progress, then we do not address the fundamental issue of what sets our culture against the Earth and so many of its nonhuman inhabitants.

So, from the standpoint of environmental ethics, it may seem that we have come far by showing that these animals count, and nature in general counts. Given the choice between something that counts and what is vain and pointless, the correct ethical choice should not only be obvious but easy. However, the choice is far more of a dilemma than this characterization of it. Most of people are pulled by culture *and* by the environment. Bringing this point home to wilderness, Rolston, for a variety of good ethical reasons, argues that since merely two percent of the contiguous U.S. remains wilderness while ninety-eight percent has been developed, no more wild land ought to be lost.[33] When it comes to talk of compromise, wild land has already suffered too much compromise. "One should remember the score—*humans 98; wilderness 2* . . . and set an ethic in that context."[34]

As reasonable as this position sounds, it should be juxtaposed to the current debate over the Montana Wilderness bill. Of the nine million acres of unprotected de facto wilderness on public lands in Montana, 6.9 million of these are on Forest Service land.[35] In 1994, each member of the Montana Delegation introduced a wilderness bill regarding this roadless Forest Service land. Democratic Representative Pat Williams' bill (the only one to protect the Crazies) would protect the most wilderness at meager 1.7 million acres. Democratic Senator Max Baucus would protect less, only 1.2 million acres. Republican Senator Conrad Burns, in a bill he admits industry wrote, would protect a mere 778,000 acres of the 6.9 million remaining facto wilderness and actually encourage, in the "Multiple Use Recovery Areas" of his bill, industrial development of more than five million acres this land, including the Crazies. If the Baucus bill—touted as a compromise—passed, it would release more than four million acres of wildland for management by the Forest Service (which is bias toward development). Over ninety-eight percent of the suitable timber base lies outside Baucus's proposed boundaries. People persuaded of Rolston's reasonable position are labeled extremist and dismissed.[36]

So the *character of human happiness* in a technological society needs to be examined and evaluated. "Sure nature counts; but what we want counts even more." It just may be that people have not given sufficient thought to the quality of their lives. Perhaps happiness understood as consumption is misleading and does not carry enough weight to outweigh the harm consumption inflicts upon natural things and nature. If our culture can come to understand freedom and happiness differently than is now assumed, the most significant gains can be made regarding our manipulation of and harm to the natural world, for then respecting natural things will no longer be or be conceived to be at a sacrifice to our well-being, at least for the most part.[37]

Having It Both Ways: The Standard Counter of Environmentalists

Returning now to the Crazy Mountains, we see that the usual attempt to resolve the conflict between wild nature and technological culture is to dissolve it. Politically, the Montana Congressional delegation has laid down the terms that any new legal wilderness must not cost jobs. And considering our general implicit assent to the culture of technology, the most popular wilderness position would be to find a way to have jobs, a rising standard of living, and wilderness, too. Thus, although conservationists may not agree with it, they have learned to construct arguments which speak to that basic cultural condition. Generally, the counters they present to the Forest Service's plans agree with its objectives and show how these objectives can be better met in other ways.

Environmentalists point out that the timber industry is generally on the skids in Montana: Production is up but employment is down because of new, more efficient, mechanization in the industry. The industry is cutting the private lands much faster than those lands can sustain yields of raw material over the long term. For instance, the Gallatin Forest has supplied to area mills an annual average of fifteen million boardfeet of timber over the past twenty years, but mill capacity (claimed to be need) of just the area's two largest mills alone exceeds eighty-five million boardfeet. Thus, the Forest has supplied less than one-sixth of what the mills claim they need. It is impossible for the Gallatin Forest and the state and private timber lands to approach meeting even a small fraction of the present needs of the area mills on a sustained-yield basis. Moreover, the Gallatin has been rampantly overcutting during the past four decades, argue organizations such as the Greater Yellowstone Coalition. So, environmentalists claim, a crisis is inevitable, either now or when the forest has nothing left to supply.[38]

In past years, environmentalists followed this up by maintaining that only 6.25 percent of the timber base is included within their wilderness proposal.[39] Such an amount, such a small area of conflict between timber and wilderness interest, either would not affect a mill or if a mill is "that close," then leaving the suitable timber out of the proposal will not keep the mill in business long anyway. For example, they show that leaving areas, such as Cottonwood Canyon, out of their wilderness proposal would last the mill merely a month or two or even a week in some cases. Why is it, they ask rhetorically, economically or otherwise sound to destroy a place such as Cowboy's Heaven in the Spanish Peaks range to supply two months work at the mill?[40]

The void created by this negative argument against the timber industry is filled by discussing the positive economic worth of wilderness. The $25 million below-cost timber program in Montana is mostly spent on building roads in roadless or wild lands; some argue that this subsidy is simply and straightforwardly bad for the American economy and ought to be cut.[41] Others think that at least it's imaginable that the money or even a portion of it could be spent in better alternative ways to stabilize the economy and make it compatible with the wild land.[42] Most argue that the timber industry is highly unstable, that attempting to cultivate timber in southwestern Montana's lodgepole pine forest is analogous to trying to raise tomatoes commercially in the surrounding mountain valleys, and that the vast majority of the jobs related to the Gallatin Forest, some ninety-three percent, are recreational and not wood products in nature.[43] Moreover, some of the recreational jobs, such as guiding businesses, will be lost as a result of logging. They argue that wilderness and its associated amenities are thought to be an area mostly unexploited for getting business's tourists into Montana.[44] Finally, recent studies show that rural counties near wilderness areas are increasing in population either more rapidly than other rural counties or increasing when the others have been declining.[45] The newcomers are mostly young and well-educated, and that, environmentalists argue, should give Chambers of Commerce pause.

Such is the drift of the various arguments of the environmentalists.[46] They all go to show that the wild land is *not needed* as a source of wood fiber for the health of the consumer society. Wildland may even be beneficial for the economy. Considering the area's proximity to Yellowstone Park, the world famous Yellowstone river as a trout stream, the number of forest related recreational businesses, and the fact that companies such as Patagonia are willing to locate in Bozeman for the quality of life, environmentalists probably have the soundest long-term economic picture, although their vision is hardly an exciting one to a community which routinely hears threats of closure of a mill employing 120 workers.[47]

So, it may turn out that the Crazy Mountains, preserved as wilderness, may actually benefit the economy in the long-run. I can only guess. But what if the Crazies are preserved for that reason? Of course such preservation will meet some of our concerns, but will it meet our deeper ones? At bottom, is this the real or best reason we have for protecting the Crazies? Can protection of all Montana's or America's wild lands be defended cogently in these terms?[48] What shape would the Earth itself take on were we to justify most of what we do in terms of this economic rationale? To nod in agreement with the technological project is to agree to the continuation of an unprecedented global transformation of nature. For most of those who sense that wild things and places are already as good as they can be just as they are, to want this radical change to continue and to want to keep nature wild is a contradiction in more than appearance only.

CHAPTER 4

THE OTHER STORY

The bird would cease and be as other birds
But that he knows in singing not to sing.
The question that he frames in all but words
Is what to make of a diminished thing.

—Robert Frost, *The Oven Bird*[1]

No ideas but in things.

—William Carlos Williams[2]

In "The Land Ethic," Aldo Leopold suggests that he is presenting a seminar which articulates for the first time an ethic already felt and beginning to be practiced in the culture at large.[3] Surely it is true that biology and ecology *can* open up nature for our care and respect in ways which would be impossible without the assistance of these sciences. Accordingly, Holmes Rolston, too, collects evidence of a shift, what might be called a postmodern shift, in attitudes and perspectives. There are reasons to feel encouraged here and reasons to encourage such a change of thinking.[4] Still, it is more likely that the better aspirations of this ethic will fail.[5] The more prevailing story of western civilization is not one of moral progression with regard to nature and natural things, but one of decline. Domination, heedlessness and shallowness are the marks of our culture's approach to the natural world. Nature is merely a resource. Yet it was not always this way in western civilization, nor in other cultures.

One day as I was working on the trail crew building the Falls Creek Trail in the Cascade Range, the supervisor paid us a visit. I spoke of the awe I felt for those ancient Douglas Firs and Cedars. He seemed to agree, then added, "But I hate to see them go to waste." Seeing five-hundred-year-old trees in terms of board feet alone is to take a silencing and shallow view of things. Yet the supervisor's remark embodies an appeal, an ethical appeal. People *ought not* to leave these trees alone; they *ought* to use them. They ought to use them to build. Our culture ought to use them for production and consumption. The ethic at work here counters an environmental ethic. Technology competes with nature. So we need to see through this ethic, its shallow conception of things, and its vision—before we can become released from it. If we do not dig to the root of the matter, we will merely repeat one or another variant of this same story of decline. An environmental ethic will move us beyond a superficial view of things, but because it takes its bearings in mere opposition to the exploitive view, it cannot render an account of things in their full depth.

Observations of Decline: Heedlessness

Many in the nineteenth century saw historical time as progressive while others, at the margins, suspected that the story of progress was less true than the optimists thought or that it was an unfinished story that could go either way. Henry David Thoreau belongs to this latter group. If human beings learn to live deliberately, Thoreau holds out much hope for the future, but he is highly critical of his present and finds it unequal to the past. He finds that in earlier periods a world of considerations went into working with nature and living on the land, translating Cato, "When you think of getting a farm turn it thus in your mind, not to buy greedily; nor spare your pains to look at it, and do not think it enough to go around it once. The oftener you go there the more it will please you, if it is good."[6] As a guide to his criticism of farming practices in his day, Thoreau notes that in the past agricultural holy days suggest the celebration of husbandry as a sacred calling. Although his point may not be universally true of pretechnology, it was more than occasionally true that the pretechnological farmer was interested in the prosperity of an entire way of life and not in maximizing merely one aspect of it. To the contrary, the context of consideration out of which the farmer moved and to which he gave deliberation in planting, harvesting and sacrificing gave a shape to the land, crops, and inhabitants which seemed as richly determined as the natural formations themselves. As a steward of the land, "This broad field which I have looked at so long looks not to me as the principle cultivator, but away from me to influences more genial to it, which water and make it green."[7] By taking account of so many natural determinants, this kind of agriculture did not superimpose a structure upon the landscape, but merged with and emerged out of nature. A hiddenness of nature is thereby brought forth and disclosed by the farmer.

Meanwhile, "husbandry is degraded with us" and "the landscape is deformed."[8] Thoreau sees farmers pursuing their vocation with a kind of what I will call *heedless thinking* that narrows the object of husbandry to large farms, large crops, and monetary profit. Agriculture has become here a mere means to some other and more important end. In the narrow light of this one-dimensional thinking, many of the tasks undertaken by husbandry, such as raising grain partly for the birds, look irrational—unprofitable ways of filling one's time. Thoreau writes, "He knows nature but as a robber." Of a certain farmer he writes, "He regarded even the wild ducks that settled in (his lake) as trespassers."[9] Therefore, in contrast to the contextual thinking of traditional husbandry, heedless thinking is shallow, narrow and flattened.

Wendell Berry, in *The Unsettling of America*, has substantiated and developed this idea.[10] He finds that Americans have generally exploited the land, and in particular agribusiness has unsettled America with its heedless thinking narrowed to making a profit from the land rather than farming as nurturing a way of life. Apart from the ensuing environmental and social problems, the unsettling, Berry shows, is one people have done to themselves as well. Domination has been at the expense of the cultivation of rich relationships to the land and to each other. Destruction of the land is simultaneously self-destruction.

Heedlessness is not difficult to achieve in our culture. It comes to people very 'naturally.' In fact, it informs the way they see: trees are sawtimber, rock is ore, meadows are range for livestock, the river is a power source, the hills promise oil and gas, and the high plains roll over coalfields. So a heedless, shallow seeing is connected with heedless thinking.

We share a basic framework of understanding in our culture from which we interpret and take up the world. Martin Heidegger has characterized this framework as one in which we see everything as resources charged with a challenge to bring them under control.[11] Heedlessly, we see only the raw material of things. These things seem to challenge us in an unusual way, to "set upon" them to get them under control; in turn, we challenge them to produce. It seems only natural for us to be involved in a systematic collective effort to bring everything under control. Naming a space shuttle "The Challenger" resonates well with this framework of understanding, and the shuttle's destruction brings the framework into relief.

To treat the land as a mere resource is, of course, to constrict and impoverish the land. Even further, to treat the land as resource is to treat it as something less than raw material, for raw material, traditionally, was something to be struggled with at least as an object. As resource, people today do not struggle with and against the land as artisans or peasant farmers; they overpower it with more and more powerful machinery and techniques of control. The material advent of modern technology, signaled by the invention of the steam engine, yielded a kind of *heedless power* over nature. No longer did humans have to wait upon wind and water, day and night, summer and winter, for the machinery runs regardless of these. As resource, nature no longer stands against them even as an object (German *Gegenstand:* literally, something that stands against). People's relationship to nature has changed from where they must rise to the occasion to be a match for it to a relationship where it is always already at their command. Hence, the land no longer demands them to consider it in its own right as something for which people need skills, attention and other virtues in order to be equal to it. Loggers do not doubt that they have the technology to bring the forest of Cottonwood Canyon to the mill. Because of the controlling power of technology, resources do not call for any other consideration than this heedless one. To be a resource is to be mere raw material ready to be commanded.

Clearly here our age may not be on the threshold of a higher plane of extending respect to the land. The dominant story is one of decline of respect for nature and, finally, the entire loss of respect when thinking becomes merely heedless. These insights into exploitation and heedlessness toward nature are evidence that in the modern period our basic framework assumptions have become so entrenched that they are concealed, unquestioned and unquestionable. So the framework reigns as common sense. When I worked a summer job in Oregon doing timber "stand exams" for the Forest Service in its silviculture division, I was not ultimately involved in a task of helping this country to understand its forest better, although the experience had that effect on me. The information was supposed to be used for improved control over timber production. Why else would we spend money?

Given that we want to get everything under control, it follows that *everything* is not limited to nature. In fact, the commonplace thought that people just need to get technology under control springs from the same source, and, when seen in this light, shows up as self-contradictory. The reform called for in the following pages will not follow this pattern. Importantly, "everything" applies to cultural things, too. Rainer Marie Rilke is horrified by this heedless approach to cultural things—artifacts and the built environment. America, for him, forecasts the change of weather. He finds,

> . . . the ever swifter vanishing of so much that is visible, whose place will not be supplied. Even for our grandparents a 'House', a 'Well', a familiar tower, their very dress, their cloak was infinitely more, infinitely more intimate: almost everything a vessel in which they found and stored humanity. Now there come crowding over from America empty indifferent

things, pseudo-things, *dummy-life* . . . A house in the American understanding, and American apple or vine, has *nothing* in common with the
house, fruit, the grape into which the hope and meditation of our fore-
fathers had entered . . . The animated, experienced things that *share our
lives* are coming to an end and cannot be replaced. *We are perhaps the
last to have still known such things.*[12]

Influenced by Rilke and other German poets, Heidegger, too, is even
more concerned about cultural things than about natural ones. "The hydroelectric plant is not built into the Rhine as was the old wooden bridge
that joined bank with bank for hundreds of years."[13] In "Building Dwelling
Thinking" he shows how the bridge as thing allows the landscape, stream
and beings to come forth. The bridge is the locus of what he calls the
fourfold of Earth, sky, mortals and divinities. It "brings stream and bank
and land into each other's neighborhood. The bridge gathers the Earth as
landscape around the stream."[14] In its source and rhythms, the stream
itself ties together the sky and Earth, and so too the bridge brings the
stream into a renewed relation with the sky and is "ready for the sky's
weather and its fickle nature."[15] The bridge provides mortals passage, joins
communities, and is a reminder of the last bridge one must cross. The
medieval bridge bears divinity in the figure of the saint to which it is
dedicated. By carefully taking into account each of these four regions—
Earth, sky, mortals and divinities—the thing joins harmoniously the fourfold of a unified world. Stepping into a different tradition, we may think of
how bridges in China bring into relief in streams and their surroundings
the Taoist cosmology of nature.

Now the Interstate highway system bridge often passes by streams
without even naming them. Its bridges are more on the order of over-
passes. From the Yellowstone to the Bitterroot, streams around Montana
are eyed for the tourist and real estate dollars they will bring into the state.
These dollars, in turn, will enable people to buy other "goods." In the next
chapter, we will sharpen our idea of the cultural framework indicated here.
The full story and big picture of this reduction is one of resources, and
machinery and commodities.

Correlational Coexistence

Where do Thoreau, Berry, Heidegger, and Rilke get their bearings?
What provides them with the standards against which they measure as
heedless this approach to nature and to cultural things? Ultimately, they
take their bearings from things, and in this work, too, things provide us

with our standards and guidance. Things gather and present a world, and they engage us in manifold ways. Our very being is tied to things in a relationship I call correlational coexistence.

For example, work with stock animals, things in the sense I use the word, can generate correlational coexistence. I think of a particular man, Keith Neal, who I worked with on trail crew in Yellowstone when just out of high school. From his voice to the way his hands spoke, Keith had a rapport with horses and mules such as I had never seen. He communicated, corresponded completely with the animals. Through him, I saw their character in a much different light. Indeed, they often acted almost magically in his presence. A horse rolling back its eyes in fright could be calmed immediately when he took the lead rope. Through them, I saw his childhood and youth on a Nebraska ranch, saw how his character and virtues—his evenness—had been molded to agree with his vocation, and saw through his handling of them his direct love for horses and hitches.

To get clear about just what things are and how they enlighten us will take us to the end—here we will begin by focusing on the thing's part in correlational coexistence. Heidegger has attempted to provide us with a language for articulating the thinglyness of things, so we will turn first to his work. Taking his cue from the etymological sense of the word "thing," he finds that things *gather*.[16] They gather the fourfold of Earth, sky, divinities, and mortals. Accounting for each of these four regions in manifold ways, the thing joins the fourfold into a unified world. Considering the thing, we, thus, can understand its world. In fact, more strongly, things keep us mindful of the fourfold, and so the very intelligibility of the world is stored in things. And so it is that things locate the character of thoughtful authentic human dwelling.

Developing this fourfoldness of things in a less metaphorical manner, Albert Borgmann suggests that things, especially centering things, are deep in that "nearly every discernible property is significant and an essential tie to the world of the thing."[17] No wonder, then, I was taken back to my basic premises, to a basic conflict of visions, when the ancient trees of Falls Creek were superficially conceived in terms of their volume of raw material alone. This supervisor's view considers only one aspect of the entire thing to be important. Similarly, white hunters killed many of the bison for their tongues alone. To the Plains Indians, who were taken aback by such waste, the bison was a powerful focal thing. Joseph Epes Brown said he began to count the material uses the Indians made of the bison and quit when he had listed over three hundred.[18] These uses, of course, are ones aside from the ways the bison shows up in mythology, symbols, and the background experience of the tribe. When a bison is painted around a lodge, for instance, those entering the lodge are entering the bison and, thereby, "entering the cosmos" according to Brown.[19] A careful examination of most Plains Indian artifacts will show them to be webbed to their world in similar manifold ways, often displaying the seven directions sacred to them, east, south, west, north, sky, Earth and center.

Things, allowed their fullness, take into account a world of considerations. Means and ends are interwoven in them, and so too are nature and culture, shared and personal experience. This world of considerations I call the *considerability of things*.

So seen, the depth of things correlates to the complexity of the world. *Things are rich in their capacity to reciprocate each and every tie to the world.* To try to sort out what is "in the thing" and what is "from the culture," for instance, is to mistake this correspondence between the thing and its world. Rather, things must be equal to that world in order to bear that world. To take away any of these relations, as projected by humans, for instance, is to put into the dark some of the depth of the thing. Hence, it is to impoverish it and not to let it be.

Human beings and things are correlated in correlational coexistence. Because of the equality of the two sides of this relationship and so the seeming sufficiency of each side, it is easy and, given the particular setting and issue, often appropriate to neglect one side of the relationship and focus on the other, especially the human side. Here, in one form or another, one is concerned about human capacities, e.g., self-development, the objectivity of our subjectivity, the human socio-historical setting. From this standpoint, the western tradition, even the naturalist Aristotle in his ethics,[20] has generally been a *psychocentric* tradition to the neglect of things. On the other hand, poets and artists seem to be especially sensitive to the opposite alternative, the thing's side of the relationship. In his essay on *Hamlet*, T. S. Eliot uses the term "objective correlative" to force us to reflect on the tight fit between the way we feel, think and act (the subjective correlative) and the material conditions which evoke those different feelings, thoughts and actions:

> . . . a set of objects, a situation, a chain of events . . . shall be the formula of that *particular* emotion; such that when the external facts, which must terminate in sensory experience, are given, the emotion is immediately evoked. If you examine any of Shakespeare's more successful tragedies, you will find this exact equivalence; you will find that the state of mind of Lady Macbeth walking in her sleep has been communicated to you by a skillful accumulation of imagined sensory impressions; the words of Macbeth on hearing of his wife's death strike us as if, given the sequence of events, these words were automatically released by the last event in the series. The artistic "inevitability" lies in this complete adequacy of the external to the emotion . . .[21]

Extending his insight, we may say that humans are always and already correlated with materiality. We can account for feelings in two ways—by giving an account of the feeling *or* by giving an account of what evokes the feeling. Similarly, we can speak of interests, desires and motives *or* we can speak of what is attractive, appeals to us or moves us. From the standpoint of being in the world, the former are accounts of the self, the latter accounts of the world.

In the past, the objective correlative to human existence has been a world of things. As people feel, think, act and develop in relation to things, the things themselves are also disclosed in their manifold depths. So, both what people are capable of and what things are capable of are simultaneously disclosed in this relation. Since both human beings and things emerge into being at the same time in this process, and since there is no conflict between the two but actually the two require each other, this symmetrical relationship is a *correlational coexistence*. By responding to things in their full dimensions, I too emerge in the fullness of my dimensions. If I lack the power to be equal to them, neither do things emerge into the fullness of what they can be. If things are not allowed to be, neither am I allowed to be. If I sever my bonds with things by dominating them, I too am diminished. Realizing that human beings and things require and can harmonize with one another is the basis for a respectful and harmonious relationship with our surroundings.

We need to contrast the two stories of progress and decline by juxtaposing this considerability of things, the fourfold world of considerations that are gathered in things, with what environmental ethicists call moral considerability. Only the approach which use the considerablity of things is likely to counter the culture of technology.

Moral Considerability and the Problem of Petty Homocentrism

If I am correct about the dominance of the story of decline, then we should not expect our age to have increased its consideration for nature and natural beings. The considerability of things, the way things are taken into account, is instead greatly impoverished so that a shallow vision of things prevails in the age of technology. Heedless thinking seems only normal. Unlike the sequence of expanding ethical concern seen by Leopold, this other story finds that consideration given to the environment has reached a low point. When the environmental ethicists of the previous chapter imagine themselves writing a story about a sequence of expanding ethical concern, they see as their chief task the overcoming of this minimal regard for the environment. However, if the story is quite different—if our culture has arrived not at a higher state of progression but, ironically, at a lowpoint in our regard for the natural world, then to move beyond this nadir is not necessarily to arrive at anything like a full respect for nature. We can now summarize how this plays out with environmental ethics.

Kenneth Goodpaster suggests, as a first step toward laying the groundwork for an environmental ethic, that a line of demarcation be drawn between what counts morally and what does not count morally. The former deserves what he calls "moral considerability."[22] The latter does not.[23] The virtue of such a distinction, he thinks, is that one does not have to be committed, at least immediately, to any further specification concerning how much and what kind of consideration and obligation humans owe to this or that individual, kind of being, or natural system.[24]

The purpose of moral considerability, seen from the standpoint developed above, is to check or constrain heedless thinking. Because heedless thinking regards everything as a mere resource to be made over for human use and the satisfaction of human needs and wants regardless of any other considerations for things in their own right, it exerts coercive power heedlessly, over the natural world. It is homocentric in an extreme. "Humans are not the only species, we just act like it." Nothing else counts. Thus, it is tyrannical. I call this exertion of tyrannical heedless power *petty homocentrism*. How well will a principle of moral considerability meet our concerns with petty homocentrism?

The realm of moral considerability is invoked to protect those beings within its domain. For Goodpaster, all living beings are morally considerable; for him, all nonliving beings lie outside its scope.[25] Grass and trees are in; rocks and streams are out. So, for these nonliving beings petty homocentric regardless power has free reign unimpeded by other considerations. Nonliving nature, interpreted as mere resource to be reshaped for human want satisfactions, warrants no further consideration. Following his criterion, it would seem no further considerations need to be made, other than economic ones by industry, in deciding whether or not to place a telecommunications relay station on a mountain peak, so long as the structure does not affect lichens, mosses, grasses, marmots, goats or eagles. However, from the standpoint of the *considerablity of things*, Earth and sky and even day and night deserve thoughtful, circumspective consideration which they are not now receiving under the ruling vision of technology and the petty homocentrism entailed by it.

Typically, environmental ethicists respond to the criticism that nonliving nature, such as landscapes, deserves something more—i.e., more consideration—by expanding the realm of moral considerability to include these other things and places, such as landscapes. However, even if these things are included within the domain of moral considerability, the prospects are bleak that they will get much more consideration than that given by heedless thinking because such principles do not radically challenge people's petty homocentric stance but only seek to constrain it. The moral considerations they confront our petty homocentrism with are altruistic or "other-regarding" (as opposed to "self-regarding"). Viewed in this way, a stream, for example, because it has its own project to fulfill, ought to be able to follow its course to the sea without interference from our human petty homocentric projects. Apart from "balancing" this altruistic consideration for the stream against what the consumer society wants, there is, from the perspective of moral considerability, nothing more to be taken into account. Thus, such an altruistic principle fails to account for the overlooked significance of these things—in their own right—*for human life and culture*. Moral considerability alone will *remain heedless* of these other culture considerations, the fourfold world of things. In other words, to maintain that things are morally considerable does not say nearly enough about what it means to consider them as things. Yet, only if these cultural regions of Earth, sky, divinity and mortals are brought to bear as well as the other altruistic considerations will things be considered in a rich worldful way and really be respected for what they are.

We must not, then, take our bearings from our age and its minimal, resource-view of nature; rather, we need to reconsider in a profound way what it means for things *to be* before we can consider either what it means to be adequate to them or how to act in relation to them. Our deeper concerns about petty homocentrism cannot be met, as Rolston and Goodpaster hope to do, by constraining it in some domains. Rather petty homocentrism needs to be challenged as a worthwhile mode of being in the world. Only a more profound contextual consideration of things can present such a challenge.

The Crossroads

As well as reconsider things, we need, secondly, to understand the pull of technology *against* treating nature with respect. Something else is being considered by people which challenges them to dominate nature in a heedless way. Even if they consider things morally, many people will dominate them anyway because they see that the benefits of domination outweigh the damages. What we need to take account of here is the pull of technology. A philosophy dealing with the protection of the environment must also be a philosophy of technological culture.

So the task confronting our age is not fundamentally to extend altruistic ethical regard to nature and natural beings; rather, our problem is to confront the guiding vision of technology. Under the sway of this vision we as a culture assume that the challenge of our age is to get everything under control as resources. Such heedless understanding impoverishes what it touches: the farm field, the river, the forest, and the planet itself. Freeing ourselves from this general orientation in the world is the chief and most difficult task before us if we are to recover and renew deeper and more complex bonds with nature. We are not in the latter stages of a progression; we are at a crossroads of a fundamental choice. Either we go forward with the technological project and continue to rearrange the Earth in accordance with the demands of petty homocentrism on a collective scale, or we rescue and discover things and ways of life which will help us move beyond this age. The attractiveness of the first alternative and its influence on the way we take up with things calls for much more thought than is currently being devoted to it in the field of environmental ethics. So, too, letting ourselves in on what is at stake for the second alternative calls for more radical ways of disclosing the significance of things than are presently being pursued. A disclosure of what is, of these things, may indeed teach us what ought to be.

CHAPTER 5

THE TECHNOLOGICAL SUBVERSION OF ENVIRONMENTAL ETHICS

The unexamined life is not worth living.

—Socrates

We don't want to exaggerate our degrees of freedom. But they are not zero.

—Charles Taylor[1]

How do we get beyond this other story of our age, this regressive story of technological impoverishment? We need to clarify and deepen our understanding of this fundamental choice our culture is facing. Things will play a key role, but we also need to understand technology differently and better than we have so far. To feel uncomfortable amidst all our comfort is not enough. We want to know what is the point of getting everything under control. Humans are not merely puppets in the unfolding of the age. Coming to terms with why we do what we do has often been cathartic in the maturation of humans. Understanding how technological culture hangs together will enable us to foresee its ultimate shape, intelligently evaluate it, and find its pivots of reform.

I

The Underlying Ethic of Technology

Some have argued that we live in an invisible iron cage.[2] Indeed, technological forces are shaping people's lives in ways that they have little or no control over, especially if the basic framework of technology goes unchallenged; but, as Charles Taylor points out, the conquest of nature had a benevolent point to it. It was to serve humanity. So, he finds that, along with other forces, there are moral forces at work here shaping our lives. We live neither in an iron cage nor in an arena of unconstrained choice; we inhabit a possibility space where some moral choices are being made.[3] We did see earlier that there is a kind of ethical appeal to not letting our resources go to waste. So what ethical forces might be called upon to reform technology in a deep way? How should we understand the basic choice we face? For developing what I call the vision and underlying ethic of technology, I will draw heavily upon Albert Borgmann's theory of technology, the best account of the character of the technological culture we have so far. Then we will use this vision of technology to show that the concerns of environmental ethics and people's better concerns for nature generally will be subverted by technology unless we as a culture come to grips with the irony of this vision and begin to make a fundamentally different choice, that is, choose things over consumption.

Making the Appeal of Technology Intelligible: The Promise of Technology

Neither Heidegger nor Thoreau makes clear what it is about technology that is attractive to people. Claiming that we delight in the exercise of power seems correct enough when we think of the enormous amount of power we wield with technology, yet this view does not address our more intelligible motives and, therefore, does not really address many of the proponents of technology without trivializing their concerns. In one way or another, most of us, if not all, see technology as good. What is at the heart of our petty homocentrism? What good is technology?

Typically people articulate what good technology is when they say that something is better or improved and demonstrate that "that's progress." Advertisements are continually pointing out what is better about the product advertised, even if the chief "advantage" is two for the price of one. Although they may well dupe us, these advertisements normally appeal to standards that at least on a deep and general level are already in place and widely shared in consumer culture. We hear everywhere around us, not just in advertisements, what better is. "It means less work." "It's more comfortable." "It's convenient." "It's healthier." "It's faster and more productive." "It's less of a hassle." "Sleeker looks better." "It's lighter." "It doesn't get in your way." "You don't have to wait on anyone else." "It's exciting." When we see the very latest devices, often our expressions are on the order of "Wow!" or "That's great!" or "Look at that, would you?" So, at deeper levels, there seems to be a good deal of likemindedness about what constitutes better in our culture.

Another approach is to consider what people think of as clear examples of progress. Television today is far different from what it was in the past. In the early 50s, one was lucky to own a television. Reception was poor, the picture rough and in black and white; the screen was small, the set large; the number of programs was very limited. In addition to other obvious improvements, now the sets come on instantly, are controlled from the couch, can be found in all sizes and nearly everywhere, and have access to a vast number and variety of programs, especially with video cassette recorders. Even if they are not willing to pay the price for all of them, most count these changes as improvements, and rarely do we find people watching a black and white set any longer. What are the standards which make these changes count as improvements?

Television as a clear example of technology will play a key role in our understanding of the nature of the fundamental choice we face, but Borgmann uses another paradigmatic example of technology, the central heating system, to disclose most of these standards of technology.[4] We can easily trace the development of central heating systems back to the wood-burning stove or the hearth. The chief advantages of the heating system over these latter two are various. Central heating is *easier*. We do not have to gather, stack, chop or carry the wood. An automatic thermostat means that we do not have to trouble ourselves in the morning or evening with setting a thermostat. Central heating is more *instantaneous*. We do not have to wait for the house to warm up. It's *ubiquitous*. Warmth is provided to each corner of the room, to every room, and everywhere equally well. Finally, a central heating system is *safer* than a hearth. My grandmother was born in a newly built chicken coop because three weeks earlier her family's house burnt down from a chimney fire. So the standards by which people judge central heating to be better than a woodburning stove are ease, instantaneity, ubiquity and safety or some combination of these, for example, convenience. These four "technological standards" can be collected under the more general notion of technological availability. To be more *available* is to be an improvement, then, in terms of one or more of the four above standards.

Why does it seem to people that this availability is good? From one perspective, this availability relieves people of burdens: less effort, less time and less learning skills are required. Available anytime and anyplace, they are disburdened of the constraints of time and place. They are disburdened of having to take risks. Historically, modern technology was envisioned as enabling people not just to subjugate nature, but to do so for the purpose of freeing humanity from misery and toil. To be relieved of these burdens then, fulfills this vision of technology. *To the degree people personally share this vision,* they will also see its concrete manifestations, such as central heating, as unquestionably good. Compared to older versions, the latest portable computers exemplify this relief from burdens and are attractive to many for this reason.

. By overcoming nature, technology would, as some in the seventeenth century foresaw, not only relieve humans of burdens, but it would make available to them—easier, safer, quicker, and more ubiquitous—all the goods of the Earth. So, technological availability negatively disburdens people of misery and toil, and positively enriches their lives, makes them happy, it seems. So seen, technology has an attractive glow about it.

> Technology promises to bring the forces of nature and culture under control, to liberate us from misery and toil, and to enrich our lives . . . [More accurately], implied in the technological mode of taking up with the world there is a promise that this approach to reality will, by way of the domination of nature, yield liberation and enrichment.[5]

Borgmann calls this "the promise of technology."

Clearly those below the middle-class of advanced industrialized countries and those outside those countries do not derive the benefits of technology, although many do feel the pull of its promise. As I outlined in chapter 1 and will argue later here, the claims of social justice will not likely be met until the more privileged ones, the middle and higher classes of these industrialized countries, come to terms with the questionable character of technology's promise. So, the critique of technology I am developing here does not apply to those in poverty. It applies only to those who have too much.

For these latter, technology has made good on its promise in important ways. My grandmother's father died from what she believes was pneumonia when she was eleven, leaving her and her younger sister to perform heroic feats to save the cattle from starvation in the rough times of an extended winter that followed. Often hitching the team up before dawn and returning hours after dark, especially in winter, her family took an entire day to get to and from town sixteen miles away. For the privileged, then, many past hardships have now been conquered. Although we may have legitimate concerns about whether there is too much medical technology, no one could reasonably refuse every advance of modern medical technology. The weather will never be brought under control, but, via comfortable structures, nature's heat and cold, rain and snow are controlled as well as darkness and drought. Toilsome labor is largely eliminated within the culture of technology.

A reasonable person may reject motorcycles in favor of horses to do ranch work, but that person still rides to town on paved roads in a car, has parts shipped by air, reads a newspaper and books, transacts business over the phone, and owns at least a radio. No thoughtful person will want to turn her back on technology entirely. Thus, technology, by conquering nature, has relieved humans of severe burdens. Today we are still working to overcome those, such as cancer and AIDS, that remain. So, if technology does not saddle us in the long run with more than it has relieved us from, it will have made good on this aspect of what at first seemed and still does seem promising about it. It could turn out that ozone depletion, global warming, ecosystem destruction, the population explosion, polluted land, air, streams and oceans, and human and mechanical errors will impose burdens far greater than those we were relieved from in the first place. To meet these problems certainly calls for a reform of present practices. We read or hear of these calls for reform nearly every day. More common critiques of technology, such as David Ehrenfeld's *The Arrogance of Humanism*, attempt to show that technology will fail by its own standards, bringing disaster upon us.[6]

Much as reform in these areas is needed and much as these pessimistic critiques deserve thoughtful consideration, the present work will turn to a uniquely different task. It grants and, in fact, seeks to have the reader appreciate, the genuine success of modern technology. Technology has relieved, and technology will, I assume for the purposes at hand, continue to relieve, humans of many hardships of the human condition.

So what is wrong with technology for those within the realm of its benefits? Underlying these standards of availability is really a vision of a good life that is free and prosperous. What is at the bottom of concern with technological availability is an aspiration for freedom and happiness. Most people, at least in the Western tradition, are concerned with liberty and prosperity. For Aristotle only the Greek free man was able to have sufficient time and sufficient wherewithal to develop the moral and intellectual virtues he thought to be required for happiness or eudaemonia. The Hebrew people's understanding of the covenant centered on an idea of prosperity. Jesus preached of a free and abundant life. The Enlightenment, as we see its results in "the pursuit of happiness" in our Declaration of Independence, is fully within this tradition. But to find agreement at this high level of abstraction is not to see that the crucial differences lie with the particular versions of freedom and prosperity. For Socrates living well had to do with human excellence and living a just life, not with materialism. The blessed life and the abundant life of the Hebrews and of Jesus was not commodity happiness. So, too, we must look carefully at the particular idea of freedom and prosperity governing people's attraction to technology, for only at this level of particularity will its misleading and harmful features begin to show. In other words, one can criticize the trivialized forms of freedom and prosperity on which the technological society is centered

without, at the same time, criticizing freedom and prosperity more generally as a vision of the good life. Quite the contrary, we can call technology
into question even more sharply by showing that technology fails to provide the free, prosperous, and good life we want in our waking moments.

Technological society offers a flattened vision of freedom and prosperity. The more disburdened, the better off I am according to this vision. So,
the technological idea of freedom is really one of disburdenment. What
about prosperity? Cellular phones are currently a status symbol. These devices which disburden people of the constraints of place are taken to be a
sign of affluence because, generally, only the more prosperous have them.
So, in part, to be prosperous is to have the latest, most refined device. A
sign of affluence, too, is to be able to go to an undiscovered exotic place,
have the most channels and compact disks, own specially designed
clothing, own what no one else has yet. Thus, in part, to be prosperous is
to own the most varied, the widest assortment of commodities. Finally,
when people buy a product on sale they get both the commodity they
purchased and still have money left over. Why is that attractive? Because
they can buy something else with the money saved. They are better off that
way, they think, because they get more items for the money. Thus people
pursue prosperity through the standards of owning the *most numerous,
widest variety, and the very latest (most refined)* commodities. The powers
that be in the technological society own and control the most of these
items. Such is the picture of the good life envied by those keeping up with
the Joneses. Our culture's vision of the good life is the goods life.

Does this vision really deliver a good life? If we say no merely because
it differs from the blessed life according to Abraham, Moses, and the
prophets, or from the Greeks' eudaemonia, our analysis would be dogmatic
and presumptuous. Technology must be thought through; it will not be
met by simply reacting against it. So, if we answer "no," as I will, then we
must be able to provide good reasons.

The Technological Means to Freedom and Happiness: The Device

The ironic consequences of this vision of freedom and prosperity can
be drawn out through a careful analysis of the peculiar way technology
transforms or, more specifically, dominates nature and culture. Technology
does not dominate these in the traditional manner of lording it over them;
rather, as Albert Borgmann shows, technology follows a pattern, unique to
the modern era, in the way it gets everything under control. We can expose
this pattern by examining instances of it.

The central heating system dominates warmth; it brings warmth under control in ways that the wood-burning stoves do not. To show its unique form of domination, Borgmann distinguishes between "things" and "devices." A thing in his sense

> is inseparable from its context, namely its world, and from our commerce with the thing and its world, namely, engagement. The experience of a thing is always and also a bodily and social engagement with the thing's world . . . Thus a stove used to furnish more than mere warmth. It was a *focus*, a hearth, a place that gathered the work and leisure of a family and gave the house a center. Its coldness marked the morning, and the spreading of its warmth marked the beginning of the day. It assigned to various family members tasks that defined their place in the household . . . It provided the entire family a regular and bodily engagement with the rhythm of the seasons that was woven together with the threat of cold and the solace of warmth, the smell of wood smoke, the exertion of sawing and carrying, the teaching of skills, and the fidelity to daily tasks . . . Physical engagement is not simply physical contact but the experience of the world through the manifold sensibility of the body. That sensibility is sharpened and strengthened in skill. Skill is intensive and refined world engagement.[7]

Here, in his retrieval of the thing's world and our engagement with the thing, Borgmann has been influenced by Heidegger's fourfold account of things. Obviously, Earth and sky are woven together with mortals. He points out that in Roman times the hearth was the abode of household gods, though he does not make much of it.[8] Borgmann's account goes beyond Heidegger in emphasizing social and bodily engagement to a degree to which Heidegger seems insensitive. He also steps beyond Heidegger by highlighting the way things focus practices.[9] Practices call for skills and the development of character; the diversity of different characters is joined to each other through participating in a world of practices. In our terms developed earlier, the hearth is the correlational coexistent thing which establishes the world of the household and, correlatively, calls forth its members and calls on their deeper capacities.

Today the hearth, if it exists at all, is no longer the central location in the house although the mantel still remains a place of honor. What has replaced the thing is the "device." The device (the central heating system) provides a commodity, one element of the original thing (warmth alone) and disburdens people of all the elements that compose the world and engaging character of the thing. This world of the thing, its ties to the natural and cultural world and our engagement with that many-dimensional world on bodily, cerebral and social levels, is taken over by the *machinery* (the central heating plant itself) of the device.

The machinery makes no demands on our skill, strength, or attention, and it is less demanding the less it makes its presence felt. In the progress of technology, the machinery of the device has therefore a tendency to become concealed or to shrink. Of all the physical properties of a device, those alone are crucial and prominent which constitute the commodity that the device procures.[10]

To make the commodity even more technologically available, the machinery varies radically in the history of technology (wood or coal or oil or electricity or gas). Owing to this radical variability and to this concealment, the machinery becomes necessarily *unfamiliar.* I probably do not know by what means the water is heated in a building. But the device is not just machinery or even most importantly machinery. The device makes available a commodity—warmth. Warmth is what the central heating system is for. Just the opposite of the machinery, the commodity tends to *expand* (become ubiquitous in the house), to remain relatively *fixed* as the means change (from coal to electricity) and to be *familiar.* It follows that—unlike with things—there is a wide division between what a device provides, the commodity, and how it provides this commodity, the machinery. Hence, and this is Borgmann's central insight we saw illustrated earlier with second homes, devices *split* means and ends into mere means and mere ends.

Even though these claims that a thing makes on people are not always experienced as burdensome (as we see from the above account), this very world of the thing and the engagement it calls for can be felt at times as a burden or hassle. The technological device and its refinement *disburdens* people of all these problems by expanding the commodity, so that the world of the thing no longer determines when, in what way, and where it is available. Thus, it disburdens them of the claims that call for engagement. In short, the technological device disburdens people of the thing's world and its claims upon them. The device is considered the more refined the more it lifts these burdens from them. The ideal device is one where, from an experiential standpoint, a commodity can be enjoyed unencumbered by means. A reliable self-regulating central heating system whose maintenance and energy bill are taken care of by a management agency can be taken as a paradigmatic example.

The peculiar way technology dominates things is not limited, of course, to the central heating system. Considering how household technologies have changed, Witold Rybczynski in *Home: A Short History of An Idea* writes.

> The evolution of domestic technology . . . demonstrates that the history of physical amenities can be divided into two major phases: all the years

leading up to 1890, and the three following decades. If this sounds out-landish, it is worth reminding ourselves that all the "modern" devices that contribute to our domestic comfort—central heating, indoor plumb-ing, running hot and cold water, electric light and power and elevators—were unavailable before 1890, and were well known by 1920. We live, like it or not, on the far side of a great technological divide. As John Lukacs reminds us, although the home of 1930 would be familiar to us, it would have been unrecognizable to the citizen of 1885.[11]

Just as with household technologies, so too with other features of our surroundings and our cultural and natural environment generally. This thing-to-device example is representative of the pattern of the technologi-cal transformations of the Earth. Generally then, this transformation is one in which:

> Devices . . . dissolve the coherent and engaging character of the pre-technological world of things. In a device, the relatedness of the world is replaced by a machinery, but the machinery is concealed, and the com-modities, which are made available by a device, are enjoyed without the encumbrance of or the engagement with a context [that is, the world of the thing].[12]

Borgmann calls this pattern the *device paradigm*. At times I will call it the separation pattern of technology. (See diagram on the following page.)

In chapter 4, we characterized our age as one in which we reduce everything to resources that we want to control. Now we can see that the device pattern is used to get control of these resources. The purpose of the device is to supply people with unencumbered commodities. So now we can develop this picture of our age further. The fuller vision is one in which everything gets reduced to resources, machinery and commodities.

Ironic Consequences

So far we have developed a theory by which we can interpret what has taken and is taking place with regard to the technological transformation in our time. Using this theory we can pass from technological object to technological object, seeing how they more or less fit the pattern. The illustration of the pattern does not commit us as yet to an evaluation of the good or bad of what has taken place. Now we are in a position to begin that task. What are the consequences of this change from things to de-vices?

Don Ihde finds that technologies transform experience in a "non-neu-tral" manner. A tool always amplifies in some way certain aspects of nor-

The Pattern of Technological Domination

The Transformation of Things into Devices

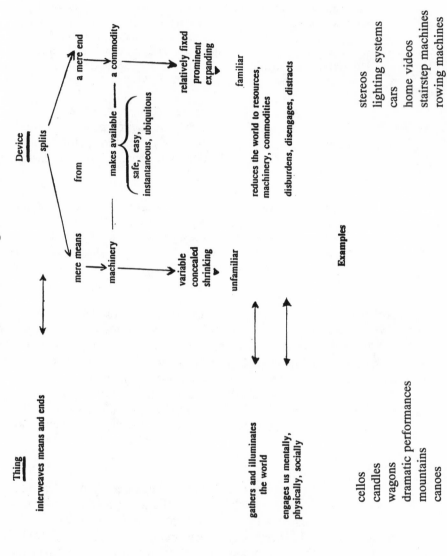

Thing

interweaves means and ends

gathers and illuminates the world

engages us mentally, physically, socially

Device

splits

a mere end → a commodity → relatively fixed prominent expanding

familiar

mere means ─ machinery

variable concealed shrinking

unfamiliar

from

makes available ─ safe, easy, instantaneous, ubiquitous

reduces the world to resources, machinery, commodities

disburdens, disengages, distracts

Examples

cellos
candles
wagons
dramatic performances
mountains
canoes

stereos
lighting systems
cars
home videos
stairstep machines
rowing machines

mal embodied experience while simultaneously reducing other aspects.[13] A dentist's probe shows the hardness and cavities in a tooth to a degree fingers miss, while the wetness and warmth of the tooth felt by the fingers go undetected by probe. This change Ihde finds is non-neutral because the amplified features are heightened, drawing our attention, while the reduced features tend to go unheeded and are overlooked and often forgotten. Asked what a hearth is for, we find it logical, after having experienced central heating, to answer that it supplies heat, ignoring or not even seeing its other aspects. Extending Ihde's insight makes it more intelligible why we become fascinated with commodities, heedless of what has been reduced. Yet pointing out that this change is non-neutral is not enough. We now want to comprehend what exactly has been hidden from us. We need a language which articulates what is overlooked and forgotten, for then we can see in what ways this change is non-neutral. Our language of things retrieves and focuses this loss. It reveals the general pattern that things are transformed into devices, detaching people from things, their world and each other.

Ihde further argues that these lost features only tend to recede, thus, implying that they are retrievable. With certain kinds of instruments (not all technological objects are devices, splitting means and ends), this is true. We can easily retrieve the features missed by the dentist's probe. With devices, however, these features do not just tend to withdraw, so that a change of attitude, perception or act of will could retrieve them. Notice that mere warmth, no matter how expanded the commodity has become, is not a substitute for the thing of the wood-burning stove. Mere warmth could not be the essence of a household; it does not warrant that kind of attention or care, of heeding. Indeed the source itself is concealed and the warmth is suffused throughout the house so that it fails to provide a focus. So warmth is no substitute for the thing because it lacks a world with which to become engaged. More than this, because it is impossible to recover in the mere warmth of the central heating plant the full-bodied experience of the hearth, the machinery of devices ineluctably withdraws the world from people. A device is necessarily unfamiliar in the ways that the context of the thing was familiar. Thus the transformation of the thing into a device does not merely tend to obscure possibilities of experience, but its very material structure makes the rich experience of the thing impossible.

Another way of putting this is that devices allow the possibility of only slim points of contact with "narrowly defined aspects of what used to be things of depth."[14] Devices force people to take them as commodity bearers; they leave them no choice. So our way of taking commodities is not a psychological matter, but a real matter. Technology is not only a way of seeing (and for this reason characterizing technology as a vision is perhaps misleading), it is more importantly a way of *shaping*. The very material structure of a device is such that it can be experienced only as holding up a commodity calling for consumption and nothing more.

The implication of this change of shape is alienation. What seemed promising at the outset—relieving people of burdens—leads ironically to disengagement, diversion, distraction and loneliness. In short, we become not-at-home in the universe. But clearly, simply finding ourselves free from the exclusive use of candles and outhouses, does place us in this alienated position. So how can such positive events as electric lighting and indoor plumbing lead to these ironic results?

To be relieved of famine, cold, darkness, confinement and other genuine adversities of the human condition was an intelligible and urgent demand for the early phase of modern technology. For the middle-classes of advanced industrialized countries, most, not all, of these kinds of challenges have been met for some time. At the stage of mature technology, the challenges can be quite frivolous. Food processors, electric pencil sharpeners, prepared fishing leaders, automatic cameras, electric knives, and some pain relievers are typical. The basic question here is: Do we need to be relieved of every last and least burden? Aren't some of these burdens actually good in senses that touch our very humanity? When people reflect on these questions they may answer them differently, but when they act, they tend to act in agreement with a vision that seeks to bring everything under control. Ironically, in the wake of such technological success, in the wake of the initial excitement over owning the latest item, the item falls back into the ordinary every day and they become bored. Being bored, they become disengaged and alienated from what may have been a vital practice, such as preparing meals or gardening or photography. Accordingly, they seek diversion. Thus, ironic consequences follow from the disburdenment of every hassle, problem or felt demand. If we pursue disburdenment in this unchecked and unreflective manner, as people are doing in the stage of mature technology, then these are the results we should expect.

However, it may seem as though we have been just too nostalgic. The disburdenment devices yield "frees us up for other things" as people commonly say. Yet this perspective makes us think that technology is mostly about freedom, as Charles Taylor thinks, when the promise and vision of technology are mostly a promise of happiness. The most unique and devastating critique of technology is not centered on technological freedom, but on the fact that technology *fails most where it succeeds most* at procuring happiness, at procuring the good things of life. As a culture, we think not only that we can use technology to liberate us, but also that we can use it to fill that new possibility space with technologically available goods. In short, what people are freed up for are not other things, but *more commodities*. Then too when people imagine what they are doing as they throw food into the microwave as freeing themselves up for other and more important things, they ignore how pervasive the technological order is. The totality of technological devices is far more consequential than any particular device. The former point can be advanced best by developing the latter first.

Extensively yet unobtrusively this technological way of taking up with the world pervades and informs what people think, say and do. We need an account of technology as *correlational environment*. Organizations, institutions, the ways nature and culture are arranged and accessible all become modeled on the device. As people make more decisions for consumption against engagement, our average, everyday world is stamped more deeply with the pattern of the device. In other words, devices do not simply liberate people from some things and free them for other and better things. We are surrounded. The things enabling correlational coexistence have nearly disappeared. As the totality of our daily environment changes from an environment of things to an environment of devices, from an environment making demands on people to an environment that is more at their finger tips, this change necessarily entails heedlessness and evokes an attitude of cultural petty homocentrism. So it is important to consider not just the appropriateness of this or that device in a particular context, but to consider what the consequences are of the totality of these devices and people's *typical* use of them. We would expect the consumptive ways of life in such surroundings to be disburdened and disengaged.

So what are people finally freed up for? How do they attempt to use technological means to positively enrich their lives? Typically people use devices to procure entertainment commodities.[15] Hence our culture treats tradition, culture and nature as resources to be mined. Just as ubiquitously available warmth is not a substitute for the hearth, entertainment commodities are at best insubstantial aspects of the original things. Because they use devices here to procure the delights that matter, final things, these entertainment commodities can be thought of as final commodities. In this respect, to consume a final commodity is no different from consuming an instrumental one that disburdens us of a chore.

The Ironic Consequences of Final Consumption

Television is a clear example of a final commodity. Its refinements from the first sets to those of today fit the same pattern as the refinements in central heating and the refinements of devices in accordance with Borgmann's device paradigm in general. So television is an instance of the vision of domination, liberation, and enrichment. It does not make demands on people and is a window of the world, making all the goods of the Earth available, technologically available, to them in their living rooms.

Understandably, television has tremendous appeal to us as a culture. It's where technology comes home to people. The amount of time they spend watching it indicates its power.

> The A.C. Nielsen Company (1989) currently estimates that people in the United States view upwards of 4 hours of television each day. Given the likelihood that such estimates are inflated, let us assume a more conservative estimate of 2 1/2 hours of television viewing per day over the period of a lifetime. Even at this more conservative rate, a typical American would spend more than 7 full years watching television out of the approximately 47 waking years each of us lives by age 70—this assuming an average of 8 hours of sleep per day. Such a figure is even more striking when we consider that Americans have about 5 1/2 hours a day of free time, or approximately 16 years available for leisure of the same 47-year span. From this point of view and based on a conservative estimate, Americans are spending nearly half of their available free time watching television.[16]

Since it is the most popular way people enjoy final consumption, it is worthwhile to examine in detail the *experience* of this form of consumption as we develop the ironic consequences of final consumption. *Television and the Quality of Life* by Robert Kubey and Mihaly Csikszentmihalyi (cited above) does just that, examining systematically the reported experience of television in contrast to the reported experience of other activities people spend time on in their daily life. So we need to look closely at their findings with a view to showing how technology in the form TV does not fulfill its promise.

Kubey and Csikszentmihalyi find that television is inexpensive and is easily and quickly available for those who have time for it.[17] It helps people to relax and, at times, may help some to retreat before gathering themselves to face a difficulty.[18] People can watch it for prolonged periods without wearing themselves out physically. It tends to bring families together and family members normally do talk with each other while watching. They also feel better than when watching alone.[19] It is used for news programs, for nature shows, and to present dramas such as *Death of a Salesman*. It could be used to present lectures in chemistry and Plato.[20] It helps connect us with our culture and some of its common stories. On the other hand, "viewing is almost always mildly rewarding in that it provides relaxation, distraction, and escape with minimal effort."[21] It gives people something to do with their time and most report they do want to watch it.[22]

With so much of our leisure time taken up with television and with so many benefits, one might mistakenly conclude that people choose to watch because it is better than anything else they could be doing. Yet the actual cumulative benefits they receive from television are rather low and often negative.

Ironically, the reported experience of people viewing television often turns out to be one of disappointment.[23] Not only are chemistry courses not aired because few would watch them, not only do most people gravitate toward watching movies with light and escapist content rather than challenging dramas, but, just as important, half the people who watch television do not use television guides to help them decide what to watch.[24] The stories viewers share, then, are not those shown on public television. The shows tend to support existing beliefs. As Stu Silverman told Kubey, "Television reassures us, it's 'nice,' it doesn't offend or challenge an audience. It is designed to do just the opposite of art, to reassure rather than excite. That often is what people want."[25] Although television does help people to relax, it does not do so any more than other activities such as reading. Moreover, it helps people relax only while watching it and not later as sports and other activities do.[26] Although this study found that television is not a completely passive activity, it is comparatively so. It is not usually challenging, requires little mental alertness, and is reported to exact fewer skills than eating. Only idling was reported to be more passive.[27] Unlike activities that gather and restore a person, a "passive spillover effect" tended to follow watching television, making people feel duller, more passive, and less able to concentrate.[28] Families for which television provides a center also experience this spillover effect carried over into other family activities.[29] Finally, the positive benefits one receives from television tend to be enjoyed less the more one watches.[30] Heavy viewers are not made happy by watching it; they generally feel worse than light viewers both before and after viewing.[31] Even light viewers do not report themselves to be any happier than average while watching.[32]

Aristotle found amusement, like sleep, to be therapeutic as long as life is oriented around exertion. So, too, Kubey and Csikszentmihalyi find that those who stand to benefit most from television use and need it least.[33] More often television is used to disburden people of problems in ways that do not go to the roots of the problems, are only marginally effective, and, hence, are entirely inappropriate.[34] People disburden themselves of the problem of leisure time that their time-saving and labor-saving devices have created by killing time watching television. They disburden themselves of the problem of loneliness when devices leave them isolated by turning on a device, the television set. Heavy use is higher among singles.[35] Such an answer to loneliness is only a diversion from genuine forms of social engagement. On the other hand, television is often used as a way for family members, usually fathers, to avoid talking with other family members and avoid dealing with family problems.[36] Television resolves the problem of independently ordering ones life, of giving shape to the day. It takes care of boredom.[37] Heavy television viewing is likely driven by a wish to escape, to be disburdened of bad days and bad moods, of personal problems and of alienation from self.[38] Diverting ones attention, it tends to mask the deeper and more real problems a person is having and, hence, leaves these problems unintelligently resolved. Does it meet the task of leading a more rewarding and meaningful life? No. "Happiness is a more complex state than relaxation. It requires a more elusive set of conditions, and is therefore more difficult to obtain."[39] Television seems to "encourage a false sense of well-being in some people," distracting them from and becoming an obstacle to the hard work it takes to realize ones potentials.[40]

More indirectly, we can ask what people are missing when they watch television. When viewers are not pleased with the amount of time they watch television, the entire reason is not only that it is a low-grade activity, one that many think best fits the phrase "Am I lazy!"[41] Part of the reason, too, has to do with what television is displacing. Many report that they feel as though they should have been doing something else. College educated viewers felt this way more often than other people because "they should have been doing something more productive."[42] Television rearranges life through decreasing the amount of time spent involved with other activities. It at times provides a center for the household, but such a center seems flimsy at best, especially in comparison with other potential centers or centers of the past. In another context, Kubey and Csikszentmihalyi speak of these kinds of centers of life.

> When people are asked what they enjoy most, and enough time is left for a genuine answer to emerge, we often find that the most enjoyable things involve doing something, and usually something rather complex and demanding. Rarely does watching television get mentioned, or any other passive or consummatory activity . . . The first reflex for many people is to say that one most enjoys going on vacations, going to movies or restaurants—the typical "leisure" responses in our culture. But as people think more deeply about their real feelings they will mention enjoyable times with their families, and then there is often a point when their faces light up and they say something like: "Actually, the best times in my life have been . . ." and start talking with great enthusiasm about designing and sewing quilts, rock climbing, playing music, working on a basement lathe, or about other activities that require concentrated skill, that do not separate the individual from the end result of his or her effort, and that provide the kind of exhilaration and high focused attention of flow. So . . .

we are still able to keep in sight those *vivid signposts* that show what it is
that makes life worth living . . . [On] reflecting on such occasions, people
often say that not only was the experience enjoyable at the time, but that
it helped them grow and become more than they had been. Compared to
such optimal experiences, much television watching could be deemed a
waste of time . . . wasting it amounts to wasting life.[43]

Casting television in terms of the symmetrical relationship of correlational
coexistence developed earlier, we can see that the medium is just not
enough for humans to make the center of their lives. It does not call forth
their humanity in any depth. Hence, Kubey and Csikszentmihalyi worry
that by spending so much time viewing television "one may well lose opportunities to grow as a human being."[44]

Kubey and Csikszentmihaly find that a mistaken cultural assumption
underlies much of the appeal of television. For them the mistaken cultural
assumption is narrowly one of thinking that physical and mental exertion
are bad, and that they are unrelated to human growth and living a worthwhile life.[45] In contrast, for us, the more comprehensive mistaken assumption is that technology generally can fulfill our aspirations for freedom and
enrichment. Considered from the standpoint of the vision of technology,
television is a paradigmatic example of and not an exception to the unimpeded development of technological culture. As for liberation, it is a commodity which does not make demands—in dress, transportation, or man-
ners, or even having to be at home when a program is aired. Following the
device's split between means and ends, people exert themselves in labor
and expect to relax completely in leisure. They want amusement, not challenge or disturbance. In terms of prosperity, with video cassette players
and hundreds of channels, the most, the most varied, and the latest programs can be watched. Advertisements, too, and the settings of the programs themselves celebrate this prosperity of technology. In short, the
incredible attraction of television is that it is the homeplace of the vision
people are still spellbound by. It confirms them in that vision and tells
them what's what in the universe. Its glamour binds and soothes while
simultaneously disappointing them with the flatness and shallowness of its
nourishment, its ironic unfulfillment. Television as an exemplar of a final
commodity represents the ultimate appeal of the promise of technology. It
is, then, the success story of the technology. Television is the vision of
technological culture.
Much of the remainder of our leisure time is spent, if not in front of a
television, then with the commodities advertised on it. But these other
forms of final consumption, technological alternatives to television, even

more interactive ones, will manifest the same basic pattern and similar ironic consequences. We have already seen how second homes can relieve people of a midlife crisis and the problems of daily life in the city, and it is now easy to see how the second homes conspicuous leisure agrees with technology. So let us look at how the wild Crazies can be packaged and sold as a commodity for final consumption without materially damaging them as clearcuts would do.

Llama trekking is becoming fashionable. Unlike packing with horses in traditional western style, llamas carry gear but not riders, and, so, trekkers must hike. Moreover, llamas are easier on the environment because they do not eat or weigh as much as a horse, and, being sure-footed with a cloven hoof, they are probably as easy on the trails as elk. What could possibly be inappropriate and insulating about their use?

They can be used appropriately, no doubt, but it pays to attend to the reasons given for using them. Consider an article entitled "Hiking with Llamas in Montana" from the travel section of the Sunday *New York Times.* Aptly enough, it is focused on a trek in the Crazies from the Cottonwood Canyon trailhead. The article begins:

> "What else can we take?" asked [the guide] . . . I need more weight to balance the llama's packs." "How about a few more liters of wine," suggested his wife . . . "How about some chairs? . . ." "Got camp chairs . . . got solar shower, got the stove and Dutch oven, got the fishing rods, got all the coolers. Got *a lot* of wine . . ."[46]

Here one stays clean and comfortable, has plenty to do, and has everything one could possibly wish for. "Released from the dread of freeze-dried lasagna and powdered lemonade," trekkers can look forward, we are told, to dinners like this one served the first night.

> We began with wine spritzers, smoked salmon and cheese. The meal progressed through a saffron-infused paella loaded with shrimp, chicken and sausage, a bottle of stream-chilled champagne, a banana concoction flambéed with a self-mocking flourish, coffee and liqueurs.[47]

Such a meal is billed to enrich the camping experience. And what about the liberation from hardship and misery? The author gives us a measure of these forces one can expect to encounter. Rising early in the morning, "I washed my face in a stream, barely suppressing a howl as the icy water hit my skin. The thought of subjecting my teeth to the same torture was too horrible to contemplate." Finally, an appeal is made directly to the vision of technology, for, while it is acknowledged that such trips are obviously costly, they are so literally disburdening that, "Llama trips are a dream come true."[48]

The problem with llama trekking in the above account is twofold. On the one hand, it insulates one from the conditions of the place, smoothing out even the forbidding ruggedness of the Crazies, narrowing ones contact with them, and making wilderness an easily consumable package. The blank spot one is freed up for is filled with such an array of goods that ones attention is directed from the place to the specialness of what is packed in. Our everyday problem-solving is never thrown radically into question—one always has something to do. In these ways, using llamas (as advertised above), impoverishes our encounter with a wild place. We experience a wilderness veneer, a wilderness completely on our own terms.

The second problem has to do with the standards to which such llama trekking appeals. They are technological through and through, valuing technological novelty and availability. Others, sharing these standards, will greet them by asking if such standards can be met better in other ways, perhaps more socially just, considering these are public lands. If disburdened hiking is all one wants and if it takes the importation of plenty of wine, French cuisine, inflatable rafts and solar showers to make the experience really attractive and palatable, then why not punch a road further into the core of the mountains, nearer to the lakes? Then such experience would be available to nearly everyone and not just yuppies.

The next step would be to put a climb up Crazy Peak in my basement or at a health club. The dream would be to mimic the sights, smells, wind, terrain and other features of the experience in uncrude ways. Where does the separation pattern's wounding split between means and ends occur here? Certainly I am not cashing in my prior exertion in labor for what could be called a passive affair such as when I drive a car. Challenge and enjoyment may occur at the same time. Certainly my mind is not reading a book while my body pedals an exercycle, splitting mind from body, myself from others. Body and mind do attend to the same pictured world of the Crazies, the same scenes and terrain. But virtual reality is at our disposal, on our turf and terms, and is disconnected from the larger, fourfold context of our lifeworld.[49] As such, it is essentially merely an instance of domination at the expense of relationship. The correlational coexistent thing has dropped away entirely. In the setting of virtual reality we may see into a playful story of Chuang Tzu's in a new and disquieting way. After having had a vivid dream the night before that he was butterfly, Chuang Tzu said he found himself puzzled about whether he was now Chuang Tzu who had dreamed he was a butterfly or a butterfly who is now dreaming it is Chuang Tzu. The vertigo we feel here is not one from heights, although it is not as safe as it might be were we merely on a flight simulator.

The old saw is that humans are acquisitive animals, and the more we have the more we want. From an ethnocentric perspective, it makes some sense why we would think this is "just human nature." Now we can see that people have an insatiable need to have more because they have so superficially. What is it to consume something? "To consume is to use up an isolated entity without preparation, resonance, or consequence."[50] A commodity made available by a device is free of preparation, does not resonate with the natural, cultural, or local world, and, since it takes so little time and makes such a muted statement, it is unlikely to turn a person's life one way or another, or affirm forcefully its present direction. A person consumes it and is ready to follow the same basic pattern in consuming more. Seeing how much consuming people can cram into their day and their life becomes a norm.

So while technology is successful on its own terms when it makes goods available, its success is merely a pyrrhic victory. What makes good things rich and involving has been lost. We have been seduced by a shallow semblance. Thus, technology fails to deliver happiness, not because it fails to make goods available, but because such goods as it does make available turn out to be merely ironic goods. What seemed promising in the appearance is disappointing in the reality. Our aspirations for freedom and happiness go awry when we attempt to procure them with devices.

So does technology deliver the goods? Does technology help people live more rewarding and meaningful lives? As people make the things that count in their lives technologically available, they empty them of depth and they lose them. It is a lesson our culture has not learned yet when we let television, like Kirkê's magic wand, turn us into something less than members of the animal kingdom.

Allegiance to the Vision

Later we will see how Thoreau provides us with a language to make the above point about the shallowness of consumption even more comprehensible when we consider what the villagers would be missing were they, following the vision of technology, to reduce Walden pond to a mere reservoir tapped with plumbing machinery to supply the commodity dishwater. For now we need to see through this vision and its trivializing underlying ethic. Why does everything get reduced to resources, machinery and commodities? What is the appeal? So long as it seems plausible to us as a culture that we can procure happiness through technological means, we will continue to rearrange nature and culture according to this vision. The final commodities that constitute this goal will be numerous, varied and highly refined in terms of the other standards of ubiquity, instantaneity, safety and ease. To procure final commodities in this way is the ideal and counts as the larger success story of technology by its own standards.

Accordingly, to be affluent is to possess and consume the most. Affluence has glamour. "It is the embodiment of the free, rich, and imperial life that technology has promised. So it appears from below whence it is seen by most people,"[51] or, as it is seen from the perspective of less affluent countries. This, then, is the goal and blueprint of the technological society our culture is so busily building. This more specifically drawn picture constitutes the *basic vision and framework* of technology.

People's agreement with the framework of technology underlies their concern with the national economy, showing a common commitment to a high and rising standard of living. An increased standard of living cashes out into more numerous, more refined, and varied commodities. Since our culture's commitment to the technological good life is so firm, political campaigns can focus on the economy without ever having to confront deeply the issue of the kind of quality of life the economy provides.

If our culture tacitly grants this commitment to the promise of technology, certain hypothetical imperatives fall out. To produce the most commodities, much of the machinery of production must be centralized, forbiddingly complex, and, by way of productive devices, it must reduce contact of the laborers within the process to narrow points. Normally people do not take up the challenge of making room for intrinsically good work at the expense of technological progress. On the contrary, the degradation of work takes the next step with the elimination of work when more productive and reliable robots take over. A union official is quoted by Borgmann as saying, "We don't like the idea of losing jobs, but it's part of life."[52] It is part of life, *granted* that technology is the goal.

Earlier we saw that these hypothetical imperatives were at work in the development of the Crazy Mountains. So much raw material would go to waste in the Crazy Mountains if the pinebark beetle infestation were to continue. The notion of waste was contingent upon the assumption that the volume of wood was needed by the technological society. Given that the technological society has consumption as its goal, that bonus pay and second homes are a standard package of a good life, and given that the raw material of Cottonwood Canyon is believed to forward this goal, then the timber of Cottonwood Canyon needs treatment, needs to be logged.

If this vision and framework has at least people's unspoken allegiance, then several consequences follow. First, consumer culture is not at bottom created by advertising as a more Marxist view might hold. To be sure, advertising does regulate, heighten, and make consumption palpable, and, it replaces art by providing us with our orientation in a technological setting where much of the traditional fabric and many of its landmarks have been dissolved by the device paradigm. Still, the basic framework condition which people move *from* when addressed by advertisements is already in place: From a historical perspective, universal consumption for all is the outcome of the vision of technology and the hold it has upon our culture.[53] Then, too, from the perspective of the structure of the device, devices provide an isolated entity to be used up and disposed of. Hence, devices call forth a life of consumption and nothing more. Consumer culture is, thus, a consequence of the vision of technology and of the technological device.

This prior cultural condition advertising addresses shows tellingly when people make genuine decisions for consumption. Where do these choice points occur? Most people do not have choices whether they can become potters, poets, wheelwrights, musicians, or follow out liberal arts vocations, whether they can buy from a shoemaker or shoestore, whether they can remain farmers in the face of low product prices and high machinery and energy costs, or whether a nuclear plant gets built near them. But the absence of these kinds of choices rests on a prior agreement to consumption as a way of life. More to the point here, there are occasions when these outside constraints are missing, times when people shape and choose, and at these moments they show how disposed they are to exchange things for commodities. Here we discover whether they are with or against the rule of the vision of technology.

> It is to take a condescending view if one excuses families who surrender and betray their tradition by saying that advertisements told them to eat out more often and to refurbish their homes according to the dictates of the Sears catalogue.[54]

When things and engagement are exchanged for commodities and consumption,

> what moves one to take the step, so firsthand experience tends to show, is the persistent glamour of the promise of technology; the relief that one looks forward to in having the burden of preparing another meal lifted from one's shoulders; the hope of richer engagement with the world on the basis of greater affluence; the desire to provide one's child with the fullest and easiest means of development; the impatience with things that require constant care and frequent repair; and the wish to affirm one's existence through the acquisition of property that commands respect.[55]

Statistically as well, people do continue to adhere to the promise of liberation and enrichment.[56] These, then, are those moments when we choose technology over what Kubey and Csikszentmihalyi spoke of as those vivid signposts that show what it is that makes life worth living.

III

Technological Subversion

Technology subverts in two different ways. On the one hand, technology subverts things when it procures a mere aspect of a thing of depth. Koolwhip replaces whipped cream. This happens, importantly, when we speak abstractly of valuable things, for technologists are apt to present us with an alternative means to the same end. That is, technologists seek functional equivalents for the same value, e.g., a wilderness experience substitute. So value talk, raising the value question, does not cut deeply enough since it likely already assumes the means/end split of the technological framework. If we assume this split, we will be subverted by the device pattern. Technology's underlying ethic of freedom and prosperity has been subverted in this way. So too Charles Taylor's ideals of self-realization, regardless of how well-articulated, will meet a similar fate, becoming subverted to trivialized and deviant modes, unless such ideals of authenticity remain tethered to correlational coexistent things.

In this same fashion, Leopold's land ethic, abstractly conceived outside the context of his book, is subverted by today's Forest Service. Leopold writes:

> The 'key-log' which must be moved to release the evolutionary process for an ethic is simply this: quit thinking about decent land-use as solely an economic problem. Examine each question in terms of what is ethically and aesthetically right, as well as what is economically expedient. A thing is right when it tends to preserve the integrity, stability, and beauty of the biotic community. It is wrong when it tends otherwise.[57]

As we saw earlier, the Forest Service by law is required to manage the forest in terms other than economic expediency alone. The doctrine of multiple use, for instance, makes it consider other uses for the forest than those we typically associate with economic expediency, such as timber, grazing and mining. Recreation and big game habitat are the dominant goals for some areas. We saw that timber and hunting were supposed to be treated as equally important in the management plans for part of Cottonwood Canyon. Even if an area is selected to be managed primarily for timber, economic expediency is not the only factor taken into account.

Environmental Impact Statements and Assessments are undertaken so that factors of biological uniqueness, diversity and stability constrain the final management plans and their specifications such as the size, shape and placement of clearcuts. Finally, aesthetics and cultural factors get taken into account in the planning process and can constrain the final management of an area, such as Cottonwood Canyon. The timber sale proposal for Cottonwood Canyon leaves a strip of trees between the road and the clearcuts so that recreationists driving the road will not witness what, to the "average forest visitor," is ugly. And, of course, the clearcuts shaped like avalanche chutes are more costly than they would be if the agency were completely insensitive to beauty. So the Forest Service in a technologically subversive manner is employing the principles set forth by Leopold; yet most people who turn to Leopold's land ethic for guidance are not happy with the way the land is treated by the agency. The Forest Service may maintain some of the scenic factors of the canyon, but the real beauty and special character of the place will have been destroyed.

Technology subverts in a second way when heeding its pull overrides all other commitments and claims. If technology is the agreed upon cultural goal, then whatever comes into conflict with the steps thought to be necessary to achieve that goal will normally be defeated. We saw this defeat and subversion in our culture's willingness to destroy good work for the sake of production, and in choices of commodities over things. The same subversive force undermines the claims of social justice. In this area people do not need to develop an ethic from the ground up as Rolston does for the environment. Respect for the equality of persons in this country has been a force since the beginning, yet glaring inequality persists. Borgmann argues that our society believes that "pervasive relative deprivation fuels the motor of technological advancement."[58] They think that what the rich have today they will have tomorrow. Hence, so long as they continue to hold this belief, and so long as they are enthralled by the promise of technology, people will tolerate inequality. Global problems of misery and poverty claim people in affluent countries, too. Yet, with too few exceptions, they callously disregard these people in poverty so long the well-off are within the framework of the blessings of technology and continue to be fascinated with affluence.[59] Living with less affluence will seem to them a sacrifice of their prosperity as long as the vision of technology has their allegiance.

We see this subversion when people face the claims of excellence. People are still somewhat claimed by standards of traditional excellence. Often these standards are at the heart of the kind of life they would have liked to lead if less constrained or wish their children might.[60] However, our society does not act on behalf of this concern for excellence, e.g., people's command of science is weak, participation in politics is minimal, television programs which critics like least are being watched most and so on. Moreover, although people have room and means to shape their leisure, they do not spend their time at those kinds of activities which could suggest a dedication to the pursuit of excellence. Rather all activities suggesting a tie to excellence constitute less than a quarter of the time spent watching television.[61] This means that over eighty-five percent of their leisure time is devoted to something other than traditional excellence, that is, mostly consumption. So here again technology subverts the claims people still feel.

The Underlying Pull to Dominate Nature

Importantly for the task at hand—although it is only one case among many such subversions—technology subverts all other claims of nature and the natural world. From the standpoint of the device paradigm, the environment and nature are areas to bring under control and secure. Nature can be made available in the form of final commodities through roads, trains, the tourist industry, game farms, Disney movies and so forth. It can be brought under control in a defensive and insulating way through securing health, shelter, warmth, clothing and food. It can be brought under control for production through the exploitation of timber, oil, coal, and mineral resources. In bringing nature under control, technology has very often been voracious and short-sighted, yet, when technology proceeds this way, it fails by its own standards of safety and ease. It may saddle us with greater hardships than it relieves us from. Hence, the environmental crisis resulting from the physical limits to growth is not simply a point of concern raised by those living at the margins of the ruling paradigm. A telling sign of this is the fact that it has come to the center of attention. Everyone understands the need for trade-offs, achieving balance between environmental concerns and future growth. We need to live between the rims. This means that the environmental crisis is not radically a challenge *to* the framework of technology from outside its own terms, but rather challenges the framework *from within* to become more comprehensive.

How will environmental stability be sought in terms of the vision of technology? For this safety and ease, the device paradigm must be extended to the whole globe and take an enlightened, long-term view. This may fail, but how is it likely to succeed were it to succeed? Apart from economizing through engineering ingenuity and the elimination of wasteful practices, citizens of advanced countries, Borgmann believes alarmingly enough, will make the poor, and poor from other countries, pay the price of coming to terms with our physical limits. If successful, the technology

society's global future will tend toward a physically homeostatic equilib-
rium, though this is not likely soon.[62] (Even if scientists and engineers save
the planet, the question for us, unlike other critics of technology, always
is: will it be a planet worth living on?)

If this goal and its blueprint have people's tacit if not explicit assent,
what else will matter about nature? Clearly, nature from this standpoint is
viewed with merely sophisticated, enlightened self-interest. Clearly, just as
in the cases cited earlier, whatever other claims are registered from nature
and natural things in their own right, so long as people remain in agreement with and enthralled by the promise of technology, these claims will
not be heard and made room for, especially when making room for them
would entail some *sacrifice* of a high and rising standard of living and
hence to the good life of consumption. We found this agreement with
technology to be at the bottom of the imperatives to develop Cottonwood
Canyon. Then, too, the initial road bulldozed into Cottonwood Canyon
makes the wilderness more commodiously available for a summer home.
As should be clear by now, the underlying ethic of technology competes
with and defeats an environmental ethic, and so the claims made upon
people by nature and natural beings in accordance with Rolston's environmental altruism are likely to fare worse than the claims of social justice.
So long as the glamorous appeal of consumption has their ears, their heeding, the story of the domination of nature, in one variant or another, will
subvert the story of a new respect for nature. When environmentalists
argue people can have it both ways, both the environment they want and
the technological good life, the contradiction, when spelled out by a theory
of technology, becomes obvious. So, if the claims of nature and natural
things in their own right are to be respected, honored, and acted upon
with consequence, the ruling vision of technology must be protested and
successfully challenged.

How can this challenge take place? How can we begin to initiate a
reform of technology? We have taken a major step in this direction by
locating the fundamental problem as technology and by evaluating crit-
ically the vision of technology in terms of what it does to things and its
ironic consequences. Reflection enables us to step back and regard the
appeal of consumption as glamorously attractive but disappointing. The
hold that the vision of technology has upon us is thereby weakened, yet
more needs to be and can be done. It is not enough merely to cut back or
cut out entirely the amount of leisure time devoted to television, for otherwise we will easily fall back into its spell or that of another form of consumption. To counter consumption more generally we need to find attractive and substantial alternative things.

Things need more of a say in our lives. What we have yet to learn is the complete force of the appeal of things and appropriate ways to communicate that appeal. So that we may heed them, their voices must be given a hearing again and for the first time. Then, unlike those choice-points illustrated above, when we choose between technology and things of final importance, we will know the full weight of what we are agreeing to and protesting.

Technology will subvert us if we speak abstractly of correlational coexistent things, so how can we better awaken an understanding of the force of the appeal of these things? How best can we speak of *the things that matter* in the ways they matter? Over a cup of coffee in graduate school, I fell to reminiscing about the Crazies with a fellow student. As I stumbled about seeking the right words, I was surprised to learn that she understood well enough; she could see what mattered to me, that this came to life in my manner of speaking. Isn't that the way of it so often? To be intelligible the felt presence of the thing exacts a kind of showing. In chapter 11, "Learning to Speak Again," I will develop this idea. In the next chapter, I will exhibit it. My signpost will be an actual landmark, the Crazy Mountains themselves. When it comes to bringing home to us the full appeal, the real force of correlational coexistent things, philosophy and theory need to give way to narrative and poetry. Ultimately, it will be these powers of things and what they tell us that enable us to turn technology.

CHAPTER 6

GRANTING THE THING ITS ELOQUENCE

. . . the figure of a labourer—some furrows in a plowed field—a bit of sand, sea, and sky—are serious subjects, so difficult, but at the same time so beautiful, that it is indeed worth while to devote one's life to the task of expressing the poetry hidden in them.

—Vincent van Gogh[1]

He laughed. "They don't understand. We know these hills, and we are comfortable here." There was something about the way the old man said the word "comfortable." It had a different meaning—not the comfort of big houses or rich food or even clean streets, but the comfort of belonging with the land, and the peace of being with these hills.

—Leslie Marmon Silko *Ceremony*[2]

If anyone comes to the halls of poetry without the madness of the Muses, convinced that technique alone will make one a good poet, both the poetry of this man who is in possession of his senses and the man himself will fall short of perfection and be eclipsed by the poetry of those who are mad.

—Plato[3]

Beginnings

My first experiences with mountains were in the Crazies, where my family hunted. Their primary, though not exclusive, contact with the natural world was with rifles slung on their backs. Hunting stories were among the few in those years that my father found worth telling.

Our family must have hunted deer up Duck Creek in the Crazies, though for me at age three or four, the name itself was a much more concrete location than anything I could point to outside or locate on a map. I don't remember all that much about the trips we took—how many times we went or who shot what. I do remember I was drawn to my mother's rifle with its lever action and open sights because it seemed like the real thing.

The trip I cannot forget is one I did not take. When the light came on in the room I shared with my older brother I remember it was pitch black out, and it felt like the middle of the night, not morning at all. I asked how early it was. "Are you still going?" my mother asked. "I'm too tired," I said. Probably my parents were relieved. When I woke next it was bright out and they were long gone. I moped about the house all day behind my sisters who no longer went hunting after my father shot a soft-eyed deer. These Crazy mountains, wherever they were, were both near and distant to me that day—near because that's where my parents and brother were, distant because I'd let them leave without me.

"Up Duck Creek in the Crazies," I kept thinking. The next time I was up and ready. To this day, in the predawn hours, this memory or an unremembered stirring, nudges me out of sleep in order to meet the event of the day. Yes, I do have a sense of having missed something important; I could have, I should have done something about it. My life is in bad shape when I do not care enough to rise early for the event of the dawning day.

There are six mountain ranges within the region where I grew up: The Absarokas, Crazies, Beartooths, Gallatins, Bridgers, and the Bangtails. I spent time in all of them as a young boy. Not all of these were best known to me or my family and friends as ranges; some were mostly known by more local names: up Fleshman Creek, in Tom Miner Basin, on the Wineglass mountain. Having come to know them from the inside out, it takes a visual imagination to see them from outside in, to tie these places together as ranges. From town, however, the dramatic Absarokas and Crazies stood out distinct and unmistakable. The Absarokas, just across the river, were the most dear to me, and it was in them that I had my most decisive beginnings with mountains.

This time it was summer and I was four. My father and his friend took their sons—my brother Bill, and his friend Tom—on a pack trip. I was too young to go; I would get my chance, I was promised, when I was Bill's age. I fought it. But, in the end, I stayed home five days, sore the entire time.

I heard the stories about mules that were hard to handle, steep trails which turned back upon themselves called switchbacks, a pass called "The Saddle" up the South Fork of Deep Creek, a basin in Davis Creek with grassy meadows where they picketed the horses and mules, a secret shortcut to the Twin Lakes where one had to jump from one huge boulder to another, and, finally, the two magnificent ten pound trout my father caught there and brought back, and, the one, nearly as big, he got to shore before the hook pulled loose. The fish were put in the freezer, where they were taken out to be admired from time to time until the freezer quit one summer afternoon a few years later.

These fish and those stories embodied the presence of wilderness and its attraction for me. They spoke of a mysterious world I did not know yet longed to be immersed in. They seemed to be the key to it all. I lived for the time I would experience firsthand what I could only imagine from these stories.

To my disappointment three years later, my father was too busy to take me. Fortunately, the year after that, my sister, back from college in Iowa and missing the mountains, decided she wanted to hike some of this country. With Cheryl and my brother Bill, I took my first day-long hike up the South Fork of Deep Creek. We retraced the first part of Bill's earlier trip. I stood by the quiet Blue Spring, saw my first bear in the wild outside of Yellowstone, climbed the switchbacks, drank from the plentiful cold springs, and was shown the places and things my brother and my father had spoken of in their stories.

We were only strong enough to reach the Davis Creek divide, The Saddle, so named (by my family anyway) because of its deep, gentle, symmetrical sway so obviously a pass when viewed from the river valley below. From this pass I looked into a promised land. Below, bright with life, were the meadows with the meandering stream where my father and the others had camped and picketed the horses. The place was aptly called a basin, having a rounded, wide floor enclosed by abrupt walls. I learned then about avalanches and found it hard to imagine this warm, green place in winter, more difficult still to imagine snow having the force to snap trees I saw clipped off in strips.

Beyond the basin was Davis Creek, which I had heard so much about, not only from that trip four years ago, but because it was where my Uncle Louie, a Norwegian, herded sheep many seasons, back in the days when my grandparents knew these places. Louie once caught fish in a stream with his pants, tying the legs in knots. Somewhere between Davis Creek and where I was standing, through these surrounding walls of stone, was the short-cut where one had to jump from rock to rock to get through. There, somewhere out of sight would be those Twin Lakes and at least the one ten pounder that got away. One day I would return.

Again and again I do return. And always in wilderness I am returning to this place.

When I was thirteen I hunted mountain goats in the Crazies. Here again the stories preceded the experience. The same crew that had gone to the Twin Lakes in the Absarokas had hunted goats in the Crazies two years before. My brother had taken a big billy goat. I had heard about the rugged, trailless country, the tremendous cliffs, lakes above treeline, and goats that proved impossible to see after an October snowstorm. These stories did not quite ring like morning on my ear the same way the others had, but I idolized my brother and wanted to be the hunter and shot he was. So I put in for a goat permit.

This time my father took me. We were turned back on two trips by mountain fog. Though it had snowed a skiff the evening before, the day of this final effort dawned blue, and we started up Trespass Creek. Near the head, we followed a branch of it into a small cirque and began climbing the steep side. Midway up we faced unclimbable cliffs and had to sidehill below them quite a distance on a slope of small, pebbly rocks under which was a hard base, maybe frozen ground. The angle of the slope with its skiff of snow would not have been unnerving if it had ended fifty feet below in a swimming hole, but we were hundreds of feet up and the jags of the rocks at the bottom looked like the bared teeth of a vicious dog. I could not get solid footholds, though my father, ahead of me, seemed to be having no trouble even with his hands in his pockets. More than once I called for him to stop, which only earned me a scolding on the topic of toughness. He showed his disgust when he had to take my rifle at one point. I wanted no part of this anymore and, except for his presence, would not have gone on. Finally, the cliffs above us gave way and we climbed to the top of the ridge. I forgot about everything else and felt relief, huge relief, at being able to put my feet side by side and not having to cock them at an angle, always threatening to give out and send me sliding to the rocks below. Just at that moment Dad noticed the goats above us.

I guess they were an easy shot at first but I wasn't ready. By the time I ran to a good place to shoot from and rested my rifle against a snag, they were further away but still within range. I missed more than a couple shots. Then they were gone. I had blown it. I had moved too slowly, had been out of breath, had not held steady enough, had jerked the trigger. I have often been a good enough shot, but never have become a genuine marksman like my brother, nor a genuine hunter either. I don't care enough. The game never calls my aim to kill into the necessary resolve. I have gone through the motions, but it is not in my blood. I don't really want to shoot one of them. In these mountains, that has become clear.

Disappointing my father and not measuring up to my brother could have turned me to safer grounds, but these mountains did not send me away. I have come to accept now that I am no hunter; hunting is not what makes my breath worth the breathing. I don't have to prove differently to others. But when I get into rugged country, I discover the measure of what a long way I've come. I feel as sure-footed as a goat. I avoid taking genuine chances with falls when hiking alone, but I do not back away from places most would back away from simply because they look scary. This groove in the rockface will hold. That rock is not going anywhere. I am somewhat afraid of heights, but I have learned to trust rock and feet, hand and hold. If I came that way again, I, too, could put my hands in my pockets and let my mind drift to the realm of the forms. I delight in the feel of slanting rock under foot. My father worries about me now.

We followed the ridge to the notch-like pass where the goats had disappeared. It was the top of the world up there, an impressive view, and my first view of the Crazies from that height. We looked into the eastern side of the range, the Sweet Grass country. Below shimmered Moose and Campfire Lakes. Everywhere ridges rose, turned, arched, peaked, and dipped out of sight like the backs of a school of churning, frenzied fish breaking from the surface of the water. Some ridges had spines, others looked like blades chipped from stone, while still others rose friendlier, like a shoulder, with wide, rounded tops. It was crazy country to put together—valleys going this way and that way, each with a mind of its own. None ran straight. Some elbowed around as if lost. Some curved elegantly, like the spiraling horn of a Bighorn ram, only to be cut off abruptly by the thoughtless intrusion of another. These ridges did not fall out into the relaxed harmonious patterns of bigger country river drainages—there the Stillwater, there the Boulder, there the Yellowstone. By comparison, this place looked like the poet Richard Hugo's Philipsburg with streets laid out by the insane.

Once in Yellowstone Park I rounded a large boulder only to startle a grazing Bighorn ram at close range. In an instant, his head was up and he froze. The great eye of the far-seeing ram locked with mine, drew my soul back not only to Pharaoh, Egypt and echoing monuments, but back further still beyond mind and memory, past even animal life, to stone, earth and water. A life looked back out of life to elemental eternity. The magical, telescopic eye of the Pharaoh horned ram held me, and slung me out of time. Like a comet, I returned to a life beyond, a life restored, rapt, serene, complete, whole. Man, ram, rock, one.

Nimble as dancers, innocent as children, carefree as birds, goats are little white mustard seeds high up in the impossible cliffs. Shooting goats is ridiculous.

Lessons

What is really learned by walking over grassy hills, through sagebrush, in river bottoms, beneath the crowns of a forest? What is learned wading rivers, hiking ridges, climbing mountains, listening to waterfalls, swimming in lakes, lying beneath the stars? There is not a simple answer to these questions. Perhaps it is misguided to think there are any essential answers, however some seem to clue us in.

"Many an irksome noise, go a long way off, is heard as music, a proud satire on the meanness of our lives," wrote Thoreau. I remember hunting for elk when I was fourteen. We camped out below the Davis Creek divide in the Absarokas at about nine thousand feet during the last week of October. It snowed and was very cold that night making it impossible to sleep in my light sleeping bag. At four o'clock we got up, fixed breakfast, climbed to the pass and waited for daylight to show us the basin and, we hoped, elk below. Dawn came but we could make out only momentary glimpses of the basin below between periods of gale driven snow and cloud cover. There would be no elk. That was plain. I was miserably cold and the wind was my enemy. I just wanted to get out of there.

The wind always seemed to be an adversary in Livingston, one of the windiest places in the nation. As a kid I had to put my head down and stand on the pedals riding my bike home from school. It roughened the ice for skating. It drifted snow in the road in winter so we had to walk. Later, it ruined flyfishing and snowskiing, and made me flinch when gusts pelted my cheeks with sand. I was surprised to hear a friend in high school say she loved the wind.

Then something happened in my senior year of college to let me know all that had changed. I had cut out in the late afternoon to drive up a nearby canyon and hike. While climbing a ridge to the top of the mountain I heard the winds far off rushing through the trees toward me. Suddenly I heard and felt in those winds the same winds blowing in my face on Davis Creek divide. Only this time they came free and lifted me with them. They made me glad to have been there. This wind was my friend and I had come to love it.

Wind is not always pleasant. But I know if I went back to that pass again, my heart would laugh with the cold, and snow and howling wind. This time I would be older.

In the Crazies, I go a long way off, I achieve distance.

I like to think of a particular gunsight pass between the two highest peaks in the Crazies. If I could see the wind and it were water, behind the Crazies to the southwest would be a lake stretching all the way to Old Faithful and further. And through this low gap would be such a torrent as exists nowhere on Earth.

"And what you thought you came here for, is only a shell, a husk of meaning," T.S. Eliot wrote. The first time I hiked to Cottonwood Lake I did not make it. The trail gave out about the time the legs of the friend I was with did. We lost the trail and headed back down, but we stumbled upon a lake tucked away in the cirque walled in with the high cliffs. The Crow called these Bird Home Mountains. This lake with no name is a sacred place. I often go there to renew again my understanding of how the world is put together. One time I was there it was the final day of an eight-day backpack that took me round the Crazies. Two eagles drifted into the cirque, circled the lake, and flew back down Cottonwood Canyon. I took heart at that good sign and followed them out.

When Cottonwood Canyon was first slated for a timber sale, I took a photographer friend up to get a few pictures of the place. Paul was not an early riser and we arrived about thirty minutes too late for what I would sometime in my life like to see. Often when a big storm pulls out, those underneath don't perceive any weather change has occurred until the sun burns the lower mists off. Above this mass, the mountains can be glistening under a blue sky, looking simultaneously heavy and floating like islands in the sky. The Crazies may have had this look that morning had we arrived sooner and climbed the knob we did.

I talked Paul into hiking to the lake. We arrived, went swimming, ate lunch, talked, climbed around in the rocks, glissaded down the snowfields and took photographs. Only in the most real sense, we never got there. Everything was too self-consciously accomplished to be really in touch with what I had felt about this place. Everything had a film on it I could not rip away. No wild goats danced high in the impossible cliffs that day.

On another occasion I forgot my binoculars four miles back on the trail in the Absarokas. It was already dusk when I discovered their absence by trying to find out what that dark object was ahead in the willowed meadows. Good place for a grizzly. There was no time to go back then, and my two companions, already miffed because I had fished too long at Silver Lake, insisted we begin hiking out early in order to make it to the trailhead and back to town on schedule. Scheduled time and mountain time grate on one another to my way of thinking. Anyway, I rose with the first hints of dawn, put on my pants stiff with frost, and hiked back there. As soon as I had shaken off my drowsiness I noticed it was a fine morning and I was glad to be up with it. Wilderness time is dawn time. The air, the clarity, the fragrances, the sounds all rise into being and are not yet messed up, so to speak, by the day.

I found the glasses and looked for a new way back, a shortcut. The trail actually followed the ridge a couple miles below a long wall of cliffs before topping the ridge and doubling back to where we camped. All I had to do was go over the ridge if I could find a way through the cliffs. As luck would have it, there was a break in the first row not far from where I found the binoculars. After a couple of attempts, I found a way to the top and chuckled at my good fortune. The night before I had calculated that if I could just make it to the top the other side would be easy.

What I did not anticipate was the astounding view of Pyramid Peak I found to the south when I broke over the ridge. This lone, tall, glacier-carved peak caught the first rays of the rising sun. Down ridge was back to camp and my waiting companions, but up the other way the ridge I was on culminated in a lower, climbable peak and possibly a better view of Pyramid. There was nothing between it and me except distance and time. I did not resist. I found Pyramid across the way standing calmly in an unforgettably clear light, casting a tremendous dark shadow for miles across the wide valley to the west below. Though I knew it would not last, peak and shadow seemed to stand there at rest as they had done for ten thousand years.

On my way down I spooked a buck deer. As he turned to look at me, his antlers flared with morning light.

"Teach us to care and not to care. Teach us to sit still," wrote Eliot in "Ash Wednesday." Wilderness is not only a place you go. Wilderness is what happens to you. Shivered, sweated, baked, bathed, often not knowing when, not knowing where, only knowing it happened somewhere along this song called trail, I wash away all my old outworn skin and am now fresh, clean, whole and happy.

Wilderness distance is not just the country mile, though it is that. Wilderness distance is not a distance traversable by steps alone. Wilderness distance is indirect distance. You must be called up and called out as you move along. You must ascend, somehow always miraculously, your own inward mountain if you are to greet these mountains as they greet you. To be small in mountains is to feel the loneliness of the withheld.

Traversing wilderness distance can be assisted, though not guaranteed, with practices. Streams have taught me to meditate. Listen, hear, and see. Streams come from above, wash by, wash away. What arises let play in currents, wash by, wash away down stream. Listen. See. Hear. Concentrate. Let it wash by, wash away having had its say. Again and again.

Sweet Grass Creek. Delicate, worn, rounded, pooled. Echoing, carved pools. Pools remembering the spring dripping centuries. Thin, graceful drips. Water dropped to the pool below from the long longing moss above, dropped to the quieted pool; pool held up to light; held up to forest and sky, cloud and sun. It says, "Look here to see!" Pool holds up rock, sand, and fish, not just to green forest but to watercolored trees. Bottom and sky in transparent display. Distorted, brought forth in liquid being. Down tumbling, whitewater stilled in the pool. Quieted, transparent, made clear.

Being

While fishing the Yellowstone without much luck one early May, I fell to contemplating the Crazies, bright with new spring snow against a cloudless sky. I followed a ridge up from the foothills to where it disappeared, suggesting a passable route to the peak behind it. And so I awoke early at Rock Creek trailhead in the middle of July. Before I was ready to leave, a farmer appeared on his four-wheeler to check the irrigation ditches nearby. I enjoy the playful headshaking that goes on between people bent over shovels and people bent under packs, each pretending not to understand how the other "could do that sort of thing."

Leaving the trailhead, I soon left the trail, too, for the ridge, and by late morning stood at the top. I saw I could not get to Fairview peak from there, the connecting ridge was a smile of sheer cliffs, but a new route opened up to the north and so I hiked down into the cirque below, followed the stream down and up another to its headwall, crossed it, another down and up, and I was at Crazy Lake to camp for the night. It had been a long day, and the mountains had impressed me with their moodiness. The Crazies gather and they scatter. The peaks, ridges, and canyons twist off every which way and, so, too, does one's mood when hiking in them. At times I soared with the view; other times, feeling weak (sometimes I don't eat much while backpacking), I clung to a hard-won truth: "Mountains have tops." But at the top, amidst cirques, peaks and ridges, there is so much rock and the rock is overwhelmingly grey. I like shrubs and trees, meadows, dark earth, meandering streams and the fragrance of bottomlands. High in the Crazies even the lakes can be surrounded entirely by grey rock, and more than once I thought: next time I will choose a place with more life.

I had just poured a cup of coffee the next morning when the sun's first rays fell on the lake and me. Suddenly again I knew why the Crow people prayed to the sun, smoked the sacred pipe, and acknowledged the four directions and Mother Earth at sunrise. The Crazies teach me to be alert to the joints of the day. We would do well to pause and linger before what gathers. Yet when I began to ascend a steep ridge out of the cirque my oppressive mood returned. It seemed to hang in the air. But I kept climbing, thinking, "rhythm . . . rhythm." It came to me as a kind of helper being.

Changing moods, changing weather, the sun and clouds played chess with one another. Reaching the ridge top near Crazy Peak, I waited a few hours to discover if the clouds would clear or settle in. They did neither, so I worked my way down through the cliffs, letting my pack go first over the tougher drops, glad I hadn't known how hairy the cliffs looked from below. I decided to camp in an alpine meadow above Pear Lake. After a brief afternoon thundershower, the sky began to clear. "I won't put up the tent," I thought. Then at twilight I noticed a small sheet of mist, a mere clue, drifting in from the north, a long way off. "Better put up my tent." Before I had it up and got the camp in order, the valleys below had filled with an ocean of white fog that now rushed toward me, bending up and flowing down the ridges, surf of a fast rising tide. Soon I could not even make out the pass behind me and I had to check my bearings by the way I had set up the tent. That night a blast of wind that crackled the fly of the tent awakened me. The stars were out.

I did not sleep well, dreaming of an avalanche burying me alive. Above me spread a large snowfield with a sizable cornice perched at the top. In summer they do not slide, especially at night, but try to convince your dreaming mind. Being buried alive in snow, perhaps only a couple feet below the surface, not knowing which way is up or down, east or west, north or south, not knowing where to begin to dig a way out: this seemed a terrible way to die. It seemed to define what it means to be disoriented.

Tired, I fell fast asleep at dawn. When I woke, the clouds overhead, now coming from their usual southwest, were dark and heavy. As I finished rolling up my tent the rain began, hesitated and then stopped. Groggy, not eager to begin the climb to the ridge or to cross the large and possibly dangerously steep snowfield, I stopped packing to make my morning coffee.

In the few minutes it took to boil water, the sun came out, the sky cleared, and my mood lifted. These peaks, meadows, lakes, this sunlight and sky filled me with light and life. Some shy and wary spirit in me could relax here, wander out freely without threat or fear. This clean, vast country danced my dance. Its distances were my distances. Its peaks, my peaks. Its beauty, my own. This country allowed me to breathe, to be. "This is exactly the right place." Whenever you go out of it, which ever way you travel, you fare worse. This is the way the world was created: these morning lit peaks, meadows, lakes, this newly cleared sky, this freshness, my joy; nothing out of place.

My heavy boots proved their worth by notching out solid steps across the top of the steep snowfield in those morning hours as I climbed to the pass. I knew of a waterfall down in the next valley and decided to make it my destination for the day. Sometimes I get on a roll and can't seem to stop, but the Crazies do not let me be that way for long. Why not rest here at this deep pool, take the pack and these clothes off, bathe in snowmelt water? Sun warms. Breezes cool. Clouds tell me when to move. I am always, already in nature here. It initiates what I do and think and feel. Nature imagines my life and I delight in weaving the unforeseeable patterns.

I made camp in the trees at the edge of the meadow beside the waterfall and followed the stream up to a perch above. Earlier that day at the pass I had picked up an ice ax. As a friend later put it, "That was a find." Why should we think to report the finding of equipment and take that to be the definitive find? I could buy the ax for not much over $50. I spent four days in the Crazies and brought back an ice ax. I would not even be working for minimum wage, and much less, if I counted the times I brought back nothing but dried sweat and words. What do we find in wilderness that we have such a difficult time communicating to each other? Why are our lives better for wilderness? It is not the wages nor the products. I've had little call for an ice ax.

There were a few more minutes of sunlight left before the sun fell behind a ridge. What do I see, think, say in the midst of this joint of the day? Thanks to the meadow, I had seen this waterfall before and made up my mind to spend some time here on this backpack trip. Thanks to the waterfall, I saw this vantage point from which I survey the meadow, the valley, the ridges and peaks beyond. Thanks to this passing and splendid light, I am drawn out of myself to see what there is. Thanks to the long shadows and soft light, the greenest of plants brighten. Paint Brushes flame. Birds fly and sing. Word things. Bird friends. Wild ones.

In the shadows and evening light, two ancient pines stood out in the distance in the swathes cut by avalanches. Withstanding these avalanches year after year, they grew strong, large and old. Because of these trees, I knew what I would do first thing in the morning.

I have never seen and never will see a house grander than these trees. Rocks have gashed them. Avalanches have uprooted or snapped every tree around them. Lightning twice has spiraled down the trunk of one tree. Claw marks of a bear have made their way up the other. Porcupines have scarred them. Disease and old age have found their ways into them. Wind has shaped their branches into blown hair. Still they endure, like the face in a photograph of an old, frowning Indian warrior.

Thanks to these pines I found another tree, not far away among the younger firs. Beside it I discovered another of these pines which had crashed to the Earth, how long ago I could not say, though more than a year. What I heard in what I saw was a silence, a terrible crack, boom and silence again. Limbs, branches and twigs were shattered by the fall but not scattered. Fallen pieces lay as if caught and held in a painting. This dead, barkless, awesome, fallen tree evoked and defined the words of *Eccle-siastes*. "If the tree falls toward the south, or toward the north, in the place where the tree falleth, there it shall be." That was a find.

I sat beside the waterfall that morning and watched these Crazy Mountains spin memories I did not know I had and weave them into place. Watching the wave at the tail of the pool above the falls curl over, back, and crest, I see the wake behind the open aluminum motorboat our family owned. In the steady drumming of the plummeting water below I hear again the steady buzz of the outboard motor at full throttle. As a child, on Lewis Lake in Yellowstone, I would lie crossways in the curve of the bottom of the boat as we returned to camp at the day's end. The boat bottom was cold to the touch but out of the wind, and I could feel against my back the water seeming to rush beneath as we sped on. Here too I was curled in a notch of rock as I had been once in that boat—a little cold but out of the wind, watching the wave crest, letting my thoughts drift with an even-keeled mood, feeling all is well. These were good times. These are good times.

Later I made my way out.

Just being. Not very self-conscious, not pretending, simply corresponding, just being. Slinging this pack on my back I feel I am lifting the great song again. Feels good to be in my boots. Rock, dirt, boot, foot, leg and muscle join without gap—belong to each other, belong here. This morning I move through these trees resolute. Sharp-eyed, lion-like, I prowl this unpathed landscape, not knowing where I am or where I am going. Walking firm, hands bending branches out of the way, feet not missing a step. I am wild again. I am made for this place and this place is made for me.

Being, not thinking. Not saying, just being. I follow this landscape like a song. Watchful, moving, being, not rigidly destined. Moving with things calling out to move. Branches and clearings show the way. Here is the elemental, the wild, the old. Here are well-worn clothes with a comfortable fit. Here I become one of the old people.

Conclusions

We are a people on this side of the divide, the Enlightenment. We cannot be satisfied to watch suffering and hardship that can be relieved. We cannot be satisfied with figurative justice. Nor can we be satisfied to remain ignorant of matters we can bring to light using science. We do not want either superstition or the marvelous. But should we cut down what others have called sacred just because we lack the language for what is intimated to us by these things? The Earth is not a miserable green rock we are making a better place to live, though we live as though it were. The Earth is the center, the sacred center of the universe. Why change it when it is already as good as it can be? Humans need to learn to know what they love and care for, and its irreplaceable worth, if the given arrangement of our planet is to remain valuable, valuable enough to make human life here worth it. We can want every step we take on this planet if we live carefully, deliberately.

Crazy in name, crazy in character, crazy in legend. The god whose work these mountains are may have been good, may have been powerful, but certainly that god could not have had a designing mind. These mountains were stirred not with care but indifference. And with indifference they treat all who come and exist here. Wind, rock, sky, cloud mix here mechanically. Sharp rock pitted against gale-driven snow. More eternal is this gnawing than the damned of Dante's last circle. More eternal because more uncaring, completely indifferent—they are not even defiant, inhuman in striving. Shoved by indifference into one another's presence, there they seem to war when actually we have no word to render what is so completely without form except for the indifference that holds it together for a time.

Where in this deranged tangle of rock is there reason for us to care? Why should we treat with care something so uncaring? Isn't this just neutral rock? Couldn't its arrangement be otherwise? Shouldn't it be otherwise? What in this indifferent deranged range wants us to want it the way it is?

The lightning and hail storm that kills eight head of cattle in the river valley nearby and now crackles about my storm-flattened tent does not intend to harm or benefit me, these mountains, or the cattle below. Lightning and mountains are givens without a giver.

The universe is very large and mostly cold. Often we would wish-believe this away. But the prayers go out and do not return—that heaven is empty. In my wakeful moments I realize that things are better without a giver, better to be impersonal givens. I am not safe or unsafe because of any divine plan. Seeing lightning as planned is not to see it at all, but to skip over it and become uneasily comforted by a superstition. Not the supernatural, but the natural makes us free. I do not blame lightning when it harms. It is not directed and controlled, bears no message like that for us. Yet, only as lightning remains impersonal can I receive its gift. In it, I sometimes find a splendor and release, blessed with a prosperity beyond what I willed. If lightning flashes, the thunder claps, and the chasm grown in me is healed for a time, if I am moved from estrangement to intimacy, that is their good gift to me, an unintended outcome. And this too—after the storm, the morning order is restored and sometimes passes, without noticeable break, into twilight. The Crazies are generous. These givens without a giver are its good gifts. Even here we can be at home like nowhere else.

Gentle water flowing freely over glacier smoothed rock. Wild water. Water not channeled, canalled, reservoired, piped, bottled, drunk without sight, smell, sound. Water falling through sunlight. Falling uncaring. Uncaring meeting of sunlight and water. Just being. Being whether I am, whether I deserve. These mountains are not mountains of merit or design. These mountains are kind, kind with uncaring grace.

PART II

LEARNING FROM WILDERNESS

We can *talk about* how things gather a world and how they engage us in many ways and on many levels, or we can *show* this in the way we have come to witness it and to understand it. In the preceding chapter I have attempted to show it, not talk about it. My contention is that this disclosive discourse is necessary for a more complete understanding of what things are and how important and appealing they are.

Throughout Part I we have moved from Cottonwood Canyon to its recent road, from pinebark beetles to planned clearcuts, from Livingston, Montana to Livingston, New Jersey, from the story of progress to the story of decline, from environmental ethics to the philosophy of technology, from the exploitation of resources to the consumption of final commodities, from climbing Crazy Peak to stair step machines, from things to commodities, and then from commodities to things, from television to the visions of beauty in the Crazy Mountains, and so we have located the crux of the issue for our culture. Things are now beacons in a wilderness of technology gone wild. Will we continue to agree with the vision of technology or will we affirm the vision of things and make room for them? Since this issue is so basic, it is difficult to grasp what turns on it and difficult to weigh it reflectively. Nonetheless, like Odysseus, before we can come home, what we need to learn must come home to us, and so the first four chapters of Part II weigh the implication of technology and the absence of things against the presence of things and the quality of life they sponsor and inform. Here we will learn to listen to, consider and experience things again. Wild things and wilderness remain our chief focus. Chapter 11, "To Speak Again," shows why and how we must present things in disclosive discourse. The final chapter, "To Build Again," presents the new challenge to the culture of technology. To come to inhabit the Earth we must relinquish the vision of technology and its old challenge, and learn to build in a technological setting a culture of correlation—of things and humans.

CHAPTER 7

TO LISTEN AGAIN

I wondered if Mose and First Raise were comfortable. They were the only ones I really loved, I thought, the only ones who were good to be with. At least the rain wouldn't bother them. But they would probably like it; they were that way, good to be with, even on a rainy day.

—James Welch, *Winter in the Blood*[1]

Where wast thou . . . when the morning stars sang together?

—*Job*

Must you always have battle in your heart?

—Kirkê's question to Odysseus

Reading our age in terms of the story of moral progression has misled many writers in environmental ethics, such as Leopold, to think that our specific form of domination, technological domination, is present in both our Greek and Judeo-Christian heritage.[2] These writers tend to *read back* into the tradition the same heedlessness found in our own time. For instance, William Aiken writes,

> If only human interests are of moral worth then it makes little moral difference how we treat other animals. Provided that human interests are promoted then we can use animals any way we desire. Traditionally, animal husbandry is an important part of agriculture . . . Since the well-being of the animal is often crucial to the survival of these farmers they are not likely to mistreat them (for instance, by making them work too long in the hot sun or carry too heavy loads). Yet their interests are clearly being subordinated to human interests.[3]

Such a reading of husbandry reduces all concerns to those of the dear self. However, to look at agriculture in terms of food production, pigs in terms

of pork production, and chickens as mere egg-producing machines is characteristic *only* of the technological age.[4] One can imagine horses being
used in the expedient way Aiken speaks of. Considered carefully, however,
horses are not merely less powerful, less efficient and more of a hassle
than the tractors which replaced them. Wendell Berry, for instance, shows
that a culture and way of speaking grew up around the plowhorse. A boy
became a "teamster," "an accomplished man" because of them.[5] Berry ap-
preciates their beauty. Like the animals themselves, he finds the work not
a mere means but valuable in its own right. Horse and work bring him to a
homecoming,

> . . . Now every move
> answers what is still.
> This work of love rhymes
> living and dead. A dance
> is what this plodding is.
> A song, whatever is said.[6]

Whatever else may be said about the above, this treatment of animals is
not that of the shallowly considered heedless thinking of petty homocentrism. Both human and horse are brought forth in the way of correlational
coexistence. Berry's treatment of horses is certainly considerate in a
thingly way, and ultimately it steps in the right direction for resolving the
profound problem of technology, for finding a real way of inhabiting the
Earth which is compatible with and respectful of all its beings.

We must be careful, then, not to take our bearings from the shallow
view of our time and read that back into other epochs of our tradition. It is
easy to blame the way we dominate nature in our age on our Greek, Jew-
ish, and Christian roots. Yet it may be time to remind ourselves that no
one in these earlier traditions would have predicted that we would interpret the texts of these traditions the way we do since there are so many
other possible interpretations of them. For instance, I think we need to be
reminded that none of the Hebrews would have guessed that the 'message'
of the *Genesis 1* creation story would have been heard by the movers and
stompers of our age as: "In the beginning God formed a big ball of raw
material. On the sixth day God put humans on the Earth and said, 'I didn't
quite finish the job. Have at it! I hate to see it go to waste. Build! Reshape
it. Develop it into something.'" The better question for us to ask ourselves
is why we read this kind of interpretation back into the tradition.
Thoughtfully considered, our western traditions, even our American pioneering tradition, may teach us a great deal about meeting the deeper
issues of our age more resourcefully. Nearly everywhere in them we can

learn more *respectful* ways of being with nature and natural beings than we commonly display today.

I

Creation, Wilderness, and the Possibility of a Good World

Our culture has made an implicit covenant with technology. Cast into Bible-like terms, the covenant might read something like this: If you dominate nature, you will live a free and prosperous life. How? By becoming liberated from suffering and toil and by being able to be provided with all the fruits of the Earth. However, many of us have serious reservations about this trivialized view of freedom and happiness, and some of those reservations arise because of the teachings of the Bible. There we are not told to consume in order to be happy, but we are admonished that we cannot serve both God and mammon.[7]

Following the promise of technology, we seek the blessed life through items that are possessed and under our control. We have them at will. Yet the things most traditional religions point to are beyond the will, and much religious language focuses on the renunciation of control and an openness to events that are beyond our control, that are more and other than we expected. Hence, religious language is the language of inspiration and insight, healing of spirit, gift, creation, blessing, miracle and grace. In contrast, the language of commodities is that of bargain, possession and fingertip control. The only trait that the promise and goods of technology shares with the promise and blessings of the Bible is people's devotion to them as ways of life.

Still one may wonder if the Judeo-Christian tradition is too other-worldly to affirm life on Earth. Taken literally, nothing seems more unnatural than miracles or God's intervention in history. It may seem that the Judeo-Christian tradition, trying to avoid idolatry, deliberately downplays the importance of 'things', yet it is the transformation of and loss of these special things and places which is at the heart of the problem with the technological transformation of the Earth. *The Book of Job* gives us an opportunity to see how important these things (and in Job it is 'wild things') are in one strand of this tradition.

Job. Rather than a meditation on divine justice—on how, in a creation by an omnipotent, omniscient, and good God calamity and affliction can come to an upright and innocent man—that is, rather than an attempt to justify the ways of God to humans, *Job* seems to me as a meditation on the character of divine power. Divine power is assumed to be manifested as the ability to manipulate, control and, generally, overpower nature and natural beings. God seems to be able to coerce anything at will, when, as it turns out, power which is experienced as genuinely divine is found from an entirely unsuspected direction.

The prologue of *Job* is written in the style of myth. Job is portrayed as a righteous man who sacrifices even for his sons and daughters, lest they have sinned. Satan gets God to allow him to test Job's righteousness by having Job suffer first a calamity in which he loses his property and his children and then a calamity in which his body is afflicted with sores and disease. Changing styles to a dramatic dialogue, the book has Job defend his righteousness to his friends as he pleas to God for a justification for his plight. After this dialogue ends, God answers Job out of a whirlwind. Through this revelation, Job is healed, although its difficult to see why or how. The epilogue, returning to the style myth, reinforces this sense of healing by having his calamitous conditions reversed.

In the prologue and epilogue, God's power is made out to be the exercise of this coercive power overpowering creation. God grants permission to Satan to bring on calamity and touch the body of Job; God restores Job's body, brings him new children, and doubles his wealth. Both Job and his friends assume God exercises this kind of power over creation. Because God is in control, what good and evil, rewards and punishments, come to humans is justly deserved by them. The righteous and good supposedly are benefited and prosper, while the wicked are punished and perish. Were not such the order of the creation, something would be wrong with God in terms either of goodness or of the power to control.

His friends seem to read Job's condition by way of their theory of God and the universe. Here is an instance of punishment and perishing; therefore, great wickedness must have preceded it. More deeply, *Job* shows these men to be worried about themselves. His affliction presents them with a possibility of being they are vulnerable to and wish to avoid. They do so by setting Job apart from themselves. There *must* be something wrong with him.[8]

At first, Job, too, tries to set this possibility of being away from himself when he rationalizes the first calamity that befalls him. "The Lord gave, and the Lord hath taken away; blessed be the name of the Lord." But the second calamity will not allow him to stand at this safe distance that his friends do. Suffering now touches his body inescapably as affliction, rendering this possibility of being undeniable for him. Job, who maintains and defends his integrity, cannot deny this possibility of being which should be impossible within the framework of a good God exerting cverpowering control of creation. The greatness of Job is his unwillingness to accept a false answer, and yet, in these impossible conditions, he still believes that an answer is possible, and it is only this possibility that keeps him alive.

Somehow, the revelation of the voice out of the whirlwind makes the difference to him. The character of this difference needs careful analysis. First, according to the text, Job repents of what "I uttered that I understood not."[9] The text implies he understood something through direct acquaintance rather than merely by assenting to tradition. Secondly, Job has been healed, although what that healing means remains a question. Merely having his sores removed, recovering his wealth, etc., would not fully heal a person of Job's integrity in his position. On the contrary, these restorations are unnecessary to a true healing in the sense Job's condition requires. So, thirdly, if a healing takes place, it does so because Job is somehow answered. His friends recognize his having been healed and having been answered. Finally, whatever answer Job finds in the revelation it is certainly not from an expected direction, not that of a God exerting absolute control explaining (and justifying) to Job why he suffers.

If this is good drama—that is, if a warrant for Job's affirmation and healing is generated in the *Book of Job*—then there must be something in the revelation that answers a person of Job's integrity. It seems unintelligible to me that such a person could be healed through an overwhelming display of coercive power. Humiliation is not what heals Job; that would only compound his affliction.

We need to attend closely to the whirlwind's address to Job. It begins by invoking creation and remains throughout a kind of creation story. We notice, surprisingly, the creation in the revelation is not anthropocentric. "Who hath divided a water course for the overwhelming of waters, or a way for the lightning of thunder; to cause it to rain on the earth, where no man is: on wilderness, wherein there is no man."[10] Neither is sentient life the center of creation. "Who provideth the raven with his food? When the young ones cry unto God, they wander for lack of meat."[11] In fact, this is not even a biocentric creation. "Who can number the clouds in his wisdom? or who can stay the bottles of heaven, when the dust growth into hardness, and clods cleave fast together."[12] It would be more accurate to say that this is a world without center where things are as they are without reason:

> Gavest thou the goodly wings unto the peacocks? or wings and feathers unto the ostrich? which leaveth her eggs in the earth, and warmeth them in dust, And forgetteth that the foot may crush them, or that the wild beast may break them. She is hardened against her young ones, as though they were not hers: her labor is vain without fear.[13]

If this is a creation where intention is absent, it could not, then, aim at touching Job with affliction. The coercive, regardless force of nature is indeed regardless. Fine, one may rejoin. The world may be this way, but only at the price of its divine or religious character. The problem of evil is resolved through a dissolution of its premises. Indeed we may expect Job to take just such a position.

But such resignation on the part of Job would preclude the possibility of remaining open to what can speak to his condition. At the same moment that these negating steps are carried out in the revelation, something unexpected is coming to be. We see in fact that the rain which falls on the desolate ground also causes "the bud of the tender herb to spring forth."[14] Here we are presented not with a biocentric universe, but with poetry. The effect of this line is like that of a passage near the ending of James Welch's novel, *Winter in the Blood,* in which, after a long, dry summer in the enormous distances of Montana plains, a miserable, estranged, and resigned man finds a healing touch in a rainstorm and thereby a determination to live. "Some people, I thought, will never know how pleasant it is to be distant in a clean rain, the driving rain of a summer storm. It's not like you'd expect, nothing like you'd expect."[15] Similarly, we are not simply left with the ostrich crushing her eggs, suggesting the nonsense of creation. "What time she lifteth up herself on high, she scorneth the horse and the rider." Things have a dignity which calls on us to behold them. "Things too wonderful for me, which I knew not."[16]

The vision Job has is essentially a vision of wilderness and wild things: "Doth the eagle mount up at thy command, and make her nest on high?"[17] Wild country and wild things are what they are quite apart from human assistance. In a culture where things are viewed as needing to be reshaped, the wild is seen either as so much raw material or worthless. "What good is it?" And yet for Job they do not have to be made over. The fresh vision of things in their created wildness, in their being what they are quite apart from both being *for us* or being *assisted by* us, is what, I take it, heals Job. What is this fresh vision of things stripped of their everydayness?

In Job's vision, creatures and creation are realized as wondrous not by dominating nature but by respecting wild creatures in their own right. Yet to say this is the key is not yet to enact it. Job comes to insights neither by theoretical speculation nor by observation and inductive reasoning. He could not have grasped them at first because he lacks both the preparation that readies him and the experience that funds these insights. Accordingly, Job's friends may not have heard the voice from the whirlwind at all, although they may well have registered its significance in the eyes and face of Job. The reader is in the same position. We may not be ready for nor have we had the kind of experience which would yield the disclosures presented to Job by the voice from the whirlwind. Certainly the answer is not arrived at either by a careful analysis of the text alone or by following an experimental procedure properly. Rather the revelation and its healing effect on Job are set forth as something to be realized only by living the questions themselves. Otherwise, how can we come to terms with Leviathan and Behometh, those strange monsters? Why are they included in the whirlwind's revelation? What effect do they have on the healing of Job?

Once, on a hike, I startled a massive bull moose in a small meadow. After the initial jump, which alerted me, his head swung around to eye, with what felt like anger and contempt, this undersized creature who had surprised him. "Behemoth" leaped to my mind. I was ready to drop my pack and run for safety, yet I found myself overtaken with awe and fascination. Not the fearful, but the beautiful, held me there. Delicate yellow pollen lightly dusted the gleaming black hair of his powerful shoulders and back.

Such an experience may transport us to a different place and let us know all is well. Job is healed, I believe, because he is restored to the goodness of creation, a sense of goodness resonant with the *Genesis 1* creation story. What restores him to this sense of creation is a vision of wild things in their own right. Divine power here is not the exercise of heedless coercive power over creation. The mightiness of divine power is seen by what it can do in a spiritual way, that is, heal this person suffering affliction. This power is known, not by mere belief or theory, but by direct acquaintance.

The sense of being found in *Job* is a sense of wild things. It is a staying with creation and creatures. In fact, it is the renewing and restoration of the *with-relation* where divine power is most manifest. Wild things in *Job* have re-creating powers. Stripped of their everydayness, they stand out as independent, wild, wondrous, and not susceptible to possession. In their revealed re-created presence they reach Job in a way that recreates him and makes him whole. Wild things help Job find his way into being again, or for the first time. Correlationally coexistent, creation is restored for both creatures and self.

These re-creating powers of things do not play the only role in Job's enlightenment. Adversity plays an essential role, too, forcing him to confront possibilities of being with which he would otherwise be too patient, as he was in the prologue. Affliction forces the assumptions of his thinking forward to be challenged. Ultimately, affliction empties and opens him to hear the re-creating address of wild things.

The Pioneers and Wilderness. How can this sense of revealed wholeness and restored creation, this healing, inform our existence in today's world? Before we can make headway here, we must be sure that we have come to terms with another, earlier way that the wild land and wild things appealed to many of our ancestors.

The wild country of the American West confronted the pioneers of

European ancestry as an adversary to be struggled with and overcome. Usually we view the pioneers' relationship to the land as consistent with the domination of nature in our time. Indeed, theirs was a time when the wild land was tamed. So, just we can blame our attitudes towards nature on the Bible, so too we can blame them on the pioneers. However, the conquest of nature at this early time is very different from the domination of nature in the late twentieth century, for nature had not yet diminished to a mere resource. Wild things and the wild land still had to be heeded, still had not lost these re-creating powers for the pioneers, even when they did not formally understand this as an aspect of divine power.

The novelist-historian Marie Sandoz's account of her pioneering father in *Old Jules* exemplifies the most profound attraction of the wild country. We find in her narrative not merely actions undertaken or behavior recorded, but a man whose ambivalence, impetuousness, and violence might have time and again carried him away back to Zurich, or on to Canada, Mexico, or South America had not the land itself (he had no religious convictions) claimed him, and renewed and deepened its claim upon him after each estrangement. Not unlike Plenty Coups, Jules, too, had a vision.

> But the land straight ahead, The Flats, as the Hunter cook called it, was absolutely bare, without a house, even a tree—a faint yellow-green that broke here and there into shifting aspects of small shimmering lakes, rudimentary mirages. There, close enough to the river for game and wood, on the hard land that must be black and fertile, where corn and fruit trees would surely grow, Jules saw his house and around him a community of countrymen and other home seekers, refugees from oppression and poverty, intermingled in peace and contentment. There would grow up a place of orderliness, with sturdy women and strong children to swing the hayfork and the hoe.[18]

Yet within a few days he gets discouraged.

> Suddenly he flung the dark liquid and cup from him, and piled his plough, his axe, and his spade into the wagon. In the morning he would go back, not to Estelle and Knox county, to Neuchatel and to Zurich . . .[19]

Still renewal occurs that very night. A wagon with a husband and pregnant wife emerge from the shadows. Jules (he was trained as a doctor in Switzerland) is called upon by the circumstances to deliver the baby. In a later incident Jules himself, like Job, suffers calamity. As his two friends pull him to the top of a sixty foot well he just finished digging they jest with him, the rope breaks, and his foot is crushed in the fall. Eighteen days later, as the young Dr. Walter Reed prepared to amputate it, the nearly unconscious Jules came alive. "His gaunt cheeks flushed a violent red under his beard, his bloodshot eyes glittering. 'You cut off my foot, doctor, and I shoot you so dead you stink before you hit the ground.'"[20] Against his better medical judgment, Reed did not amputate. Five months later, returning to the site of his homestead, Jules thought of himself as a "miserable cripple." His spirit broken for pioneering, he was even unwilling to go back to Europe, thinking,

> Even an animal hid from its kind when injured . . . He did not see the brilliant web of prairie sun, the tinge of green spreading over the buffalo-grassed hills, the antelope bounding away from the trail, to stop curiously on a knoll when there was no pursuit . . . There was nothing but his clumpy foot . . . Suddenly a little valley opened before them, with a long, thin strip of sod stretching over the prairie; a bug-like speck that was a team with a ploughman creeping along the edge. Jules saw that and sat up.[21]

Here we see a valley and a person plowing the land bringing Jules back to life. A few pages later, relating a reunion with his brother, Sandoz writes, "And the world became a good place once more, even for a man with a bad ankle."[22] This good world and his affirmation of it echoes the *Genesis 1* creation story. So, here we see the kinship of Jules with Job, both of whom suffer and yet regain a sense of the goodness of things.

Though he had periods of estrangement, Jules never lost this faith in land to the very end. As a lifelong acquaintance said of him,

> There was something of the prophet in him, a prophet who remains to make his words deed. He is rooted in a reality that will stand when the war and its hysteria are gone, a sort of Moses working the soil of his promised land.[23]

However, this does not mean he was respectful of others or other things. Often he could be quarrelsome and ruthless with others, especially women, and cruel to his family. His egotism was unsurpassable. He drove one wife insane, and living with him was possible only because leaving was impossible. Yet, in old age, even his family members do win acknowledgement in small but telling ways.

> He dropped his hand on Mary's rounded shoulder, stooping under the weight of hoe and fork. "The trees look fine, plums ripening on rows a quarter mile long. A couple of years and we'll have one of the finest plum

and cherry orchards in the state" Jules predicted. And now, at last he said
we.[24]

This is a kind of American Odyssey. Through an encounter with adversity
and adversarial nature a correlational self-transcendence and redefinition
of things takes place. The land, other things and other people steadily
deepen from adversaries to partners to beings worth welcoming in their
own right. And one is enabled to welcome them in a fresh, more mature
manner.

This redefinition and self-transcendence do not come easily. They
come about with struggle, hardship, and conditions of necessity which
exact of one what one would not give them otherwise. The land leaves its
mark hard upon them. As another character in *Old Jules* says,

> One can go into the wild country and make it tame, but, like a coat and a
> cap he can never take off, he must always carry the look of the land as it
> was. He can drive the plough . . . make fields and roads go every way,
> build him a fine house and wear the stiff collar, and yet he will always
> look like the grass where the buffalo have eaten and smell of the new
> ground his feet have walked on.[25]

One must not read these lines romantically but closer to what war means
for Heraclitus.[26] Some died. Some went insane. Others were left embittered
and with animosity toward old friends. Some became heroes.

A Sea-Change. Pretechnological perils and hardships, conditions rugged as
the mountains, called on the uncommon in people. This relationship between people and adversarial nature was prevalent in the West until recently. However, such an appeal has lost its force in our context and we
need to be self-consciously freed from what remains of its pull.

In chapter 5, "The Technological Subversion of Environmental
Ethics," it was argued that technology, to its credit, has succeeded in overcoming many of the earlier exigencies facing human beings. While this is
not true for the poor in this country or abroad, in today's postindustrial
world, unlike that of Job's, we have the technology for medical, fire and
earthquake insurance. If our skin breaks out with sores, we expect a physi-
cian to help. Expecting a further answer from God seems similar to expecting an answer from astrology. A foot and ankle injury may call for an
ambulance but possibly not much in the way of the virtue of endurance.
Likely, we would not be working or playing around with anything as unsafe as a well—or at least with unsafe climbing gear. Nor would the slen-

der shoulders of an Old Jules prove to be decisive when faced with plowing his field with a tractor. Many of us in this country, at least for the present time, have been relieved by technology of many of the genuinely harsh conditions of life. I, for one, am thankful for this change in the human condition. However, without the struggle with these threatening conditions of human existence, without the desolate and looming wild land, people seem to have lost touch with the possibility of a deeper healing and renewal. Misery and toil were good for the full maturing of human beings in past ages. In this age, what seems to have disappeared is the reliance on *any* powers other than human ones in order to be healed. Should we seek out and live with these conditions in the present so that the divine power found in *Job* can again flourish? Even if such a return were possible, it would not be intelligible or desirable. We need in our time a healing without having to pass through the fires of affliction and genuine suffering.

In the prevailing technological culture, people have not discovered this manifestation of a spiritual power in an alternative way to the pioneers and Job. Most look forward to—not many turn down—a high and rising standard of living. More commodities means they will fill their time, fill the human condition, with artifacts that are designed just for their disposal. There are always ways to use money—things to do, places to tour, shows to see. So, neither in coming to terms with frustrating, harsh conditions nor in seeking to live a good life does the power disclosed in *Job* play an important role in consumer life.

For all its thrills, frills and glamour, consumption as a way of life, however, seems to evoke only the more superficial qualities of our humanity and leave people feeling empty. Dread in the face of this emptiness calls for a different way to be with our technology. Healing this *with-relation* is where *Job* and other works in the tradition have much to offer us, if we listen to them again.

In our age, nearly everything we confront on a daily basis is either already under control or is viewed as something to bring under control and be made use of. In direct opposition to this way of seeing, interpreting and taking up with things are the creation stories of the Bible and the vision of wild creation in Job. Wild things in these passages do not need to be rearranged, "developed" or made use of before they reach the fullness of their being. Wild things in these passages are already as good as they can be on their own. Recognizing them in their own right, pausing and lingering unself-consciously before them, makes one receptive to a fresh and refreshing vision of our existence. Not the Bible alone, but the Bible surely does, through its poetic illumination of goodness, the goodness of creation and the possibility of a good world, yield insight into the wildness which preserves the world.

II

The Possibility of a Homecoming for Us

How can this healing take place in our time and in a way appropriate to the benign changes in the human condition? A transcendent encounter with wilderness and wild things is possible in our time, now and then, because we have voluntarily not brought absolutely everything under control, having protected from this unsettling, rearranging process, some wild places in the form of legal wilderness areas, wildlife reserves and national parks. For people today then the question is not so much one of *necessary* simplicity, as it was for Job and Jules, as it is *voluntary* simplicity. For people today, the basic question is: Why should we refrain in any way from using this overwhelming power technology makes available to us? While, of course, not entirely suitable to our circumstances, *The Odyssey* still provides helpful insights for our relationship to technology, for as we move beyond the modern age, we too need something like the homecoming in Homer's narrative.

"Sing in me, Muse, and through me tell the story of that man skilled in all ways of contending."[27] These first lines are usually taken to tell us what the epic will be all about. These lines *tell* us that it is a story about Odysseus' homecoming, but Homer is finally a poet and is not satisfied with this abstract mode of telling alone, and so is constantly at work showing us things which invite thought and inquiry without our being told. These first words invoke the muse, calling on powers not at Homer's command to wield, powers he must rely upon to be inspired. Otherwise, there would be no story. What is *shown* to us in these first words, the invocation of the muse, is why Odysseus is enabled to come home in the high and grand sense of mythological homecoming. *The Odyssey* is about a man who gets his homecoming, completes his destiny, finishes his story, only because he comes to understand, respect, and rely upon powers he cannot command or overpower. The overpowering life cannot come home. The unempowered life is not worth living.

The Odyssey shows us another way to be. It does so by examining the difference between the exertion of power to regardlessly overpower other things or other people and have one's way—heedless power—and the reliance upon powers which must be carefully bidden, called upon or invoked—'invocative power'. The word 'invocative' can carry religious and metaphysical connotations which may lead the reader to bring another and separate spiritual or transcendent realm into play. But thinking in terms of a nonmaterial realm would be a mistake for the purposes at hand, especially since we are concerned about the transformation of things into devices. Put simply, lighting a candle over dinner is invocative. Invoking is a kind of *calling in,* bringing into close proximity, conjuring, of powers which have the correlational effect of evoking, *calling forth,* responses on our part. To invoke is to pull together and present what would otherwise remain scattered, remote, undisclosed, out of touch. Being in touch and keeping in touch with this power is what Odysseus learns, and much can be learned from Odysseus that would teach us to restrain our exertion of heedless power.

Odysseus and Polyphemus: The Overpowering Odysseus. Odysseus blinding of the one-eyed Kyklops, Polyphemus, can be viewed from several standpoints. Of course, the school-child interpretation of the incident is that here is a hero showing his courage, guile and leadership. He just gets somewhat carried away in baiting the monster and giving out his name. For this transgression, he is kept from reaching his homeland for another nine years since Polyphemus is now able to curse him.

Approached in light of Aristotle's discussion of courage,[28] the interpretation can move on a deeper level. Odysseus and his men are faced with death in battle. Odysseus has not been coerced by a higher officer to act the way he does; he seems motivated from within for the sake of glory. He has knowledge of his situation; he knows "some towering brute would be upon us soon—all outward power, a wild man, ignorant of civility."[29] He maintains presence of mind and his actions spring not from chance or whim but from character. However, in terms of Aristotle's theory, he manifests not the right amount of fear and confidence, but a deficiency of fear and excess of confidence. His knees do not shake; there is no gathering moment of resolve. Rather, he acts rashly, foolishly, and assumes he is invulnerable, safe—perhaps even immortal. At times the text indicates that he assumes the role of Zeus as enforcer of divine law which suggests a fantasy of omnipotence.

Yet the interpretation can move on an even deeper level when we retrieve and articulate what is left in the dark in Aristotle's account of courage: correlational coexistent things. A public thing engages personal and public life in so many ways that it becomes central for the community. With Aristotle, the ideal of courage as courage in the face of battle is premised on the condition that the battle is defending some significant thing, namely, the polis, the city-state, which if defeated would mean surrendering one's loved ones, community, and culture to death, slavery, and destruction. Aristotle does not articulate why the city-state deserves such protection; to him and his fellows it is obvious the polis is the sort of thing one protects without question. For Aristotle, the polis needs no defense, only defenders.[30]

Without the city-state, courage in the face of battle would lose its grounding for Aristotle. So, too, when Odysseus "greets" Polyphemus, it is in stark contrast with the way he greets the princess Nausikaa nine years later. It is not simply that with Polyphemus he is belligerent whereas with Nausikaa he is extremely careful, sensitive, and prudent. In the latter case, Odysseus' homecoming to Ithaka hangs by the thread of this young girl. In the former case, at each juncture of choice, Odysseus chooses to go out of his way to go to the Kyklopes' island (which is unnecessary), stay in the cave, provoke the brute, and finally call out his own name. And for what? The ram he stole? "Zeus disdained my offering."[31] The suggestion here is that not only was Odysseus feeling rashly overconfident, but, more deeply, he was without reason for being where he was. It was pointless, uncalled for, ungrounded. His actions were without a coexistent thing, a polis or an Ithaka, to warrant them. In terms I will develop in a moment, his actions were not animated by things.

Sometimes it is thought that Odysseus and Polyphemus are diametrically opposed: the small, smart trickster and the towering, stupid, uncivil brute. Yet a careful reading of this story leaves one with the impression that the brute, who feels for his sweet cousin ram, and the smart man, who has made this brute suffer, are more alike than the smart man would like to pretend. One is left with the impression that here is some kind of mirror resemblance. How can that be with such obvious and important differences?

The Kyklopes are powerful giants, mountains of all outward force. Everything they own and with which they have to do is large. Their bulldozer-like power is unguided by much intelligence. They are easily fooled. Everything they own is not only large but crude from the drying racks to the dung piles Odysseus hides among in the cave. Justice is rough; might makes right. They do not live with others in a community. Their practiced life goes on without a need for a flare of thought. Good timber grows on the island but they live in caves. Rich soil goes untilled; they reap wild grain. They pluck the wild grapes but make no wine. Annexing the provident island near them is impossible for shipbuilding is beyond them. Polyphemus cannot whistle a tune. They do not have dance, fine foods, or hearths.

How do these traits hang together? George Sturt, distinguishing between craft work and machine work, provides a good clue and starting place.

> Knots here, shakes there, rindgalls, waney-edges . . . Thicknesses, thinnesses were ever affording new chances or forbidding previous solutions, whereby a fresh problem confronted the workmen's ingenuity every few

minutes. He had no band saw (as now) to drive with ruthless unintelligence, through every resistance. The timber was far from being a prey, a helpless victim to a machine . . . I don't think I ever afterwards, in the days of band saws, handled such a large number of superlatively good felloes as used to pass through my hands in the days of axe and adze.[32]

Sturt, here, observes both fine workmanship (not all craft work was of high quality) and spells out the reasons: problems confronting a limited amount of power demand resourceful, imaginative, and delicate solutions which result in finely wrought products.

The overpowering Kyklopes confront no adversarial conditions, no resistances to their practiced way of life of all outward power. Because of a provident environment and because of their physical strength which is sufficient for getting along in that environment, they do not have to think. Intelligence is uncalled for. Conversely, it would seem, with more limited power, a more vulnerable, sensitive body, and with an environment where grain does not grow uncultivated, we encounter problems, adversarial conditions, resistances which call forth greater craft.

So far, it seems that the Kyklopes have been set at an even greater distance from Odysseus. Odysseus is "small, pitiful, and twiggy"[33] and he must use intelligence or perish. But a merely smart person may be only a clever, calculating, manipulator of his or her environment, and such a relationship hardly seems sufficient to issue into genuine and high culture—fine foods and wines, poetry, temples or even genuine friendship. Odysseus is this smart manipulator of his environment, the one considering "how to win the game."[34] The terms he plots in, the actions he takes, the emotions he feels are crude, cruel, and uncivil. His self-glorying exclamations are those of an adolescent. What Polyphemus evokes from him is merely the mental equivalent of brute strength.

Odysseus at this point is a problem-solver, knowing what he wants and figuring out a way to get it, yet he is not here capable of homecoming; that is another nine years off. *The Odyssey* indicates something deeper issues out of those years of experience. We saw earlier, that, unlike his encounter with Nausikaa, Odysseus' actions were uncalled for or not animated by things. What difference does that make? Sturt, in the same passage quoted earlier, adds, "(The timber) would lend its own subtle virtues to the man who knew how to humor it: with him, as with an understanding friend, it would cooperate."[35] It is no mistake that Sturt likens this to friendship. The wood *appeals* to the wheelwright, and it is on the strength of this appeal that he is caught up in woodworking and on the way to becoming the character he is to become. The wood holds a wonder for the wheelwright that is not allayed by finishing the product and fitting it within a framework of other instruments. The activity itself is in answer to what addresses him and appeals to him in the wood. It animates him in a kind of symbiotic relationship. Sturt suggests that in this address-response activity lies a might, steadiness, and steadfastness that keeps a person alive in body, mind, and spirit.

> But no higher wage, no income, will buy for men that satisfaction which of old—until machinery made drudges of them—streamed into their muscles all day long from close contact with iron, timber, clay, wind and wave, horse-strength . . . The very ears unawares received it, as when the plane went singing over the wood, or the exact chisel went tapping into the hard ash with gentle sound.[36]

This kind of relationship makes woodworking human. Both humans and animating things emerge into being together. One may hope for genuine culture to issue from this symmetry of correlational coexistence. It is this animated life that is held up as *being* in the revealed text of *The Odyssey*, and it is what is missing both for the physically overpowering Kyklopes and the overpowering, manipulating mind of Odysseus. Without that animation by coexistent things, Odysseus' actions are uncivil, crude, cruel, insensitive and pointless—as well as rash and foolhardy.

Odysseus' Turnings. How is this correlational coexistence brought home to Odysseus? In his wanderings Odysseus actually has many incremental turning points when he moves closer to a homecoming. In the next episode, Aiolos, the wind king, directs Odyssseus how to sail to home and bottles all the storm winds into a bag for his safekeeping. Odysseus and the crew come so close that they see men building fires on the shores of Ithaka. But ironically the most extreme distance from a homecoming is depicted here by Odysseus's coming closest to it. He can't go home again that way for two reasons. He tries to go home by way of all the power he can muster, guarding the sack of wind almost jealously, and taking the sail by himself the whole way for nine days and nights. It is guaranteed that he would fall asleep and the crew would be suspicious and untie the bag, allowing the winds to escape that blow them back to Aiolos. Also, Aiolos this second time finds something wrong with Odysseus' wholehearted desire to get home. Reflection shows that his overpowering extreme actions, manifesting a kind of willed resoluteness, are not only a weakness but indicate a division and lack of resolve within himself.

 Had Odysseus gotten to Ithaka at this point, what kind of ruler would he have been? His rule might have been similar to Meneláos'. Meneláos gets home before Odysseus. He has his life, wife, household, wealth and kingdom. None are now in jeopardy. Yet his life is felt to be lacking in something, and one senses uneasiness between him and Helen. Politically, Meneláos is the most powerful man in Greece. He is a brilliant man with a tremendous spirit and a deep-lunged body to match it. It is no mistake that he is the one who wrestles with Proteus, for he exercises his massive heedless power over forces of nature, things, events and other people. Meneláos tells Telemakhos he would like to have cleaned out a town for Odysseus and moved the latter's kingdom near his palace if only Odysseus had returned. He is impetuous and careless, but he can get away with it because of his sheer strength. Meneláos has Helen back and she will stay, but he has had to exercise force in bringing her back, and perhaps, it is only by way of her tacit understanding of that force that she remains. Meneláos' life, household, and realm hang together, but the force that holds it together, his sheer strength, is less than ideal. This basic framework for understanding how the world hangs together is what Odysseus must become liberated from.

Odysseus' approach to Kirkê, the sorceress who turns men into swine, shows for the first time that he has learned to rely on invocative powers other than those he can guarantee with his wit and his own right arm. The fundamental issue with Kirkê is reliance upon powers involved in recognition. What Odysseus wins from Kirkê, and what the other innocents do not win, is recognition and respect for himself as a human capable of sustaining his presence of mind and a full range of human concerns. Once he has won that acknowledgment it serves as the tightly stretched oxhide bed, as it were, upon which he can enjoy in nakedness Kirkê's flawless bed of love without fear of being unmanned.

No animal would have left Kirkê. To be sure, Odysseus still needs to be reminded of homecoming. Ithaka pulls him away from Kirkê because he comprehends how Kirkê stands relative to Ithaka. Comprehension is different from calculating cleverness. The latter is a power we have at our disposal, more or less, most of the time whereas comprehension requires silence, stillness and time. Getting our bearings, finding our place in the world again, are insights that come to us and not thoughts we steer or contrive the conditions for. That is not to say that such powers cannot be bidden or invoked, as the Plains Indians did with the structure and symbolism of their sweatlodges.[37] But ultimately we must be at the disposal of that which reaches us from afar in its own time and way. And so when Odysseus journeys to the underworld, a kind of sweatlodge, to meditate on death he shows he has learned to invoke and rely upon the powers of human comprehension.

If the meditation on death is a story of human strength, the ability to grasp the landscape of our lives in advance, the adventure with the Sereines, by contrast, is a meditation on acknowledging human frailty. Here, although Odysseus can foresee the issue, by himself he cannot fight off the attraction of the bad homeland—the pull of nostalgia which would tease him out of time, as it were.[38] The Odysseus who relies on the mast, crew, and wax to get him through stands in sharp contrast to the Odysseus who mans the sail by himself.

Finally, the Odysseus who quietly calms his panicked men whose oars fly wildly out of control in the face of the terrorizing Drifters is an Odysseus who is on his way to understanding a strength through gentleness. Rather than wielding powers over them he puts the crew members back in touch with the powers of the situation which call for and enable resoluteness in the face of death.

However, all those trials and events are a kind of preparation for the events where the lessons of invocative power really come home to him. The island of Kalypso the nymph goddess where Odysseus spends seven years is not suffered as a prison all along. It is a success story of sorts. Far from a prison, it is a wished-for hedonistic paradise: pleasant, pleasurable, convenient, comfortable, blissful and forever. Yet, for all that, the irony is that what is promising in the wish goes unfulfilled even as the wish is finally granted. "For long ago the nymph had ceased to please."[39] In living out the wish, Odysseus lives into lack and longing. Odysseus soon discovers the sterility of the paradise, and it is this sterility compounded with the sense that what carries real weight with him lies elsewhere that makes for his thousand days of weeping. More deeply, the realization which dawns on Odysseus is not merely that he cannot get his heart into this paradise; what he recognizes as sterile is the way of life which has led to this: an isolated individual who is far from what is really dear to him.

On Kalypso's Island, Odysseus suffers a convincing catharsis of a certain mode of being in the world. It is a lesson that can be understood only as it is lived through, as something one lives into an understanding of by having undergone it. Odysseus lives into an understanding of a way of life that ultimately is not enough for him. Figuratively, as a way of life, here is not home. The kind of catharsis which takes place on the island, unlike Sandoz's Old Jules, is not in the face of adversarial powers, not in the face of that which has the power to overwhelm, injure or kill, but a catharsis in the face of lack and longing.

Irony here can be understood in relation to Aristotle's discussion of wish.[40] Aristotle argues that all people wish for what *appears good* but often when people get what they desired it is *not good in reality*. The apparent good turns out to be otherwise, turns out to be actually and recognizably bad for us. We might say that what is promised in the appearance fails to keep its promise in living it through. The first moment of irony is a kind of glamorous attraction; the second, disappointment. Here Odysseus really wished for an apparent good, Kalypso's paradise; living this wish through, however, he moves from wishing to weeping.

However, *The Odyssey* indicates that the most definitive lesson and final turning event comes just after he leaves Kalypso. If Odysseus' knees do not shake in his confrontation with Polyphemus, they certainly do, in spirit at least, when he comes within a prayer of drowning. He spends seventeen days on the open sea before the raft he built is destroyed in a storm. For two more days and nights he swims before he spies the island Skeria. But the shore line turns out to be a dangerous sheer cliff upon which Odysseus is nearly battered to death by the surge of the surf. Not even the Greek hero has the strength to endure more. As he swims along this shore his last hope is an inlet where a river flows into the sea, yet as he approaches it he finds the current of the river carrying him away, back out to sea and certain death. Only because the river's flow is suddenly reversed by the incoming tide does Odysseus make it. He does not bring himself ashore by his own right arm. And so the fabricated story he tells when he finally makes it back to Ithaka could well be (and, in a sense, is) his story.

This near-drowning convinces Odysseus of his limits in an undeniable way. This washes him clean of illusions and opens him to another way of being in the world. In contrast with the lesson on Kalypso's Island wrought by undergoing the experience of irony, this is essentially a cathartic lesson in the face of *adversity*. Through a showdown with indomitable and overwhelming powers in which one suffers undeniable defeat one is enabled to transcend an adversarial relation with the world in an unforeseen and unsuspected way. Kant uses the word 'educated' to refer to the background enabling one to experience as sublime what to others is merely terrible.[41] Odysseus's transcendence of the adversarial relationship (by undergoing undeniable defeat in the face of it) is an educated way of being in the world: what was before experienced as adversarial nature is now experienced, paradoxically, as *kind*. This transcendence is, on the one hand, self-transcendence, and, on the other, a redefinition of things and world.

The Sense of Things in *The Odyssey*. If the most radical change in Odysseus understanding of power occurs on Kalypso's Island and off the shore of Skeria, then what signs do we see of it? What is the character of this educated way of being in the world? We can begin to answer these questions by asking what kind of task the Phaiakians, the inhabitants of Skeria or Phaiakia, pose for Odysseus.

Phaiakia is a paradise, rich both in terms of a highly refined and wealthy culture and in terms of natural conditions, e.g., climate, soil, fruits, grains, etc. The Phaiakians are peaceful, harmonious and festive, yet, in the interstices of their obviously harmonious world, we can begin to detect flaws. Unlike Odysseus earlier, the Phaiakians, we are told, found themselves troubled by the Kyklopes whom they could not restrain; for this reason, they retreated to Skeria. So, as one might expect, when Poseidon turns the returning ship to stone in the harbor, they are easily frightened and react by mandating no more passage to strangers. Homeric Greeks would not like how easily these people are pushed around.

Then, too, when Odysseus enters the palace it comes as a complete surprise to them; hardly anyone knows what to do since they have not entertained any strangers for more than a generation. This indicates that the Phaiakians do not welcome otherness, difference. Accordingly, the queen Arete is both the king Alkinoos's wife and niece. And while the Phaiakians know all the islands, and especially secluded places, in their secretive night sailing, like insulated tourists, they encounter no one and no culture directly.

Nausikaa, the princess, hints that Odysseus is larger, more handsome and more godlike than any of the men on the island. This is not surprising considering how easily Phaiakians are intimidated and also that they are chiefly skilled at rowing, song, dance and ball—not warfare. In order to maintain the kind of harmony they cherish, the king Alkinoos orders a change of tune when Odysseus is found weeping over the minstrel's song about Troy. In short, Phaiakians are incestuously insulated and encounter nothing from the outside: no adventure, no adversity, no suffering, no testing. Everything happens on their own turf. There is no hidden harmony better than the obvious one.

What is the challenge of Phaiakia? Odysseus, as the first stranger in recent memory (and the last), must win the love and mercy of this timid people for his passage home. Otherwise no homecoming. For its delicacy and poetic power, Odysseus' first plea for help from Nausikaa is unsurpassed by any other greeting in *The Odyssey*. It exemplifies the above challenge of Phaiakia in the extreme. Odysseus—having just awakened in the bushes the morning after his near-drowning and looking savage, naked, starved and lion-like to his very bloodshot eyes—must win the favor of this young girl. He wins favor by a very carefully phrased invocation of her, himself and his circumstances which serves to evoke her nobility which, in turn, bestows on him the love and mercy he needs.

Odysseus is warned two times, by Nausikaa and then Athena, that everything depends on the queen. This warning seems to be forgotten unless one notices that Arete is testy, cold and brisk toward him. She is at most polite, though hardly won over. How does Odysseus win her love and mercy? By his tale showing love and pity for his mother and honoring great women of the past. So, when Odysseus cuts his story short, saying it is late, it is Arete who responds wanting him to stay another day, showering even more gifts on him, and encouraging him to go on with his story.

Ironically, after all these years of struggle, the Phaiakians deliver Odysseus to Ithaca while he is asleep. Once Odysseus is on Ithaka he again proves himself a master at invoking bonds which elicit the love, mercy, and respect of Eumaious. Contrary to what one may suspect, his actions are far from merely calculative cunning. How so? Aside from the obvious need for a disguise of some sort, and aside from the point that, in the presence a powerless beggar, people like Eurymakhos will show themselves as they are, Odysseus comes back as a beggar because it is a kind of final test for him. He must show that he is capable of an existence that is beggarly, that depends entirely on powers other than those he can wield.

The other side of his powerlessness is that he must be a receptive being, receiving compassion and generosity at the hands of others and other things. For instance, Robert Fitzgerald argues that Odysseus' plan to rout out the suitors is a very desperate one at first. Penelope supplies the crucial missing piece to the plan and puts the weapon into his hands, almost. She does so because, through an extremely subtle exchange between her and the beggar (one that takes place in front of Eurymakhos' mistress Melantho), she recognizes Odysseus. Fitzgerald's point is to illustrate Penelope's intelligence and character.[42] For my purposes here, I want to point out that she, like the tide-changed river off Skeria, supplies that which Odysseus himself, for all his proven mastery, is unable to supply. It is through a series of carefully disguised suggestions and appeals to a Penelope with such intelligence and concerns that the solution to Odysseus' desperate plan is both resolved and kept secret. It is the same Odysseus who says, following the slaughter of the suitors and knowing full well what that will mean for the other islanders, "We'll see what weapon Zeus puts into our hands."[43] The Odysseus who says this is no longer in an adversarial relation to otherness; he sees in otherness something that is generous and can be relied upon. Putting this another way, the master who gracefully strings the bow and fires the shot through the dozen axes is nearer to a Zen master of archery than he is to the man who burned Polyphemus' eye out.

The Odyssey brings this sense of correlational coexistence into higher relief in two ways, by showing yet another way Odysseus relies on invocative powers and by contrasting this sense of things with those for whom it is missing, the suitors. Thought in terms of Odysseus' increasing understanding of and reliance upon invocative power, the chief difference between Phaiakia and Ithaka is that now Odysseus is able to invoke powers that *turn against* the suitors. To show this point requires us to return to the beginning of *The Odyssey*. There the goddess Athena stirs both Zeus and Telemakhos, Odysseus's young son, into action. The way she goes about it is of interest from the standpoint of how disclosive truth works in *The Odyssey*. She comes to Telemakhos disguised as Odysseus' friend Mentes, though Telemakhos knows that someone divine has passed his way. For his part, Telemakhos has been more or less reluctantly compliant with the suitors, sometimes enjoying the wine, feasts and talk. But he has come of age and is in a position to comprehend his situation and make a fundamental choice. Mentes gathers together, on the one hand, Telemakhos' circumstances—Laertes' suffering, that Odysseus is not dead but detained, the suitors' wrongdoings, the fact that the suitors will not disperse until they have gone through his inheritance. On the other hand, he gathers Telemakhos' best sense of himself—noble like his father, heroic like Orestes. Finally, Mentes shows him in what way he can respond. And respond he does. What has occurred here is not a simple listing of reasons until one has finally had it, like filling a measuring cup by ounces until it overflows. Rather Mentes points out parts of a larger pattern the whole of which suddenly leaps into relief as a gestalt, a vision, the realization of which calls on Telemakhos to respond. This disclosive truth is brought about by invoking powers that would otherwise lie scattered and unconnected, and, therefore, unknown, unacknowledged, forgotten, or ignorable.

Similarly, Odysseus, like Mentes (and Homer with the muse), makes the suitors angry beyond all reason by telling his *story* about how he mistakenly thought his power was in his own right arm and that that had led to the downfall to his present derelict state. As he retells the story he brings it closer and closer to home. The story grates on them because it invokes and presents an understanding of being that their behavior acknowledges but which, unlike Telemakhos, they would sooner suppress and forget. Why? It is a basic premise of *The Odyssey* that, when untested, one fancies oneself to be more than one is. *The Odyssey*'s full articulation of this illusion is that of a fantasy of omnipotence and immortality. The suitors think of themselves as safe and invulnerable, having everything under control. Odysseus' reminder of the real truth challenges this assumption. Rather than become reconciled with the reminder (as Telemakhos does above) it only serves to make them take more extreme measures to suppress, deny and eradicate its truth—hot disputes, throwing footstools, plotting murders.

Accordingly, what is the ringleader Antinoos' response to the beggar's feat with the bow? Anyone in his or her right mind would be moved at least to awe and wonder if not fear. But Antinoos, with a measured degree of carelessness, uses both his hands to bring his two-handled wine cup to his lips.

Did he dream of death? How could he? In that revelry amid his throng of
friends who would imagine a single foe—through a strong foe indeed—
could dare to bring death's pain on him and darkness on his eyes?[44]

And what of the other suitors? "For they imagined as they *wished*—that it
was a wild shot, an unintended killing—fools not to comprehend they
were already in the grip of death."[45] Thus, Odysseus, even here, is able to
turn invocative power against the suitors, who, unwilling to reconcile
themselves with the possibility of being revealed to them, are forced into
ever more insistent extremes of confidence and fantasy until they are con-
fused, unprepared, and unable to respond to real danger.

Antinoos is representative of a person for whom a sense of correlational coexistence is missing. If he were to become king he would be a
tyrant. He desires the absolute or heedless power the kingship would seem
to give him. If this power were possible, it would be the actualization of
the fantasy of omnipotence and immortality; one would not be troubled
with threats and one would have what one wants, forever. Everything else
is made to serve this will—a kind of petty monocentrism. Others are
merely resources to be manipulated about for the securing of power, Penelope and the other suitors not excepted. Those, such as a beggar, outside
this framework do not count. Antinoos is ready to have his way regardless
of the feelings and concerns of others or bonds of justice between them.
Odysseus' judgment is that, like the shepherd-tyrant in Plato's Myth of
Gyges, all the suitors and their cohorts, from Antinoos to Leodes, wish
Odysseus dead, wish to lie with the Queen and wish to usurp the throne.

But it is not only that Antinoos has no respect for the intrinsic worth
of other people; *The Odyssey* shows him as having no respect for the place,
living beings, things, or, following lines developed earlier, even facts.
Ithaka is not dear to him. Argos is thrust aside and forgotten. Footstools
are thrown; stores used up. And, finally, the suitors do not see facts for
what they are: one way or another they make the facts fit (or cast them far
aside from) the framework of a situation under control.

The Odyssey's critique of this way of life is twofold. On the one hand,
it leads to literal destruction exemplified by Antinoos' death because of the
extreme difference between his illusions and actuality. On the other hand,
his way of life is seen to lead to a figurative impoverishment and destruction in the sense of being sterile, shallow and ultimately pointless in the
sense of not having enough point. Antinoos overpowers things and others.
In doing so, he loses persons as persons and things as things. He stands
outside of any profound bonds with them. Alienated and hardened, he is
without sympathy or compassion, sorrow, admiration or reverence.

The sense of things in *The Odyssey*, implicit in Odysseus' educated
way of life, is quite the opposite of the above in both regards. Unlike Anti-

noos, Odysseus' knees do go slack momentarily in the battle with the suitors. He sees real danger for what it is because he is willing to reconcile himself with the possibilities of being. More importantly, in his invoking of the bonds of compassion, justice, and piety between himself and others such as the swineherd Odysseus' motives are not reducible to cunning. He finds what genuinely enriches his life in those very bonds, and he now knows the worth of that nourishment. Now he understands that what he was able to take by way of domination was of little worth and ultimately destructive. Through a receptive mode of being in the world, enacted symbolically as the beggarly but kingly way of life, he finds enrichment in what is given. What is given surpasses will, expectation, and all bargaining as unforeseen, as more and other, as a gift of kindness. Argos graces his existence. Unlike Antinoos, he feels in his deep heart how much Ithaka matters. Similar feelings are called forth by his cherished bow, the manor and the bed which he designed and built, and, of course, Penelope.

If one does not come at the Greek text predisposed about how to conceive the cosmos, but rather attempts to understand it from the inside out, one is struck by how often the word "kind" is used to describe the beneficial effect *things have on humans,* especially in Book 23 after the household order is restored and Odysseus is reunited with Penelope.[46] Fields are seen kind with grain and, at other times, with kind furrows. Odysseus longs for his wife

> as sunwarmed earth is longed for by a swimmer spent in rough water where his ship went down under Poseidon's blows, gale winds, and tons of sea. Few men can keep alive through the big surf to crawl, clotted with brine, on kindly beaches in joy, in joy, knowing the abyss behind.[47]

Penelope too says old age may be kind to them. And when in bed, they "open glad arms to one another."[48]

Of all these, and perhaps supported upon the web these particulars suggest, the most striking is Penelope's statement, "now the kind powers have brought you home at last."[49] One may suppose that the most obvious meaning of Penelope's statement is that Zeus and Athena have been kind in bringing Odysseus home as a couple may be kind in giving a hitchhiker a ride. Yet one can understand it in a way not different from the other statements above. As shown previously, the kindnesses of others, living beings and things, have powers in them which allow Odysseus' life to prosper. These received powers uphold his life, empowering and moving him from the depths of his being. So, these kind powers are not kind in the sense of doing him a service as one human being might do for another; things are kind in the way they affect and animate us. This kindness is a kindness directly to the heart. That is the manner of their generosity and gift-giving. Without denying that the Homeric world is full of misfortune and hardship, it is also full of kindness, kind powers and kind things. Such understanding is neither mystical nor depends on taking a point of view outside lived experience and the educated understanding that can issue from within it. Ultimately, then, Ithaka's deepest appeal lies with these kind powers to which Odysseus has consented in his heart and which bring him home.

These kind powers do not affect, move and enrich everyone. *The Odyssey* teaches that the exercise of tyrannical heedless power precludes the reception of kind powers. The framework within which heedless power moves and understands itself is independent of kindness, gifts, gift-giving and reception for these are outside the realm of what one can control, demand or produce. So it is not sufficient that the world has kind powers and things in it; one must be living in such a way that one is receptive of them. This is the task essential to homecoming in *The Odyssey*.

Homecoming for Us and the Need for More Wilderness. We cannot but feel uneasy with much of *The Odyssey*. Apart from the reasons obvious to every reader, Odysseus in the end does always seem to have battle in his heart, and his first and foremost teacher is adversity. Still, no work takes more explicit account of the theme of homecoming than *The Odyssey*, and we in this age stand in need of a homecoming as many have pointed out. So we should be able learn much from it and the direction it points for another way to be. How can it show us why we should refrain, at times, from the use of the heedless power technology yields? To understand this we need to examine the direct correlation between our heedlessness and our homelessness.

Nothing accounts for the source of our homelessness more concretely and precisely than the device paradigm. The heedless power of technological machinery procures for us technological availability, which seems to fulfill all we could wish for. "I want what I want whenever I want it wherever I am." We saw that the overall result of this availability provided by devices is disengagement, especially when we try to procure the centering things of our lives. Thus when we attempt to make ourselves happy with technological means the results are ironic. We become not at home in the universe. In light of this analysis, the question of our homecoming is not one of going back to an earlier time, to a pretechnological era; rather, the issue is one of meeting the problem of disengagement by fostering, re-establishing and sustaining our bonds of engagement with the things that matter within a technological context. If that is the task, what can *The Odyssey* relevantly teach us? What analogies to the kind powers that bring Odysseus home could make sense to us?

Commodities are no substitutes for things. They cannot bear a world, nor can they engage us in a multiplicity of ways. Things are deep because they tie together a world in an indefinite number of ways and elicit many forms of engagement. Thus, unlike commodities, they are thick with meanings. This wide array of material aspects of things are the powers of the thing. However, where their strength lies also lies their weakness. Often enough, these powers are suffered as standing against us, resisting us. Commonly they are experienced as burdensome, terrible and the like. Practices are not always enjoyable. Backpackers literally carry a burden on their backs when they hike in the wilderness. While these hikers usually manage to avoid having a miserable time, not all times in the backcountry are good times. Events sometimes make them think of cars, heated rooms and beds. They sometimes dream of the burdenless availability spoken of earlier. Yet, from our encounters with these wild places, we know this burdensomeness is not the deepest level at which they can be encountered. They can also be experienced in a way which makes every step worth taking. On this level, the powers of things are no longer experienced as resisting us, but now things are found to be *appealing*. When this happens, we experience their powers as kind, and we find ourselves in a self-transcendent mode.

Here we can make connections with Odysseus' education in *The Odyssey*. The chief lesson we need to learn is not that our technology will fail like Odysseus' strength off Skeria. Technology is likely to be our context from now on. The chief lesson, it seems to me, is that technological success, like Meneláos' rule, Kalypso's Paradise and Antinoos' sterile tyranny, is just not worth it all the time. The way of life centered around the exertion of technological heedless power and availability, where everything is our way, is just not enough for us. We need islands of wilderness in our lives. Wild places and wild things are rich *metaphors* for our time, a time which, in its systematic effort to get everything under control, threatens to exclude them altogether. We need these special times and special places where the goods cannot be procured through technology or through willfulness—wild things to counter our pointless, always overtaking rushing about. We need room in our lives for places where and times when we learn, like Job, to be receptive of that which overtakes us from behind, healing, harmonizing, enlivening and enlightening us. In these encounters with the enabling powers of things we learn of another, educated way to be in the world. Like Odysseus, we need to learn to enact lives that guard and remain open to and in touch with the things whose kind powers make our lives more profoundly prosperous. Therein lies the possibility of our homecoming.

CHAPTER 8

TO CONSIDER THINGS AGAIN

The villagers, who scarcely know where it lies, instead of going to the pond itself to bathe or drink, are thinking to bring its water, which should be as sacred as the Ganges at least, to the village in a pipe, to wash their dishes with!—to earn their Walden by the turning of a cock or drawing of a plug!

—Thoreau[1]

In order that we may even remotely consider the monstrousness that reigns here, let us ponder for a moment the contrast that is spoken by the two titles: "The Rhine" as dammed up into the power works, and "The Rhine" as uttered out of the art work, in Hölderlin's hymn by that name.

—Heidegger[2]

A thing of beauty is a joy for ever.

—John Keats

By now with the aid of the device paradigm, we see fairly well how things are emptied of meaning and treated shallowly in the technological age, how our culture is losing things in their thinglyness. We have seen as well that moral considerability and environmental altruism do advance respect for nature beyond the heedlessness of petty homocentrism. Much as this should be encouraged, they still, if developed alone, remain heedless of correlational coexistent considerations of nature. A great deal can be learned concerning correlational coexistence if our culture learns to listen again not only to *Job* and *The Odyssey* but to much of the western tradition and learns to listen, perhaps for the first time, to other traditions and to recent feminist thought. For now we need to turn to the task of comprehending better the thinglyness of things, the considerability of things, for things embody the powers enabling alternatives to consumption to flourish and to turn technology from its present course. What are these *things?* What difference do they make and what does it mean to consider them? In this chapter and the next, we will approach Walden Pond as a thing and see how Thoreau in *Walden* helps us to consider it in this richer way.

Philosophy must give way to art when we want to disclose the full range of what counts about things; nevertheless, philosophy and the humanities in general can help us to look and see what art reveals. So Heidegger's language of the fourfold character of things and Borgmann's language of focal or centering things provide a way of understanding what Thoreau is showing us. Heidegger's fourfold of Earth, sky, divinity and mortals was developed in order to consider cultural things more circumspectively. An understanding of human finitude and of the divine is intentionally wrought in these artifacts, and so too, a cultural understanding of Earth and sky is depicted in them. For example, the circular design of a Sioux lodge, forming an hourglass shape reaching between Earth and sky, collects and reflects their cultural understanding of the natural world. Wild things are not designed by humans nor do they exhibit the marks of human intention. It is important to remember and to respect this altogether otherness of wild things.[3] Yet wild things are so rich, as we will see with Walden Pond, that they too gather and display the fourfold of their cultural kin. From a correlational coexistence standpoint, nature and culture are not separate. Thus we can use this language of the fourfold and of focal things to disclose these coexistent wild things.

The World of Walden Pond

Like Albert Borgmann, Henry David Thoreau offers insight into the domination taking place through devices. For example, speaking of the huckleberries and blueberries he has gathered from Fair Haven Hill, he writes,

> The fruits do not yield their true flavor to the purchaser of them, nor to him who raises them for market. There is but one way to obtain it, yet few take that way. . . . It is a vulgar error to suppose that you have tasted huckleberries who have never plucked them.[4]

Here Thoreau is criticizing the way of making huckleberries into commodities procured by alternative and artificial means. And, for the villagers who know nothing of Walden Pond and have not encountered and experienced it, he sees this shift from things to devices occurring with Walden itself, the huckleberry of huckleberries. Supposing tapwater to be the only experience we have of Walden Pond, what will we be missing? From one standpoint, what we are missing is the *world* of Walden Pond. For Thoreau, in missing the world of the thing, we miss everything.[5]

Before undertaking an exposition of this world that the villagers are missing, we need to understand just what we can and cannot expect from it. Walden Pond's beauty is easily overlooked and must be revealed or brought forth by Thoreau.

> The scenery of Walden is on a humble scale, and, though very beautiful, does not approach to grandeur, nor can it much concern one who has not frequented it or lived by its shore; yet this pond is so remarkable for its depth and its purity as to merit a particular description.[6]

Thoreau's poetic prose is the most appropriate mode of discourse for disclosing the thingly character of Walden Pond, for it alone, far better than a more abstract discourse, has the world-gathering powers necessary to do justice to all the lifeworld strands webbed together in the thing. Ultimately, only the great original text will complement the gathering and presenting powers of the thing.

Accordingly, one cannot simply begin to list physical traits of the pond. For Thoreau, nature intimates, hints, suggests, and, from beginning to end, he is one who follows out and brings to culmination its suggestions. Huckleberries do literally lose their flavor when purchased even at the farmers market. For another example, Thoreau was pleased to hear from an oldtimer of an old log canoe at Walden Pond,

> which perchance had first been a tree on the bank, and then, as it were, fell into the water, to float there for a generation, the most proper vessel for the lake . . . He did not know whose it was; it belonged to the lake.[7]

Nature is from itself, by itself, into itself, and for itself. Nature is from itself. It does not need any material imported. No one has to pipe water in or bring in a canoe. Nature orders by itself. No one has to grow the tree or fall it into the pond. Nature has its own forms to fulfill. The fallen log floating suggests its appropriate task to the nature of the fisherman. No one is needed to set upon the pond as dead, neutral nature and mine it for profit. Finally, nature has its own ends. It is not there for our house, water project, or even our enjoyment in fishing and natural beauty. Nature has its own glories to animate. Nature is generous. Thus, humans can be grateful participants in much of what comes to pass in nature.

Whatever may be the ultimate relationship between humans and nature, Thoreau shows what it is not. Unless humans follow nature's lead, a rebellion, a revolution, and a tragic fall occur—for both humans and nature. Walden Pond is secured as a device. Bad poetry gets written.

Nature loves to hide, as Heraclitus reminds us.[8] Nature comes forth and shows itself in its true character only in momentous events unanticipated and unanticipatable. These disclosures don't happen because someone picks up a bigger shovel. They happen when we let nature be as it wants to be and respond on the strength of its first faint leads. In following out—not overtaking—these leads, we discover nature is deep. It is we who must enter, explore, and come to have some understanding. "We are enabled to apprehend at all what is sublime and noble only by the perpetual instilling and drenching of the reality that surrounds us."[9]

Beginning as simply as possible, I want to *suggest* the various ways *Walden* reveals Walden Pond as gathering a world.

Earth and Sky

How does Walden Pond gather Earth and sky—the landscape, the sky, the seasons, the days and nights, the hours, the weather? This simple question takes us to the core of the book, for *Walden* is written as if Thoreau's stay was for one year from spring to spring, not two as it literally was. Throughout these seasons shine the various faces of Walden Pond. Thoreau could not say what he has to say about the natural world of Walden in half a year.

Thoreau tells us, "The pond was my well ready dug."[10] In the winter months its water is "as cold as it is pure."[11] It made him put on boots and heavy clothing, pick up his axe and shovel, and search for it in mornings. Through this task he discovers the nature of ice and the calm tranquility of the world beneath it. There he meets the servant of the Bramin, priest of Brahma and Vishnu and Indra, come to draw water for his master, "and our buckets as it were grate together in the same well."[12] During the warmest period of the summer season, Thoreau remembers to place a pailful in the cellar overnight to cool down for the next day. In this season, too, he often resorts to a spring in the neighborhood. In this way he becomes further acquainted with the place because of Walden's water.

The pond tells of Earth and sky in other ways, too. At a distance on a clear day, Walden appears blue, whereas on a stormy day it has the color of dark slate. Walden can be green one time and blue another. "Lying halfway between heaven and Earth it partakes the color of both."[13] As Thoreau invokes Walden's thingly powers, one sees that its greens and blues gather all the natural world. It is blue like the ocean, green as grass, tinted yellow like the sands. It is light green, dark green, vivid green, the color of the iris, blue and green at once, darker blue than the sky itself, and in a single glass, clear. It can have "a matchless and indescribable light blue, such as watered or changeable silks and sword blades suggest, more cerulean than the sky itself."[14] Sometimes it has the vitreous greenish blue like the winter sky in the west before sunset. Walden Pond is the intermediate third term to everything. "On land only the grass and trees wave, but the water itself is rippled by the wind."[15] Soil remains too opaque and heavy to be moved by spirit. However, lest we think Walden is suggestible or given to whims, its depth makes its spring thaw "indicate better than any water hereabouts the absolute progress of the season, being least affected by transient changes of temperature."[16]

When the ice freezes across Walden, it first covers and, hence, discloses the shallowest and shadiest waters first. This new ice is clear and invites Thoreau to look through it at the bottom as through an aquarium. He discovers new creatures and their paths on the bottom. But what Thoreau finds most interesting is the study of ice itself, as a kind of counter theme to the theme of dawn and morning.

The depth of Walden is such that even in the coldest part of winter, vivid green plants can be hauled up from the bottom, reminding Thoreau that Walden yet lives in winter. It has its own fire, hearth, seed of faith, or, in Albert Camus' words, "invincible summer."[17] For Thoreau says of himself: "I withdrew yet farther into my shell and endeavored to keep a bright fire both within my house and within my breast."[18] Here, too, in things dwell the gods who can console and befriend when the cold and dark could otherwise find us full of uncertainty and despair. "Things do not change; we change."[19]

In one of his first images, Thoreau brings Walden into close proximity with us by personifying it. Like humans, it awakens to the sun. From it Thoreau learns that all of us, in our individual ways, are claimed by the great things of the universe and sway with them. The great simplicities of existence make for the simplicity of all things held in their sway.

Walden Pond's irregular but agreeable shoreline takes the eye in small steps along the forest edge, not allowing the eye to slide past any important but shy feature. Like a painting, the pond gives prominence to the noble. The beauty of the forest, for example, comes home to the observer both from the foreground reflection and the distance from which one necessarily beholds it. With additional light from the pond's opening, trees near the shore grow larger than normal, seem taller, fuller, and reach out over the pond. The pond allows the world of the forest to come forth. "There Nature has woven a natural selvage, and the eye rises by just gradations from the lowest shrubs of the shore to the highest trees."[20] Furthermore, it allows the scene to resonate with the timeless truth of great art. "The water laves the shore as it did a thousand years ago."[21] In the fall, writes Thoreau, "Gradually, from week to week the character of each tree came out, and it admired itself reflected in the smooth mirror of the lake."[22]

Mortals

Walden Pond gathers mortals too. Heidegger's account of mortals lacks sufficient emphasis on the way things gather us bodily and the way they gather other people. These ways things engage humans, certainly consistent with his view of mortals, is suggested by the text itself.

Bodily Engagement

Living at the pond teaches Thoreau the skills and know-how necessary for self-sufficiency. The place, remote and secluded, assigns what tasks are to be done, when and how they are to be done, and what must be their outcome. And so Thoreau learns about housebuilding, hearths, chopping wood, growing a garden, keeping vegetables, baking bread, and preparing for winter, for a storm, for night.

The pond encourages Thoreau to establish a practice of bathing. Bathing was not simply a task to perform with the function of eliminating dirt, sweat, and odors. Sponging off his skin would not do. Neither would a shower, a bath in a regular tub, nor even bathing in Walden Pond at midday. No, the focal thing, Walden Pond, gathers to it other focal practices which cannot, like Walden, be transformed without loss.

> Every morning was a cheerful invitation to make my life of equal simplicity, and I may say, innocence, with Nature herself. I have been as sincere a worshiper of Aurora as the Greeks. I got up early and bathed in the pond; that was a religious exercise, and one of the best things which I did. They say that characters were engraven on the bathing tub of King Tching-thang to this effect: "Renew thyself completely each day; do it again, and again, and forever again." I can understand that.[23]

In bathing and drawing water, Thoreau discovers that this water which looks now blue and now green to one on shore, is quite transparent up close. Moreover,

> This water is of such crystalline purity that the body of the bather appears of an alabaster whiteness, still more unnatural, which, as the limbs are

magnified and distorted withal, produces a monstrous effect, making fit studies for a Michelangelo.[24]

Similar remarks could be made about other focal practices such as walking, fishing, drawing water, and gardening.

Importantly, the pond engages Thoreau in an active sensuous contemplation.

> I did not read books the first summer; I hoed beans. Nay, I often did better than this. There were times when I could not afford to sacrifice the bloom of the present moment to any work, whether of the head or hands. I love a broad margin to my life . . . (These times) were not subtracted from my life, but so much over and above my usual allowance. I realized what the Orientals mean by contemplation and the forsaking of works.[25]

These blooms of the present moment animate his life, his love for nature, his thinking and his writing. That Walden Pond can invite again and again Thoreau's contemplation shows what a deep thing it is. As a kind of side effect, and for the most part wholly unintended, Walden in these defining moments reminds him of the more original, sponsored meanings of words: ". . . we are in danger of forgetting the language which all things and events speak without metaphor, which alone is copious and standard."[26]

Others and Mortality

A thing focuses social engagement. Thoreau was hardly a hermit. From beginning to end he is encountering people. (Also, one is apt to overlook the way that Walden Pond reaches out and gathers to it people through Thoreau's book.) Within *Walden,* how does Walden Pond gather people to it? Thoreau had to chop some live trees in order to construct his house, but "before I had done I was more a friend than a foe of the pine tree, having become better acquainted with it."[27] As Thoreau becomes acquainted with other things, other people, too, are gathered. "Sometimes a rambler in the woods was attracted by the sound of my axe, and we chatted pleasantly over the chips which I had made."[28] These encounters are the birds that have come to reside in the branches of the tree which has grown from the initial seed—his contact with the pond.

Walden has always attracted human beings. A skiff of snow reveals to Thoreau an ancient path near the shoreline encircling it. Perhaps this path was "worn by the feet of aboriginal hunters."[29] It still is unwittingly trodden by the present day occupants. In the future Thoreau foresees that this path, first suggested by the shoreline itself, that is, by nature, will still be followed to some extent, no matter how rebelliously. (Even Manhattan takes into account to some extent its landscape, its waterways, though in a much more heavy-handed fashion than the Toledo portrayed by El Greco.)

Walden's society is not just human. The pond is a gathering place for fish, frogs, fowl, tortoises and other animals. Thoreau knows the full range of its fishes and the extent of their respective populations. "Its pickerel, though not abundant, are its chief boast."[30] Because of the extraordinary purity of Walden's water, its fish are "much cleaner, handsomer, and firmer fleshed than most."[31] For the same reason, all the animals seem cleaner. In "Sounds," Thoreau finds that some of these same creatures voice or articulate nature. That is, all of nature's simplicity and wholesomeness comes to be voiced by these creatures recognized in their distinct individuality. The "clean race of frogs and tortoises" emerge from and become definitive of the larger purity of Walden Pond and nature itself.[32] The nature which tends to hide makes its appearance in these creatures. They are the pure sounds emerging from the vast silence.

These wild things of course gather hunters and fishermen.

> Early in the morning, while things are crisp with frost, men come with fishing reels and slender lunch, and let down their fine lines through the snowy field to take pickerel and perch; wild men, who instinctively follow other fashions and trust other authorities than their townsmen, and by their goings and comings stitch towns together where else they would be ripped. They sit and eat their luncheon in stout fear-noughts on dry oak leaves on the shore, as wise in natural lore as the citizen is in artificial. They never consulted with books, and know and can tell much less than they have done. The things they practice are said not yet to be known . . . (The fisherman's) life passes deeper in Nature than the studies of the naturalist penetrate . . . such a man has some right to fish and I love to see nature carried out in him.[33]

Fishing is not a distraction or diversion from these people's everyday lives. They have a right to it. Being at one with the wild, they realize the true state of things: the primacy of being over knowledge which civilized people tend to forget and not face. These resolute wild men define the basic condition of mortals. Walden Pond, drawing out the stuff these people are made of, mediates these insights to Thoreau.

The Divine: Piety and Impiety

In the *Genesis* Fall Story, both human beings and all of nature fall together. Thoreau thinks that Walden Pond perhaps "had not heard of the fall."[34] Its water is still "green and pellucid as ever." Oldtimers recall that ducks and eagles inhabited it at one time. Even bear and lynx roamed its woods. The anchor cable for the old log canoe was made of "strips of hickory tied together."[35] The native peoples in America did it no harm. They lived according to nature's suggestions. Hence, Walden Pond never suffered the fall and remained "distiller of celestial dews."[36] However, with the advent of the Revolution, that is, the American Revolution and its re-echo in the Industrial Revolution, Walden begins to decline. No longer are there grape vines in some coves forming bowers under which a boat may pass. No longer does it have the appearance of an amphitheater for some kind of sylvan spectacle. Why? Because since Thoreau left those shores "the woodchoppers have still further laid waste."[37] The trees are gone. The forest is gone. No longer do the gods find a place to dwell. The muse is silent. "How can you expect the birds to sing when their groves are cut down?" The trees were cut down for railroad ties. The villagers want to tap it with a pipe for dishwater. The icemen skim its ice for cooling summer drinks.

Nevertheless, Thoreau's mind floats optimistically about the purity, serenity, and simplicity of the pond. He wishes to see it as an instance of the higher law: things do not change; we change. "It is itself unchanged, the same water which my youthful eyes fell upon; all change is in me. It has not acquired one permanent wrinkle after all its ripples. It is perennially young."[38] The trees will grow back, etc. One has seen that argument so often it appears that some think the reality could be propped up simply by the vertical lines of our written words. Thoreau hopes that the engineer of the train that does not pause will not forget at night "he has beheld this vision of serenity and purity once at least during the day."[39] He may as well be drinking a beer in front of a TV set watching a beer advertisement saying, "It's the water." For my part, I do not want to visit what is left of Walden Pond today.

Having invoked the world of Walden Pond, we can now see that things gather the world differently than a clue or a symptom of a disease. Clues can be almost unnoticeable. Symptoms often merely hint and do not concentrate everything we know about the underlying disease, and so we need a highly abstract and sophisticated interpretive framework in order to connect the symptoms with the disease. On the other hand, things gather a world because they stand in the foreground and concentrate the world in themselves. This concentrated gathering is focalized in Walden Pond. From this standpoint, what the villagers are missing with their piped Walden water are all the elements that compose the world of Walden Pond. They are missing the tonic that comes from an intimacy with that world.

CHAPTER 9

TO EXPERIENCE THINGS AGAIN

We, however, are not prisoners. No traps or snares are set about us, and there is nothing which should intimidate or worry us. We are set down in life as in the element to which we best correspond, and over and above this we have through thousands of years of accommodation become so like this life, that when we hold still we are, through a happy mimicry, scarcely to be distinguished from all that surrounds us. We have no reason to mistrust our world, for it is not against us. Has it terrors, they are our terrors; has it abysses, those abysses belong to us; are dangers at hand, we must try to love them . . . Perhaps everything terrible is in its deepest being something helpless that wants help from us.

—Rainer Maria Rilke[1]

Only on the profound unbounded sea, can the fully invested whale be truly and livingly found out.

—Herman Melville[2]

Correlational coexistence forces us to think of the tight fit between the way we feel, think and act and the material conditions which evoke these feelings, thoughts and actions. We can speak either of our *experience of* things or, correlatively, of the *things* of experience. We can speak either of how the hearth engages us, or of the way the hearth gathers and bears a world by centering a home and a tradition, and by telling of the seasons. Of course these correlations are not, finally, separable. The difference between them is a matter of emphasis, for, in the last chapter, addressing the thing of our experience, Walden Pond, we saw, too, how Walden engaged Thoreau. Yet much more needs to be said about our unique experiences of things. Devices, products of our technological culture, fail to evoke and, in fact, preclude vitally important experiences that things offer. Things bring the world home to us and make us at home in it. Experiencing things

155

enlightens us and enables us to affirm life in a profound way. Without such experiences, we are apt to maintain superficial standards and fail to win through to deeper experiential truths.

I

Experience and Technology

Since we will be contrasting the experience of things with the experience of technological culture, it is necessary first to examine our situation. How does it *feel* to be ensconced in technological culture, to live lives in agreement with that framework?

Situated in Technology. When a paradigm becomes dominant, it provides an entire culture with a framework for understanding the world. It provides a culture with its "common sense"; anything outside this framework is marginalized, and all other interpretations, all other visions, of the world are viewed as nonsense, backward, foolish, "not with it." To understand how we as a culture are situated in technology, it is helpful to review this rational-seeming framework. It is held together by the promise of technology. Aligning ourselves with that promise, we adopt its standards for conquest, liberation, and prosperity. "Better" means what is technologically available in accordance with standards of ease, instantaneity, ubiquity, safety, comfort, convenience, and so on. Enriching ourselves means creating more numerous and novel commodities. One may vary the styles of the production and consumption, but everything we do in accordance with these standards is obvious, rational and powerfully sanctioned. This is what it means to be *situated* in technology.

Aldous Huxley's *Brave New World*[3] presents an imaginative version of the culture we are constructing—complete fulfillment of the promise of technology. Here life contains no adversity or any resistance whatsoever. From birth and child-rearing to sexuality, family, society, labor and leisure, through death, all problems have been resolved in advance. Unexpected problems merely call for a drug—"soma"—high. Everyone seems happy because each moment is filled with novel and undemanding stimulation (although more interactive than television). To enjoy what fun-bundles this society has to offer, no one needs to transcend infantile or adolescent states. Of all its many flaws the gravest flaw in this work is the mistaken assumption that this totalitarian order would have to be imposed from without by world controllers; rather, we now can see that this order arises from within, through the general, tacit agreement of its citizens with technology.

Huxley's work is deeply pessimistic concerning reformation of a technological society as advanced as Brave New World. A correlational environment consisting entirely of devices offers these citizens no opportunity to encounter things; they encounter objects which bid only to consume and dispose. Uneasy feelings of dread that might surface are held in abeyance through soma or other distractions. In short, these citizens are insulated from any claims calling them into the world, and they are not capable of responding even if these claims arose. From this standpoint, the real danger of technology is the possibility that it becomes totalized, entirely eclipsing things, and that we derive all our standards on its basis. Thus we as a culture forget any other way to be.[4]

In contrast, what is *our* experience of being situated in and by technology? Heidegger notes the experiential ironies of technological culture. "All distances in time and space are shrinking . . . yet the abolition of all distance brings no nearness."[5] We may add to this that the ease we pursue makes us feel uneasy, comfort brings no comfort, speed brings no rest, everywhereness is present as nowhereness, safety is pursued yet we suffer profound injury, the novelty is all the same, and mutual undertakings leave us lonely. Such is the experience of *technological irony*. This experience stems from the divisions caused by devices, and, unlike the citizens of a society where technology is totalized, from the sense that we are letting the good things of our life go. Things yield a momentous counterexperience to this disquieting technological irony. Things *bring the world near* and teach us to be at home here. To develop this essential counterexperience we need to examine first how experience helps to enlighten us and to examine why this decisive, irreplaceable experience is missing in the technological situation.

Enlightenment and Experience of the Wild. Immanuel Kant's discussion of the sublime is helpful here for understanding what experience can teach us and how the same circumstances can evoke quite different responses. Now, it is certainly true, Kant points out, that objects of overwhelming might in nature can terrorize us and cause us to flee before them. Such a reaction seems natural enough; it is what we expect, as Kant sees it, from the sensible self, the gratification-seeking self. In the face of such power, the self so understood has nothing to gain and everything to lose. Yet humans can respond in an entirely different way to the sight of a mighty object:

> The more attractive, the more fearful it is, provided only we are in security; and we willingly call these objects sublime, because they raise the energies of the soul above their accustomed height and discover in us a

faculty of resistance of a quite different kind, which gives us courage to measure ourselves against the apparent almightiness in nature.[6]

What interests us here is not Kant's analysis of the faculties required for such courage, nor the significance of calling them into play, but rather, the two opposing ways of experiencing the same mighty thing. To one it appears crazy not to flee, while the other is attracted and stands firm. What underlies the difference between the two responses?

Kant remarks, "Without development of moral ideas, that which we, prepared by culture, call sublime presents itself to the uneducated man merely as terrible."[7] To Kant the key is education. It is a matter of cultural preparation whether we become a match for (or cognitively superior to, as Kant would have it) the mighty things of nature. But education can take many forms. Education by culture alone cannot prepare us to experience the sublime. However helpful or even necessary cultural preparation may be, experience itself plays a decisive role in our becoming educated in Kant's sense.

Experience is the origin of cultural preparation concerning profound experiences. Without an experiential basis, talk of the sublime is merely nonsense, an imaginative construction of forms without the possibility of content. Cultural preparation must be born of and answer to experience. From this point of view, Kant's remarks can be recast. That which the experienced person calls sublime presents itself to the inexperienced person merely as terrible. The difference in standards by which each judges is contingent upon his or her depth of acquaintance with the thing.

What role experience plays in funding education in an essential and irreplaceable way finds its most articulate expression in the satori traditions of Eastern thought, yet, because of the subtleties involved, it is often misleading or perhaps impossible for us in the west to appropriate this thinking in an unmystifying way even when steps are taken to reach out to those in the western tradition, as Eugen Herrigel does in *Zen and The Art of Archery*.[8] For our purposes, it will be sufficient to turn to William Faulkner's "The Old People," in *Go Down Moses*. Taking the reader in small steps, this story begins simply and ends profoundly, offering the reader a glimpse of what is at issue with Issac McCaslin's relinquishment of his inherited property.

Issac does have a teacher, Sam Fathers, who is the son of a Chickasaw chief. Sam is able to show and articulate subtleties in experience which would go unrealized but for his teaching. In this regard, we can agree with Kant on the need for cultural preparation. Yet, as maintained above, experience itself must be *marked* so as to receive the *remarks*. Sam tells Issac,

"Now shoot quick and slow."[9] Such directions do not come out of hundreds of years of gun-handling experience for the Indians; nonetheless, they are born of experience and wisely characterize that experience in such as a way that a hunter will soon come to appreciate. However, the explicit paradox is nonsense to a complete outsider who has no experience akin to shooting. I will call this deeper kind of lived experience, metaphorically, the *experience of the wild*. Experience of the wild makes the paradox intelligible.

For Faulkner, this simple paradox is just the beginning, a way of making the reader charitable and establishing a direction to look for answers. Having killed the buck, Sam, with bloody hands "merely formally consecrated him (Issac) to that which he had accepted, humbly and joyfully, with abnegation and pride, too."[10] Here is a more subtle blend of seeming opposites, one which some of us may have a feel for, but also one which today's common experience fails to render comprehensible. Further,

> Because he was just twelve then, and that morning something had happened to him: in less than a second he had ceased forever to be the child he was yesterday. Or perhaps that made no difference, perhaps even a city-bred man, let alone a child, could not have understood it: perhaps only a country-bred one could comprehend loving the life he spills.[11]

With this event in the background warranting his insight, Issac intuits that shared experience of the wild, which here, grouped in terms of age and place—country-bred one—undergirds shared understanding.

Finally, on the same hunting trip, by waiting and not shooting, not shooting that which presents itself as something to be shot to the ordinary hunter—the "Grandfather" buck—Isaac learns to acknowledge the buck and all animals in the manner of a true hunter and noble human being. Paradoxically put, in the literal renunciation of killing he becomes a hunter like Sam Fathers. Such a transcendent regard for both human nobility and for the animals, wilderness, and Earth is not found even among most practitioners of hunting. And so Issac is exasperated when his cousin McCaslin pretends to be uncharitable toward his story of the buck: "Suppose they don't have substance, can't cast a shadow." The story ends with McCaslin confessing in response to Issac's exasperation, "Steady, steady. I know you did. So did I. Sam took me there once after I killed my first deer."[12] Not simply shared age, place, or even practice or family are sufficient grounds for sympathetic understanding between these two—only a specific shared experience of the wild will do.

A large portion of *Go Down Moses* works toward building up the intelligibility of and sympathy for the key act, which others deem silly, foolhardy, and crazy—the relinquishment of the land that is legally Issac's inheritance. If the ambiguity of the rightness of the action does not tease the reader, the reader has not plunged to the level where this text is working. The work seeks to educate the reader, not didactically, but by recalling and reflecting upon shared experiences of the wild so that one is enabled to understand what is difficult or impossible to understand without one's equally intense experience.

We began by reflecting on the role of experience in enlightenment and, to some extent, in culture. Sam Fathers' teaching ran ahead of Issac's experience but nevertheless was born of the Sam's profound experience of the wild. For that reason, Issac was able through participating in the practice of hunting to reclaim Sam Fathers' teaching as his own understanding now warranted by his own new experience of the wild. To be fully educated like Sam Fathers, to be able to teach what one understands, one must have this wild basis to one's understanding. If either experience of the wild or its possibility is missing, the meanings of such paradoxes as Kant's sublime, Faulkner's shooting quick and slow, as well as not-shooting-hunting decline to the flimsiness of rumor, then become bankrupt. Seeming nonsense becomes outright nonsense. In regard to the language of paradoxes involving the wild—realizations which must be lived into in order to be understood—cultural preparation must be born of and answer to the experience of the wild.

It is things that yield these deeper experiences of the wild. Since these experiences are paradoxical, it is as though one crosses a threshold into a new and unknown country. So I will call this hidden side to things the *wilderness of things.* One must cross the threshold of things into the wilderness, passing through the apparent contradiction of paradox into its concealed reasonableness. So profound experience of the wild is essential for the intelligibility of this wild sense of things. Imagination alone, though essential for articulating this experience in a way that can make its presence felt, will not do. The experience of that other shore is essentially unimaginable—it always overtakes us from behind in a manner unsuspected, as something more and something other than anticipated. For acquiring a sense of the wilderness of things, direct acquaintance is necessary and decisive.

Devices and the Wilderness of Things. We tend to use the time and effort saved by our use of devices only to consume more. We spend our time primarily in contact with familiar commodities resting upon inaccessible machinery. Now it is time to analyze in detail how contact with the final goods of technology significantly shapes our experience. Do devices and commodities exclude us from the wilderness of things?

I once made the glamorous choice to go salmon fishing from a charter boat off the Pacific coast. All that was demanded of our party for preparation was a phone call for reservations, showing up at the dock at 7 A.M., and having our money in hand. The boathands set up, baited and let out the complicated gear for us. A device kept the bait at just the right depth while radio contact with other boats and a fish scanner on our boat searched out schools of salmon and indicated the right depth at which to troll our bait. A rod holder held the rod for the clients—the others grinned at my sentimentality at holding my rod. The largest fish of the day, the only king salmon, was caught by someone who had never fished before and who had fallen asleep; he nearly wasn't allowed to reel it in himself. His seasickness from having fallen asleep was taken care of with a pill. This was device-procured fishing: easy, quick, safe, and almost guaranteed. And, aside from our being on the ocean, it was much like watching television for hours. I have never been back, and I am sure that the others in our party would acknowledge that such an experience is not what they live for. It was merely consumed.

Perhaps this example is extreme. Yet, without any more deliberation than deciding "I want to do that," one can buy a graphite flyrod at a shop where experts outfit one with everything to fit ones needs and wants, from technical manuals and videos on flyfishing to tapered leaders, to signing one up for a casting clinic, to putting one in contact with a fishing guide so that, on ones first day on the stream, one will be just in the right place at the right time with the right gear used in the right way to guarantee catching a trout. This way of experiencing fishing will not engage one lastingly.

Even where fishing has become a settled practice, the trend is toward selecting devices that disengage people and impoverish their experience. Take the difference between bamboo flyrods and the graphite rods that have come to replace them. The rodmaker's name on the bamboo rod bespeaks a history, a tradition of workmanship, and leads one to expect a rod of a certain character, such as hollow fluting in R. L. Winston rods, the light color of Leonard rods, and the parabolic action of a Pezon et Michelle. With a graphite rod, the brand means relatively little. Little personal workmanship surfaces on it and there is no tradition of rodmaking. The graphite rod embodies no history and repels any bread and wine mythology. Its tough surface requires little maintenance and many times such rods are stored carelessly. Sometimes lead-core lines are used without fear of injuring the rod. On the other hand, bamboo rods are often sent away to be refinished sometime during their long lifetime. They must be thoughtfully treated and carefully stored. Often as many used ones as new ones are shown in a flyshop. Used graphite rods are not usually resold in these shops. The graphite rod may last a lifetime but it is not treasured as a lifelong possession.

The graphite rod casts its longest casts best with a short, fast punch. It does not teach the fisherman what it means not to overpower, but to wait and work gracefully with the smooth, empowering arcs of the bamboo rod. One must take care not to injure the bamboo when landing a large trout. In the fine wood grains of the bamboo reside the green of grasses and willows, the earth of riverbanks, the growing powers of the sun's light, and the nodding of plants in the stream's cool breeze on a bright day. The graphite rod—which one manufacturer calls "The Ugly Stick"—is surely not the image of the universe nor a fleeting manifestation of the Tao. It casts as far as a bamboo rod without requiring the skill the latter does, and, because of its lightness, it can be cast with graceless ease all day long.

These three illustrations exemplify the tendency to dominate technologically a centering thing and practice, fishing. In each case, experience is occluded and impoverished by devices. With experience blocked, the ways in which fishing can benefit us, especially in unforeseen ways, are reduced. Fishing may be much of what we live for or at least may restore what we are about (as hunting often was for Mari Sandoz's Old Jules when he had become angered or disappointed or felt like giving up) but such devices prevent us from crossing the threshold into the wilderness of things. They diminish the extent to which a sense of wilderness reality is established in us. They allow fishing to become defined by technology. As such, fishing is not allowed to disclose to us its own defining moments, as David Harms' story shows.

> It was a hot, windless July afternoon, and the only motion of our boat came from our shifting bodies, sending small ripples out over the glass. I dropped my jig some sixty-five feet to the lake bottom . . . and began a slow undulating retrieve. Ten feet up one of Waterbury's innumerable five pound lake trout took the lure, and seconds later another bent Alan's rod tip to the water. Vern remained fishless in the bow. He took his pipe out of his mouth and tapped the bowl empty on the gunwale. 'What I don't get,' he said, 'is why you guides don't use depth finders. Make the fishin' a hell of a lot better.'[13]

Vern's frustration lies in the fact that a device exists, a depth finder, which could make fishing better by the technological framework's standards. Hence, it is nearly unintelligible to Vern why this device is not used. In fact, as the writer and guide, Harms, later points out, such devices are prevalently used on the Great Lakes far to the south of Waterbury, which is near the Northwest Territories.

So long as Vern's remarks and desires are not met with resistance or examination, fishing will likely be developed according to them. Increased technological domination will only close off other possibilities of the experience of fishing. By pushing technological domination to the brink, we may derive *all* our standards on its basis.

These technological standards are, of course, shallow and superficial because they make us see what first shows itself in experience as terrible, nonsense, crazy (or, alternatively, as glamorous, i.e., more fish, quicker). More generally, they are superficial because they are derived from experiences outside the wilderness of things. Vern remains unawakened to the other side of the paradox where nonsense is *redefined* as reasonable.

As devices increasingly replace things, our contact is with mere surfaces resting on now unfamiliar and *unexperienceable* machinery that occludes all further possibilities of experience. Devices then create the conditions for more shallow contact and superficial understandings. The possibility of a profound experience of the otherside, across the threshold of the wilderness of things, is blocked. Technology closes the door to the wilderness of things and entraps us on the nearside of that threshold.

How can we find our way beyond devices back into a sense of things? Is the disquieting experience of technological irony sufficient to turn our heads around, turn us homeward? On the basis of the twofold way in which Odysseus is instructed, through adversity and irony, it seems plausible that we may discover a way. Odysseus is brought back in touch with the kind powers which bring him home by having lived through the pointlessness of what Kalypso has to offer. Pleasure, comfort, ease, and safety are just not enough. Through the realization of the pointlessness of the later stages of modern technology, through the discovery of the void beneath one's activities and the experience of dread in the face of it, comes hope for turning aside from the attempt to get everything under control.

So couldn't pointlessness by itself point the way to the wilderness of things? The author of *Ecclesiastes* thought so: "All is vanity." "There is no new thing under the sun." "In much wisdom is much grief." The finished products of our labor brings no profit. The wise no less than fools, humans no less than beasts, all die. Whoever inherits your works will soon forget you or may be a fool. It seems nothing abides, that there is no reward or profit from all that is done under the sun. But all this is an appearance, a way of negating possibilities. More positively, eating and drinking are to be done in joy, a joy which answers the disquietude the earlier statements have created. "Whatsoever thy hand findeth to do, do it with thy might."[14] For this writer, the human portion under the sun lies not in the products of ones labor, not in a reward apart from action, but in the labor, the action itself. The splendor of the writings attests to it. Finally, by remembering that the days of darkness shall be many, we are turned to things in their own right, the matter-of-factness of things. "Truly the light is sweet, and a pleasant thing it is for the eyes to behold the sun."[15]

But *Ecclesiastes* comes from a pretechnological (premodern) period and relies on a different context than we can count on. For instance, assembly-line labor repels engagement that might be enacted with might and in joy. And so, too, commodification of food and drink disallow engagement. Very little in our correlational environment is left alone to astound us in its otherness. Finally, the void which *Ecclesiastes* makes one feel in order to open one to the presence of things is more likely to be handled technologically by filling it with ever new diverting and distracting commodities as in *Brave New World* with soma, or with television. So along with the realization of pointlessness there must exist the things whose kind powers call on Odysseus. Lack is instructive only together with longing. We must have a home to long for.

Hence we return to the point made at the end of chapter 5. There we saw that it is not enough to recognize how debilitating technology is. It is not enough to say no to inappropriate technology, to heedless consumption. Now we see more clearly how devices block out the experience of the wild, keeping us outside the wilderness of things. We see clearly, too, how this impoverishment of experience shapes our world view and encourages the establishment of very tame standards, indeed. We see the danger of technological totalization. Given our diminished contact with the world, it is no wonder that we are restless and uneasy. Yet our uneasiness does not arise from boredom alone, oppressed by the flatness of the surrounding plains. We are unsettled as well because the mountains still shine in the distance. We still have within our experience those things and events which once made life worthwhile. In the midst of our less than wholehearted saying yes to technology, we remember those other things we once said yes to and still feel we could say yes to again.

II

Bringing The World Near

We wish for the cushy comfort of disburdened availability and yet find ourselves ironically anxious, restless and not at home. How can we better respond to our situation? How can we come to feel really at home here on Earth? We now see that experience of the wild provides the basis for a completely different response to things and events, for when we are educated by the experience of the wild we are enabled to respond to them as sublime rather than terrible. Nothing short of the experience of the wild can make it possible for us really to understand the wilderness of things and the paradoxical language of things. However, technology locks us out of the wilderness of things, eliminating these deeper experiences. So to those who take their bearings from being situated in technology, all profound experience and understanding of things looks crazy. Here we lack a counterbalance to the ready-made framework of technology. We lack the experience of an intimacy with things and the world. Where can we encounter this missing experience again and so hope to counter living unreflectively, situated technology?

From beginning to end, *Walden* is a book dedicated to an understanding of things that is entirely warranted by firsthand experience. Thoreau tell us at the outset that he is "confined" by the narrowness of his experience. In "Where I Lived and What I Lived For," he writes that he went to the pond in order "to know . . . by experience" whether life is mean or sublime.[16] He remarks in "Walking" that a poet should nail "words to their primitive senses . . . deriv[ing] his words as often as he uses them—transplant[ing] them to his page with earth adhering to their roots."[17] So *Walden* is a good place to seek this counterexperience to technological situatedness. Where in *Walden* do we come across this experience of things and events drawing the world near? Apart from the world of Walden Pond itself, Thoreau sees that the villagers will be missing decisive experiences. Importantly for him, we "villagers" are missing the events of morning and wildness.

Morning. Morning gently invites us into correlational coexistence. "Every morning was a cheerful invitation to make my life of equal simplicity, and I may say innocence, with Nature herself."[18] Morning is both literal and more than literal. On the literal level, we can take our cue from Walden pond. "As the sun arose, I saw it throwing off its nightly clothing of mist, and here and there, by degrees, its soft ripples or its smooth reflecting surface was revealed."[19] It, too, responds to the sun's invitation. It dawns with the sun, reflects the morning, and receives the morning's simplicity. Like Thoreau's early morning outings, the pond "anticipates nature" and is not merely "present at" or "looking at" events. It too emerges with morning. Here morning, natural things and ourselves emerge and exist together in simplicity and innocence.

As its second lesson, morning teaches us that it is broader than literal morning. It is literal, exemplary, and metaphorical as well. Morning moves us, but other things move us too. "To him whose elastic and vigorous thought keeps pace with the sun, the day is perpetual morning."[20] In fact, we find out that morning is anywhere, everywhere, and forever, ever, and always so. "The morning wind forever blows, the poem of creation is uninterrupted; but few are the ears that hear it. Olympus is but the outside of the earth everywhere."[21]

So the next lesson is to learn to realize what is always present, how morning becomes an event to which we are joined in an essential way. "Morning . . . is the awakening hour."[22] "Morning is when I am awake and there is a dawn in me."[23] That is to say, the outer morning does not culminate without an inward morning. Finally, putting this together with the eternal and ubiquitous characterization of morning above, the task is not to escape to or wait for another time and place, some literal morning, but to realize the omnipresent morning. "We must learn to reawaken and keep ourselves awake . . . by an infinite expectation of the dawn."[24]

Ironically, both literal morning and literalness itself fall prey too easily to the mundane to hold up as exemplary in the final lesson. And so *Walden* concludes: "The light which puts out our eyes is darkness to us. Only that day dawns to which we are awake. There is more day to dawn. The sun is but a morning-star."[25] Following morning as deliberately as nature, we sooner or later "come to a hard bottom and rocks in place, which we call *reality*, and say, This is, and no mistake."[26] Such a consummatory disclosive event enlightens one about what it means to live, and gets one past the fear that "when I came to die, discovered that I had not lived."[27] Morning invites us to cross the threshold into the wilderness of things and, in its own time, enlightens us of that fact—shows us where we live and what we live for. It brings us home. We can see this more clearly by turning to the theme of wildness.[28]

Wildness. Thoreau writes, "Our village life would stagnate if it were not for the unexplored forests and meadows which surround it. We need the tonic of wildness."[29] For Thoreau, village life can stagnate for two quite different reasons. On the one hand, it can stagnate because it imports Old World ways which have outlived their time and have grown merely artificial. For Thoreau, practices like bathing oneself need to be renewed "completely each day; do it again, and again, and forever again." On the other hand, Thoreau thinks of the village life going stagnant as the technological society enthralled by the vision of technology. For the technological society, things and practices are merely burdensome. Hence, technology is used to disburden us of practices by having the machinery of the device take them over, but the elimination of practices also leads to stagnation or disengagement. Thus the task is not to do away with practices or the village life, but to make them appropriate and vital.

What is this tonic of wildness which Thoreau confidently believes keeps our village life from going stagnant? What is it that could freshen our technological setting and needs to freshen our practices? Approaching this experience carefully, let us first rule out one possibility: It would be too pat or *tame* to say we experience genuine unmistakable wildness in our excited sighting of larger forms of wildlife, e.g., elk or bear. Thoreau was not only interested in striking deep the roots of our lived relatedness to things, not only critical of the substitution of commodities for things, but he was equally opposed to conventions that could lead us to think we could somehow self-consciously know where the focus of wildness is, or arrange conditions to make wildness exhibit itself. He finds that nature exhibits itself unexpectedly and more often to fishermen and those spending their lives in the fields and woods than to those, such as philosophers and poets, who come at nature with expectation.[30] It is as if nature is not afraid to exhibit itself to those who are forever on the alert, in an infinite expectation of the dawn. The kind of expectation that locates and fixes the event of meaning in advance precludes it. So, sometimes the seemingly least likely wild place, such as a dismal swamp, may be most fertile with possibilities. "My spirits infallibly rise in proportion to outward dreariness."[31]

When does nature exhibit itself or wildness disclose itself? What is the tonic of wildness? Such events need invoking in order to become evocative. Surely wild geese with their flying V's gather the northern tundra with southern marshes, foretelling of fall or spring, shortening or lengthening of days, wheatfields and water. The first year I lived on Long Island I wrote of the following experience.

> One night earlier this fall when I was feeling lonely, I happened to be studying with the doors of my apartment open. Suddenly I was startled by the sound of geese for the first time. My heart skipped as if a dear friend whom I had not seen for some time was at the door. In Montana I had looked forward to the geese each fall—to seeing them on silver cold days and hearing them from out of the wind as I was falling asleep at night. Now all these memories rushed into the present sounds afresh. It seemed as if each honking evoked a memory, as if the honking called all the geese in my life to flight and follow. I found myself renewed.

Such momentous and memorable events in which wildness is exhibited are not our average encounter with wildlife. Wildness can be experienced quite differently from this as well. One night in early winter Thoreau, too, was startled by a goose and stepped to his door listening to its wings it flew so close.

> Suddenly, an unmistakable cat owl from very near me, with the most harsh and tremendous voice I ever heard from any inhabitant of the

woods, responded at regular intervals to the goose . . . 'Boo-hoo, boo-hoo, boo-hoo!' It was one of the most thrilling discords I ever heard. And yet if one had a discriminating ear, there were in it the elements of a concord such as these plains never saw nor heard.[32]

Again, wildness will not be tamed or gotten down pat. Such events do, indeed, trigger a tonic which heals, restores, refreshes, and invigorates us. They are keynotes which harmonize us.

We are now ready to follow out why "not one innocent huckleberry can be transported thither from the country's hills." The huckleberry, of course, does not show up as an expected huckleberry at all. Neither is it found in the fair weather of July. Rather it shows up when it seems nonsense to be outdoors, midwinter. All visitors to Walden Pond have been winnowed except for those who make their living barking trees and who have now come to fish. At this time the wild men come to Walden Pond who "by their goings and comings stitch towns together in parts where else they would be ripped." Again, their lives pass deeper in nature than the studies of the naturalist penetrate. What do these wild men uncover? Notice, this time at least, it is not in the hooking, leaping, landing or eating of the fish that the thing things. Here is the tonic of wildness missed when one buys huckleberries at the market or when one gets Walden's water through a pipe.

Ah, the pickerel of Walden! when I see them lying on the ice, or in the well which the fisherman cuts in the ice, making a little hole to admit the water, I am always surprised by their rare beauty, as if they were fabulous fishes, they are so foreign to the streets, even to the woods, foreign as Arabia to our Concord life. They possess a quite dazzling and transcendent beauty which separates them by a wide interval from the cadaverous cod and haddock whose fame is trumpeted in our streets. They are not green like the pines, nor gray like the stones, nor blue like the sky; but they have, to my eyes, if possible, yet rarer colors, like flowers and precious stones, as if they were the pearls, the animalized *nuclei* or crystals of Walden water. They, of course, are Walden all over and all through; are themselves small Waldens in the Animal kingdom, Waldenses. It is surprising they are caught here, that in this deep capacious spring, far beneath the rattling teams and chaises and tinkling sleighs that travel the Walden road, this great gold and emerald fish swims. I never chanced to see its kind in any market; it would be the cynosure of all eyes there. Easily, with a few convulsive quirks, they give up their watery ghosts, like a mortal translated before his time to the thin air of heaven.[33]

Here, as vividly and poetically as possible, Thoreau presents us with an event bringing the world near. The pickerel thing actively gathers and radiates Earth and sky, mortals and mortality, and, through the act of invocation and the connotations of cynosure, the divine, too. This event gathers the world from afar and puts Thoreau back in touch with it. It brings him home and makes him at home in the world, again. The night before he had spent tossing and turning in his sleep, trying to answer dark questions. This event saves Thoreau from this midwinter, midnight despair. Here, too, in this momentous consummatory event are joined the awakening of morning with this restoration of the tonic of wildness, for this event lets Thoreau and the fishermen know why they have come this way. The event, in a way, explains to them why it makes sense to be out fishing at Walden pond in midwinter. It gives them the nod to their destinies. It may not have been particularly pleasant for the fishermen, but there is no mistake about the gladness of being there.

In Wildness is the Preservation of the World. What do these world gathering events mean? What is their significance? Technology disguises nearness when it brings close merely by shortening time and distance. Hence we miss the intimacy we really want and come away with something less. In our time we have not yet comprehended how we have been duped—we do not really reach out and touch someone over the telephone. Analogously, technology can heal in terms of stitching wounds, setting bones and prescribing antibiotics. But are we always healed in a deeper sense when the cuts close and bones mend and our health is restored? Of course not. Technology injures things, denies us access to the wilderness of things, and, in a profound way, opens a wound in us. Seeing the difference between the glamorous attraction of technology and what it really does to us is pivotal for what will enable us to reform technology. Only in comprehending this can we hope to come to be at home on Earth. Does the event of bringing the world near yield this insight?

Here we can learn much by turning again to Thoreau who sees through this technological irony. In the passage preceding the pickerel, Thoreau comments on a "ruder fisherman" who cut many holes in the ice with fishing lines down each in order to maximize the number of fish he could catch in a day. Apparently he will sell these at the market. But Thoreau suggests that though this fisherman seems to move ahead in numbers, he ironically falls behind the other fishermen because, not having experienced the intimacy of things, he will not experience with any one of these pickerel the tonic of wildness. Just as huckleberries cannot be "taken" in this manner, so, too, pickerel cannot. The event of which Thoreau writes cannot be manufactured, procured with a device or ordered by setting upon the pickerel. Nor can it be bought in a market, as he notes. Not produced, not consumed, not even taken within a realm of life which is pastured by production and consumption, the event of the world gathering pickerel lies entirely outside the framework of technology, of human production and consumption. Yet it is a cynosure, a pole star, the center around which the world of these people turns, a point guiding them in building their lives.

Without the tonic of wildness, Thoreau implies that the life of the fisherman will stagnate. His fishing practices will grow stale. It would be only rational for him, for instance, to pursue another means besides fishing if it were more lucrative. But no matter how productive an alternative activity may be, its rewards will be *infinitely* less than wildness. Thus, these rewards will never satisfy him and he will remain troubled. On the other hand, Thoreau attests that such epiphanic events let him know he is alive and get him past the fear of finding he has not lived. He writes, metaphorically, "If it were not for such families as this, I think I should move out of Concord."[34] To keep him dwelling in a way that makes him at home in Concord, he must experience the nearness of things. A world worth living in must be refreshed, restored and preserved by contact with wildness.

This experience of the wild is the basis from which Thoreau makes a wild and crazy response to the culture of technology. Thoreau is able to let go of the seemingly rational dreams of the ruder fisherman and his neighbors because he has insight into the wildness that preserves the world and sees how and why that wildness is missing from technological ways of taking. He knows better than to seek what makes the world good within a life fenced in by modes of human production and consumption. Although Thoreau sees technology as a genuine improvement from the standpoint of securing basic necessities—something the affluent should extend to the poor—he does not find that it can deliver the cynosure of life. In this way, then, these world gathering events enable Thoreau to make a wilder response to life, turning away from the life of consumption his neighbors are pursuing. We will return to Thoreau's suggestion here in our concluding chapter.

CHAPTER 10

TO EXPERIENCE WILDERNESS

... Meanwhile the wild geese, high in the clean blue air,
are heading home again.
Whoever you are, no matter how lonely,
the world offers itself to your imagination,
calls to you like the wild geese, harsh and exciting—
over and over announcing your place
in the family of things.

—Mary Oliver, from "Wild Geese"[1]

This . . . theme [of wilderness] . . unifies my own life. It enfolds and
simplifies, comprehends and completes. Whenever I awaken, I awaken
into it. It carries with it the gift of life. And it lives in the authenticity of
every authentic gift, every true blessing confirms it deeper; it is always
with me when I come to myself. Through it I find my vocation, for the
wilderness is reality experienced as call and explained in responding to it
absolutely. . . . I want the truth, marrow-bone truth, and I find the intimations of it whenever I am alive to things, even the most familiar and
commonplace things, for the wilderness I take them to comprise. It
seems to me that every time I am born, the wilderness is born anew; and
every time I am born it seems to me that then, if ever, I could be content
to die.

—Henry Bugbee[2]

Can wilderness teach us what it means to be at home in the world?
We will consider wilderness and homecoming in Henry Bugbee's *The Inward Morning,* and then consider literal wilderness and the experience of
backpacking in it.

171

The Experience of Reality as Wilderness

Wilderness, like many of the other words Bugbee employs, has an experiential meaning. So we must turn to particular experiences of things to make intelligible what otherwise may be mystifying. Abstractly conceived, Bugbee's way of life and thought is to open "to the meaning of *life in the wilderness* and await with patience . . . that assurance which may overtake us in the course of our wanderings and make us at home in this condition."[3] Concretely sketched, this way of life emerges in stories of swamping, kids building a dam, rowing, fishing, boating, in listening to birds and bells, in music, and in stories of World War II at sea.[4] In the following sketch Bugbee remembers an incident with the clarity that sometimes comes to him at the moment of settling into sleep.

> For a moment just now I could remember some times at sea; especially the grey Christmas Day of 1944 on our little ship, as thirty-five of us sailed on alone over the endless swells. The land of Manus Island in the Admiralties lay behind us some days of open sea. The Philippines lay ahead, but far beyond our seeing, like whatever was in store for us there, or from there on. All that we knew of our position was like the ship's position approximately fixed on the chart. It was something else again to be there looking out over the grey sea under the grey sky, steering a course that took its direction more from the world of the chart than the world we beheld. It was Christmas in the wilderness.
>
> As the day drew to a close nearly everyone not on watch was sitting about on deck up forward of the pilot house. The sound of the engines was muted there, and the wash of the seas under the bows made it seem quite still. Only the faintest tinge of color crept into the sky as sun set. The men who talked were talking very low. Someone in a steady, quiet voice began to sing, and there were soon others singing with him. In the closing light of that day, riding the endless swells, they sang the song of men in our position. And it was Christmas in the wilderness.[5]

At the outset, we find a tension between a sense of purpose, imaged as being abstractly fixed on a chart standing within the broader context of the war, and a sense of existence, imaged as grey nowhereness—sailors longing for home but finding themselves not only not headed for home but seemingly not headed for anywhere. Their sense of existence is like that expressed by Pascal as no up nor down, no right nor left, no back nor forward. They are exiles and the objects before them are anything but near.

Yet, paradoxically, in giving over all hope of being consoled by an abstract, charted purpose or by a literal homecoming, they open to receive the gift which makes them at home in the world again. From 'inside out' and not 'outside in' they are able to take their bearings again. The ship, the closing day, and the song enfold them in an intimate presence. They remember who they are and become themselves again, steadied in the here and now. They are at home in the unknown, on the frontier, come what may. This is what it means to be restored to reality as wilderness.

All that we need to understand about ourselves, Bugbee persuades us, issues out of our lived involvement with our things. "You cannot place yourself outside it and hope to understand it; it can only be nonsense."[6] Only by giving ourselves over to things can we realize what was at first only intimated to us; things, for their part, unforeseeably overtake us with their importance. In the sketch of swamping, it seemed like nonsense to be outside, nonsense to be among dead trees, cold wind, grey sky. Yet, in giving himself over to it the boy discovers, "There was something about the water in the swamps that made it impossible to stay out . . . It was not particularly pleasant, as I recall. But there was no mistake about the gladness of being in the swamp or the immanence of the wilderness there."[7]

One may think of reality as wilderness presenting itself in wild places: the ocean or swamps or alongside streams. However, for Bugbee, "one is in this place all along" though we seldom realize it. When we do, familiar and commonplace things stand out in "wonderful matter-of-factness."[8] Common things become everything and the commonplace becomes a holy place.

The key to the experience of reality as wilderness is not in arranging or rearranging our conditions, for instance, by going somewhere: "it is, rather, a coming to meet them, a welcoming of them, an acknowledgment of them."[9] So, Bugbee speaks of the need for patience and openness. Patience because things take time to intimate their meanings. Openness, because mere intellectual receptiveness is not enough. Following Gabriel Marcel, he means the openness of the person in his or her entirety. In part this means the candor involved in recollecting oneself. In part this means extending oneself in a *welcoming* of persons and of things—receptivity in participation with them. Insofar as this openness is lacking on our part, as when we refuse the gift of things, reality is experienced not as a wilderness but as wasteland. One can imagine a sailor, like the "sullen" in Dante's *Inferno*,[10] refusing the Christmas gift in Bugbee's sketch. Less extreme, an objective or reportorial attitude may make the things which should be experienced as presences into mere objects. Nothing that is merely looked at, as opposed to actively received, can make its 'necessity' felt by us.

The Need for Literal Wilderness

For Bugbee, awakening to reality as wilderness is always awakening to things in their here and now importance. It is not a matter of transcending things because we have become disillusioned with how fickle and unsatisfying they are; it is much more a matter of *transcending our way of taking* things, a way which fixes on, clings to, or takes control of them. Things rightly realized bless us. True existence is coexistence with them and other people. Any time, any place, and any thing can beckon us to awaken. In a world of genuine things this emphasis is appropriate. However, our technological situation requires us to ponder this further. We need to retrieve things literally.

Looking once again at Bugbee's sketch, the ship's position is a mere X marked on a chart. That X could be almost anywhere at sea and all would be the same: the endless swells and the landless horizon. Temporally, the succession of days seems to be marked merely by X's as well. The day is neither bright and clear nor torn by storms, but merely grey. The sunset is remarkable only for its absence of color. It surely seems an unlikely time to find something remarkable. Yet, the crew is not aboard a nuclear submarine nor living underground where days and nights could be mere conventions. They are not just anywhere on the ship, but up forward where it is quiet. And this is not just any day; it is Christmas day. It is not just any hour, but the time when the day is gathering to a close. So too Erazim Kohák's *The Embers and the Stars* invokes the resonant meanings of dusk, evoking within the more ordinary before and after order of time a sense of the vertical order of eternity, such as we see in Bugbee's sketch.[11]

From a correlational coexistence standpoint we see that, in responding to things, humans bring into relief the special and unsuspected character of the materiality of things, making it appear and drawing it near. No work, not excepting Heidegger's, goes further to retrieve things and show their importance than *The Inward Morning*, yet, having a theory of technology enables us to understand that the character of thingly materiality needs to be highlighted more than it is in the philosophy of that work. Technology is not only a way of taking things—setting upon them—it is a way of *shaping* things. It is not a matter of taking devices as things; devices cannot be taken as things. A correlational environment consisting of commodities supplied by devices will have lost the quality necessary to engage us. On the other hand, literal wilderness has these deep, thingly qualities. Its character of materiality warrants its being experienced as wilderness in Bugbee's sense. We know it ought to be experienced that way, at least from time to time. Moreover, wilderness is a place mostly untouched by modern technology. It is not a place which has been divided into shallowly experienced surfaces and unexperienceable depths. Rather it is more than any conception could have it, indicated by how we flounder before it, how we articulate it only negatively, saying, for example, that a tree is more than boardfeet. But what more? Should we explain its moreness in scientific terms alone? These are places where animating nature still flourishes.

Animating Nature

Nature, in my account of it, is not simply observed nature. It takes hold of us, *animating* and involving us. For those of us who, like Thoreau, are indeed attracted to natural things, animating nature is merely a collective term which summarizes all the various ways nature and natural things call out to us, move us. Etymologically, 'animate' bears connotations of life and quickening; it has root meanings of air, breath, life, soul, mind as well as wind, spirit, and courage. It is also related to animal. Animating nature quickens us, nourishes us, gives us the air that makes our breath worth the breathing. Without it we may be soulless. Contact with it can remind us of our right minds. We will also find that it can be a source of encouragement.

However, most of animating nature is both more subtle and more mundane than this etymology suggests. All those various ways which Walden gathers the world are simultaneously ways in which Thoreau and other human beings can respond to—be animated by—Walden. The number of ways is indefinite and vast. Obviously, then, animating nature is a continuum admitting of a wide range of variations. Nature remains fundamentally attractive, though at times it may be experienced as neutral or unattractive and even repulsive. While animating nature may be disclosed dramatically in consummatory events, it can also appear in subtle forms, as when walking in a forest follows an unplanned course. Looking here, pausing there, sitting over there, listening to this can be so natural and unself-conscious that these do not even reach our conscious awareness. Yet these subtle ways in which we are animated by nature are importantly connected to the more dramatic events. How so?

To see this connection, we need to consider five variations out of this continuum, ranging from being faintly in touch with animating nature to being moved by its consummatory disclosures. First, with no more than faint intimations animating nature can initiate our interests or wonder. Animating nature teases us, as it were, to venture into the wilderness of things. My practice of flyfishing began innocently enough with this kind of wonder. Many of our lifelong loves of nature date from such beginnings.

Secondly, animating nature can underlie the constancy of our concern with nature without being directly the focus of attention. It is assumed rather than felt self-consciously. Steadiness and steadfastness are the marks of this variation. The other three variations are disclosive events. Animating nature can disclose itself in a fundamental way when it nearly fails to be present. Thoreau writes of this experience:

> As I was leaving the Irishman's roof after the rain, bending my steps again to the pond, my haste to catch pickerel, wading in retired meadows, in sloughs and bogholes, in forlorn and savage places, appeared for an instance trivial to me who had been sent to school and college; but as I ran down the hill toward the reddening west, with a rainbow over my shoulder, and some faint tinkling sounds borne to my ear through the cleansed air, from I know not what quarter, my Good genius seemed to say, go fish and hunt far and wide day by day—farther and wider—and rest thee by many brooks and hearthsides without misgiving.[12]

Here, Thoreau loses touch with animating nature and then regains it again, this time with more assurance. With other kinds of eventful disclosures, one often cannot say exactly where one has been reacquainted with animating nature or the tonic of wildness in a consummatory way. Hikers sometimes carry it out of the wild unconsciously. Colin Fletcher tells of meeting a pair of backpackers emerging from a wilderness. "They were weatherbeaten and distilled to bone and muscle. But what I remember best of all is that they were happy and whole. Whole and secure and content."[13] Sometimes one just wakes up to the fact of being awake after four or five days in the backcountry. Finally, there are those world gathering events we saw earlier with Thoreau's pickerel fishing and Bugbee's sailors. These consummatory disclosures of animating nature happen when things bring the world near and reality manifests as wilderness, affirming the lives of people in an unforeseen but unmistakable way.

John Dewey's analysis of "having an experience" can help us see how these consummatory events are related to larger contexts.[14] Consuming a TV dinner is contextless but consummatory events exact a setting and require time and order for preparation and celebration. A thread runs through an experience from the beginning, through the middle, and eventually is tied to the beginning and pulled together to achieve a climax. Without mixing our entire selves with the entire context this closure will not occur. Specifically, from the standpoint of Dewey's theory, the possibility of having eventful experiences at Walden Pond emerges from mixing ourselves with the practice of fishing, with the morning preparations, and also walking to Walden with other fishermen, cutting holes in the ice, letting the line out, catching fish one by one, enjoying the process and being alert to all it unexpectedly offers. Earlier variations of animating nature all assist in bringing about this eventful experience.

However, Dewey's account neglects a sense of things. He does not see how things and events are related. Yet things—Walden Pond and its pickerel—must first appeal to the fisherman before they plan to fish. Dewey descibes having an experience only from an abstract point of view: an organism with attitudes, goals, and a project undergoing a situation in a kind of bargaining arrangement. From a correlational coexistence standpoint, however, one senses not a *project* but a *calling*. Wild things tug at these people. Interaction here occurs within the larger context of being in the world—being oriented and animated by the things of that world. The wild people are already steady and steadfast in their commitment to wild things.

This means the things that animate human projects are more fundamental than the projects themselves. Mixing ourselves with animating nature is the way projects get started, take on a direction, build, and remain lastingly attractive. And, as we saw with Thoreau's momentary losing touch with animating nature, things keep appealing to us; otherwise, we would not continue to seek them out. Because things remain appealing, the fishermen return again and again, even in midwinter.

As things appeal to and animate us, things also gather us. Walden Pond draws people time and again, orienting them. For Dewey, having an experience culminates in a moment that gathers an experience together and renders an insight into the whole of it. Stepping beyond Dewey, we see that not only an experience but a complete way of life is pulled together, given insight into, and affirmed. If things did not gather and center us in this way our lives would be too fragmented to yield these events. The possibility of having profound experiences is based on the existence of things.

Without fish in the pond, no people would chop holes in the ice. If Walden Pond had been degraded to the condition of Farmer Flint's pond, Thoreau would have lived by another. If Fair Haven Hill had been replaced by a modern subdivision, a modern Thoreau would not have gathered huckleberries there. If Cottonwood Canyon is logged, it will no longer move me the way that it does now. Henry Bugbee can use the word wilderness metaphorically because literal wilderness has endeared itself to him. Though consummatory disclosures of animating nature may not invariably come with the material event of the thing, the catching of fish, it is essential to remember the things, events, and structures underlying such experiences. By becoming intimate with the world things gather, that world, now and then, is brought home to us and we are brought into agreement with it. The tonic of wildness is anchored in wild things. So, without these things and events, our lives will not be animated. Without that animation, our lives will stagnate, go dead, become soulless, be unawakened.

Enlightening, sensitive, and profound as the wilderness theme of *The Inward Morning* is, our present situation requires that we rethink it in light of the transformation of things into devices. We will follow *The Inward Morning's* wilderness theme by reconsidering the various components of its abstract characterization. "We can open ourselves to the meaning of a life in the wilderness and be patient of being overtaken in our wandering by that which can make us at home in this condition."[15] Let us consider wandering.

Wandering

The Inward Morning shows that we are wanderers with regard to life's meaning. As wanderers we are ready for and receptive to the given and the surprising as they come to pass. In the present technological setting we tend to set upon things, bending them to our projects. In advance we already seem to know the uses of things and lack the ears for hearing how things may address us in any other way. We may wander in the technological setting but we do so abstractly. Technology is likely to subvert a more profound sense of wandering, unless we take steps to guard against its seductive forces. Yet the act of guarding, too, seems opposed to that deeper sense of wandering. The problem is, once one uncovers how thoroughly our present context is oriented by the technological framework, how almost hourly we are asked to pay lip service to the ruling vision, we fear letting go, getting with it, being spontaneous, lest we sooner or later find ourselves aligned with technology's standards and chatter: envious talk of cushy jobs, second home locations, glamorous commodities. How can we both guard and wander?

A second problem has to do with context. In Bugbee's sketches, we often see people progressively moving towards being utterly immersed in a situation. At times a person is shown as withholding, then enduring, fighting and gradually being drawn into what claims the person in their entirety.[16] Again, a kind of making sense dawns through ones wholehearted involvement even though why one is on this particular ship and in the South Pacific may have been determined more by someones hangover in the Personnel Office than anything else. What is generally missing in these stories or the analysis of them is an explicit account of the larger context. It is assumed that we can basically agree with it. However, such a context cannot be assumed for us today. In today's Defense Department, a weapon's design expert may be fully immersed in applying physics to the design of plastic particles for penetrating internal organs while remaining unde-tected by x-rays. The context of the Vietnam war often precluded the possi-bility of such involvement as we see in Bugbee's sketches of war. Similarly, forest fire fighting does demand that a person give himself or herself over to it entirely, but it is sheer nonsense to risk ones life for wages and saving trees so that they can be sawed into lumber. Especially relevant to our context, members of the technostructure, engineers, managers, lawyers, have some of the best work the technological society has to offer. Unlike most of the technological society's work, much of this work does not repel engagement through the design of the surrounding devices. But it repels engagement because it serves the ironic and frivolous life of consumption. Understanding that, one cannot go home again.

We need a homeplace within which we can feel entirely good both in our immersion in present detail and in our comprehension of its larger context. We need a world within which it is really possible for us to dwell. On the other hand, dwelling in a bad sense is what Thoreau was criticiz-ing, in part, by stagnate village life. Dwelling constantly needs to be in-formed by the discoveries of wandering if it is not to go stale. In today's world, dwelling and wandering need to be joined.

In literal wilderness, we guard, wander, and dwell. Wilderness is guarded from the intrusions of mining and is a space protected from in-stantaneous satisfactions and glamorous distractions. We can wander in clean simplicity in wilderness. "When hungry I eat. When tired I sleep."[17] Wandering, ones involvement there is not broken by knowing that, in the larger context, one is complying with an order in direct opposition to ones deepest aspirations and concerns. On the contrary, one can finally let ones guard down because one is not being asked to agree with the technological order or be taken in by what one will later regret. Moreover, hiking in wilderness is not mindless escape. Comprehending how wilderness stands to the larger context can make being there more important. So, like dwellers, we understand that the important things and events lie here in this protected wandering space. Like dwellers, we have some sense that it takes a lifetime and more to bring forth the hidden character of the place. Like dwellers, we have some sense of the obligation to articulate the place into words.

Patience

Correlational coexistence shows how things elicit feelings, thoughts and actions from us. Carrying this a step further, we are in a position to see that things call for virtues. To be equal to things, we need to develop corresponding skills and other excellences. Conversely, if the virtues and skills we do develop do not have things to answer to in our current setting, they will be seen as pointless and become lost. Patience is one of these virtues that may become lost. Impatience, intemperance, willfulness, laziness and lack of skill (at least from the standpoint of ease and convenience) are not always considered vices to be overcome in a technological society. Rather than reforming themselves, people try to remold our surroundings to accord with them. Very little in today's setting calls for patience.

Some proponents of technology call for patience. Maybe centering technologies will appear. One would like to be able to affirm the technological age, but, while we patiently await the meaning of technology, we overlook its eternal repetition of the same pattern, and, worse, we fail to defend the important things that it harms. We fail to protect wild things. So a measure of impatience with technology is called for.

Literal wilderness exacts of us time and patience. At times we are not in touch with the animating nature found in wilderness. An incident relevant to this point occurred a few years ago on my third day out on a backpacking trip. For the first two days the wilderness silence had been shattered at regular intervals by B-52s and smaller jets evidently on an alert because of President Reagan's inadvertently broadcast joke about bombing the Soviet Union. After ascending and descending two high divides on the days previously, I was ascending what I knew was another high pass. I had climbed a steep incline for seven miles, and now nearing the end, so I thought, I began the steeper switchbacks in the trail. Just as I finished the first set another mountainside and another set of switchbacks appeared. This happened again and again. What comes to mind is a small meadow before yet another ascent. I was weary, sore, shaken by the jets and at the end of my patience. My heavy pack had been annoying me for some time by squeaking at its joints and rubbing on my sores. I threw it to the ground and sat down enraged. At length, I cooled off, greased the pack frame with some butter I had, stood up and slung it on again. I was all right. I went on.

Though I did not, as I recall, note anything special about this incident at the time, it seems to me now a moment of truth and decision. These kinds of events, obstacles to negotiate, can make or break it for people who have hoisted a pack on their back. From such experiences, I learn to trust in the resurgence of animating nature. We are overtaken repeatedly and unexpectedly with genuine rewards for our patience.

Wilderness' Call For Openness

Traditionally, whether we are open or not is thought to depend fundamentally on our attitude, needing a change of heart, to become empty, to suspend judgment about our beliefs and so on. Thus, the responsibility to be equal to things and circumstances was located with the self. But technology can harm things, and devices do detach us from these original things. Openness to rich and profound experiences, in a correlational environment thoroughly dominated by technology, is uncalled for and precluded. More fundamental than our openness, openness requires the conditions, the things, which evoke it. Wilderness is one of these things. Unlike devices, literal wilderness is a place we can be open to and that will not repel openness. Wilderness, even in moments of contemplation, does not divide mind and body, unlike reading a book while peddling an exercycle. Rather it unifies our mind and body. So wilderness offers us something to be open to. *What is there?* Moreover, it instructs in the way of openness by exacting openness.

Preparing To Be Open

Unlike fast food, wilderness requires that one turn toward it in preparation. Obviously, one has to decide to go for a backpack trip and that itself usually calls for a wish-list of imagined places and decisions about how much time one has and where to go. A long trip calls for much preparation; a short trip may call for an hour's preparation, given that one has an established practice of backpacking out of which one moves to retrieve equipment and knows what to bring for food.

Wilderness does not animate mind alone. Backpacking teaches one to be mindful about the body in advance. Mountains give me the measure of my physical condition. I am disgusted with myself when I am soft, weak, and breathing heavily. I resolve to stay fit over the next winter. Hence, mountains call for getting into and staying in shape: not just running but climbing muscles, and not just muscle tone but toughened feet. Backpacking makes me think of my body over a lifetime, worrying about my back and caring for my bones and knees. Alpine meadows make cigarettes and emphysema abhorrent to me.

Wilderness teaches me, while packing, to imagine the future body in various actually possible worlds. Sweating climbs, windy passes, storms, blizzards, gales, heat, evening, morning, noon, night, sleeping body, cold body, body in the dark, hungry, tired, sore, pleased, viewing, bear endangered, fall endangered, cuts and broken bones, blistered, sweaty, clean. The practice of backpacking teaches me to mind equipment ahead of time. The

boots I buy require a long break-in period if they are not to prove impossible on the trail. Mindful of this, I would rather not wear them on salt
beaches. Backpacking teaches that time has a definite character and is
consequential. What comes to pass in preparation time must be grasped
then or not at all. To forget the matches is to not have them. One cannot
run to the store or throw uncooked food in the microwave.

Beckoned To Open

But preparation is never just "body building" as on a Nautilus machine; it is preparation *for some thing*. The mindful body finds itself antici-
pating hiking with the subtle changes in light and warmth in late February. Images of past and future hikes begin drifting in and out of my mind.
As the year turns toward me, I open myself to it and become excited with
the lengthening of days.

All these February changes, however, probably would not stir the
mindful body in this way had I not already been open to mountains as a
beckoning direction in the landscape of my life. Who knows what will
speak to us and take hold? Mountains teach us that we do not know who
we are; rather, we find out who we are by living out our lives with things.
That is, openness requires us to respond affirmatively to what wonders and
animates us in order to grasp what there is and who we are. A refusing self
is indeed alone, homeless, in the universe, with some idea of its failure and
how things should have been. Mountains teach us of true wonder and
lasting mystery, of pause and humility. They make us skeptical of decisions
too rationally decided in advance—all too standardized living.

Openness Through Avoiding Misery

Misery and destitution can beget openness, yet courting this beneficial
side of the experience seems wrongheaded. No one goes to the wilderness
to have a miserable time of it if it can be avoided. A backpack trip can be
miserable for those completely out of shape. No one wants to spend the
entire time focusing on ones shaking muscles. Blisters, a heavy pack, and a
drenching cold rain all are to be avoided. Feet, legs, and body, when avoiding genuine misery, are allowed to encounter animating nature: bedrock
feels solid underfoot, a steep trail yields a splendid view, evening settles
quietly on a lake near ones campsite.

Experienced hikers are better than beginners at avoiding misery. They
have a frame of mind that takes into account the potential for misery in
the landscape, and they avoid it or risk it only for good reason. From habit
one is attuned to the environment—seeing the sunny alpine country with

the possibility of a storm in mind. Experienced hikers can enjoy a tremendous storm in a dry place, or, knowing they will be dry with extra clothes, they can risk getting drenched. Through such avoidance one is also open to equipment—a dry parka, a tent that withstands bad weather, a warm down bag, a foam sleeping pad. These are good technologies which respond to harsh, threatening, or, at least, literally hard conditions. Learning to be open to wilderness teaches us to be selective about technology, to appropriate devices. Avoiding misery does not mean avoiding frivolously every claim of inconvenience and discomfort. Such avoidance insulates one from things. Moreover, having to shoulder a pack puts 'what is really needed' in fresh light.

There are always times in wilderness in which one cannot avoid harsh claims that one would prefer to have avoided. One can get sick, hurt, lost, or drenched. Sometimes one has had to push too hard and is too tired to eat. To suffer these times and be ready for more shows moderation, authentic engagement, but to be repeatedly caught in such circumstances is inept.

Utter Containment

Sometimes in order to become open to a place we need to appreciate our utter containment in the place here and now. One must become undeceived of elsewhere and another time to come. Wilderness is like a ship in the sense that it is a place where our usual purposes and attitudes are bracketed for a time. As with boarding a ship, we don other gear, join new concerns, and leave old ones.behind us as we lift the pack to our backs. A mile or so in the wilderness and the experience of separation from cars, highways, and towns is similar to a ship undocking.

For a time, when one is adjusting to the coordinates of the mountains, what presents itself mostly is perhaps absence: absence of convenience, of news, signs directing one what to do, a hot bath, a telephone. What is present, too, is what one has not let go. On a daily walk, I may be nudged by the flying of geese, but many times my life is too noisy and too cluttered with schedules to follow their pull and come completely clean. That falls away more in wilderness, for what is presently absent fades and leaves an opening to be filled by the actual presence of wild things.

Unlike earlier times when simplicity and confinement were necessary, backpackers undertake *voluntary* containment in the wilderness. Being in wilderness is more than being confined to a homestead cabin in winter in the last century and accepting the reality of it. I know that nothing will have a more opportune moment to show itself than here. "Where if not here?" That causes me to reflect on what my life has been about. I have a strong desire to be fully in the place, and, so, I do not want a radio and seeing a Sony Walkman on a hiker indicates that the person probably fails to understand all that can be animating about nature. From this strong desire to be in place I walk, from time to time, into the presence of things again. I walk again into an understanding of what it means to treat things as ends in themselves, to acknowledge them, and not merely to treat them as means, as mere instruments.

Expectation can be a barrier to this openness. However, time and place work to break this barrier. We generally do not bring our usual projects to wilderness. Generally, meadows are not seen in terms of so many animal unit months, forest in terms of boardfeet, lakes in terms of so many acre-feet of water, or peaks in terms of so much extractable mineral. Generally, one is not concerned about legally protecting an area, and so one is not looking for reasons which count politically. Rather, the mood of the place is expansive. From clouds to critters to clover, wilderness pulses with shifting meanings. Like a room filled with people called to attention, human conversation and thought pauses before goats and cranes. One learns to become coordinated with wilderness by following its skittering stars of meaning. Perhaps not at first but after days of immersion in this sort of thing, one is here.

Pressing and Impressive Claims of Animating Nature

Unlike travelling in a car, hiking is a comparatively uninsulated way of being in the world. Avoiding misery, hikers, as pointed out, are often encountering forces that call for attention and dealing with in some way. Camping in the Salmon River canyon in Idaho, I was awakened just before daybreak by a sudden, roaring wind that flicked off the fly of my tent and hurled it straight for a rapid of that enormous river. As I bolted out to retrieve it, the entire tent, now without the weight of my body, came loose, lifted, and tumbled end to end. Moments later, I found myself stretched out on the sandy shore, one hand on the flapping fly, and my legs flopped across the tent. Animating nature laughs and plays.

Climbing mountains can be instructive concerning these pressing and impressive claims. One must find the opening in the season, day and weather. I do not usually decide to climb a mountain in any season or time of day. It is always "this summer." Occasionally I climb a mountain just because I got started up it, but even on an extended backpack trip, when I am given more to whims, a mountain-to-be-climbed usually arranges the day. It is best to remember the body in the world and climb in the cool of the morning and best to get to the top before afternoon thundershowers make it dangerous.

A large mountain usually calls for planning, at least the sighting of a good way up, and always calls for effort. Sweating is important. Unlike walking on the level, sweating from a climb brings about a welcome change in the body. Sweating is the difference, the impression, the pressing claims of the landscape make on my body. By sweating I cleanse myself of impurities and become receptive to my surroundings.

Once I have begun a climb, I am within the pull of the mountain and turning back is not an easy, arbitrary decision. It is not like tossing a stick to see which way to go: There is a definite *up* and *down*. The climb is a task and I know its general outline. Getting a second wind, breaking into a sweat, and becoming determined are all moments of a climb that remind me of a way of being I may have forgotten outside of the wilderness. Climbing teaches resoluteness and that resoluteness is possible only in responding on the strength of the claims things make upon one.

Though mountaintops are usually farther than the imagination places them, it is always slightly amazing to me how quickly I get above the treetops, the immediate landscape, and the valley floor. More and more landscape loops out before the climber like a sheet unfurling in a high wind. Unless forced, I do not like to peer around to the other side until I reach the top. Especially in glaciated high plateau country, the grassy, flowered slope I climb may tease me to the edge of an overhang, jutting out over a thousand feet of definitive nothing. Always it leads one into the sense of the sudden whole.

Yet this impressive, sudden whole can mean nothing. This can be the traditional problem of openness. Here the landscape seems near at hand and yet remains far removed. Then, too, I can be open to the unexpected and still remain detached at a mountaintop. The air is thin; it is generally windy and cold. Trees, shrubs, grass and even earth were left below, leaving only bare, weatherbeaten rock surrounding the climber. There may be a distancing, blue haze hanging in the air and the noon light is usually harsh and certainly devoid of long shadows. Snowfields glare back sterile and old, covered with rocks and windblown dirt. Far below, the landscape falls out like a fancy map. I may wonder what a bend in the river looks like down there and if the fish are feeding there in some imagined shimmering riffle, and if it has warmed enough so that the hoppers are moving in the grass of the streambanks. It is difficult not to rupture the strands of continuity between the peak and the trails below. On such a day I can take a look around but this is not the whole I welcome most.

The fragrance and soft, warm, humid air of riverbottoms must stay, stay alive in the vision from the mountaintops. When this happens, my climb is like the kneading and rising of bread. It helps if one's mindful body has mixed with the trails, meadows, cool shades, and springs until one can no longer see it like a newcomer. The mood of this kind of climbing is something I feel entrusted with and must keep in tune with. It is not something I overtake, but rather something I respond on the strength of—just as it comes to me. Mountains are difficult subjects, more difficult than mountaineers often imagine.

Descent is much different from ascent. Sometimes it is not quite clear whether I made it outside myself on the ascent. I stood at the top eyeing the landscape without knowing or possibly caring whether it had the look of being looked at or something more. The sense of harmony that overtakes me on the descent can let me know I was there while wondering about that shimmering bend in the stream below. Running down through loose talus requires physical coordination and a trust in the unknown. It requires a life instantaneous with the event of each footfall—taking up, letting go, flowing. It brings me out of myself. The sliderocks become like words that speak to the quick.

Pressing and impressive forces will not let one alone. They assist in opening one up, unlike the commodious arrangements of the technological society. They can teach us to rely on subtle powers, that the terrible is not so terrible after all, and that the world can be a good place once more. However, people who *merely* climb mountains or scale peaks are eyed with suspicion, a suspicion concerning the depth of their encounter with wilderness. The way that wilderness presents itself to them seems to be one of an adversary that they somehow have to struggle with and conquer. Bagging peaks can be a moment of self-glorification—a crude achievement over crude forces.[18]

The Gentle Claims of Animating Nature

Along with pressing and impressive claims of wild things, one may be open to the easily overlooked gentle claims of nature. One does not avoid pleasures, but rather, here, in wilderness, pleasures are let be in a respectful relation to them. Looked-forward-to pleasures are generally simple and specific. Lifting the great pack to my back at the trailhead. The feel of the trail underfoot in well-fitted boots. Setting up camp, bare feet in meadow grass at the end of a tough day's hike. Facedown, drinking cold spring water and sensing the enveloping spring-cooled air. A cleansing swim in a cold, clear lake. Warm food. The fragrance hanging in the air at sunrise. A thrush's trill in the twilight-stilled woods. The reliably fine hour beginning halfway through the first cup of morning coffee.

One learns to attend to the simple gratefully. In part, this means making efforts to become open to things. Meditating on streams and waterfalls can be as good an invocation of place as any. Some practice fasting. Sometimes I go to sleep with my glasses on, watching the stars as long as possible. When necessary to use, tents are oriented toward openings, such as downcanyon, or things, such as peaks or lakes, or events, such as sunrise. Fletcher testifies that the best dress for walking is nakedness.

> Now, nakedness is a delightful condition, and by walking you gain far more than coolness. You feel an unexpected freedom from restraint. An uplifting and almost delirious sense of simplicity. In this new simplicity you soon find you have become, in a new and surer sense, an integral part of the simple, complex world you are walking through. And then you are really walking.[19]

In part, one is taught to attend to the simple by the things themselves. Grouse, goats, porcupines; the sensuous curves shaping a valley floor; the calm stillness that descends with evening; these steal my attention away from other matters. I learn here of another companionship. No attitude change or other preparation can substitute for being immersed in this for four or more days.

Wilderness is trustworthy but, like a friend or spouse, it does not guarantee. It can be powerfully instructive, as the accounts above suggest, but ultimately it does not force openness. Wilderness in its depth demands that we learn to rely on its subtle powers. Ultimately, we must let ourselves be gentled by its more gentle claims.

Overtakenness and Wilderness

In wilderness one seems to be involved largely in getting more than one bargained for—so much so that bargaining is a poor and misleading analogy. The rewards of wilderness are not realized by pulling the knobs of a vending machine. Unless we are overtaken from behind, as it were, we do not experience wilderness as wilderness. What overtakes is not under our control. That which overtakes must be approached with patience, carefulness, humility and reverence. The Beartooth Mountains, geologically considered, are a young range which was uplifted as a mass to heights of over twelve thousand feet, then glaciated, leaving a high and broad plateau region scattered with lakes in the pockets of rolling, green alpine hills which sometimes break off with thousand foot dropoffs. When winding our way down through the switchbacks to the Boulder River canyon bottom some three thousand feet below with its gray ribbon of road finally coming into view, my companion and I realized once, after a week up on Lake Plateau, what a distance we had come since leaving the car. Both literally and figuratively it gave us the impression of descending from the Holy Land.

This encounter generates in a hiker a standard—a longing and expectation—which cannot be met within a life fenced in by production and consumption. It teaches one what it means to dwell. The danger of technological culture is that we become so ignorant of anything but modes of consuming that we are ignorant of what we are missing. Of what there is. A highway crosses the Beartooths.

At Home in this Condition

Wilderness can be somewhat foreign at first. There are moments at the beginning when one wonders if one wants to be here, especially if the first day is difficult. This foreignness is best understood by its exemplification in grizzly country. It is romantic to think grizzlies will not bother humans unless provoked; at the same time, statistically considered, such is very nearly the truth. Grizzlies, unless put on the defense or seeking food such as bacon, almost always avoid trouble with us. Still there is always an element of unpredictability in ones encounter with grizzlies, either in the chance that one may unintentionally provoke a bear or catch a bear in a bad mood. I do not want to be attacked by a grizzly and knowing how to protect my internal organs and neck by curling up in a ball and putting my hands behind my neck does not make me feel as if I have an ace in the hole.

Understandably, then, knowing I am going hiking in grizzly country makes me somewhat edgy. In winters I look at the summers I have spent in Yellowstone and wonder how I could have done it. And yet, from experience, this, too, I know: The first day and night my anxiety will be close to the surface. Morning will come as if I have passed a test. Eventually, I become more and more settled without losing appropriate caution, for example, of the trail winding through willows in a creekbottom. I know that this, too, is country where I can come to be at home. Sooner or later, I overcome the foreignness of the place and find myself agreeing with Thoreau. "This is a delicious evening, when the whole body is one sense, and imbibes delight through every pore. I go and come with a strange liberty in Nature . . ."[20] I am never really satisfied until then.

Why is literal wilderness an especially good place for finding ourselves at home? The material condition of wilderness is not that of a device where a deep and familiar intimacy is impossible. Neither is literal wilderness an average, everyday place of traditional things where a kind of familiarity resides in taking things in common ways, in taking them for granted. This is the kind of familiarity with the commonplace which a homecoming in Henry Bugbee's sense may take one beyond, where this commonplace suddenly becomes realized as a holy place. Unlike with devices, here the reach of things often goes unnoticed. But literal wilderness is no commonplace. As shown above, we are thrown out of coordination with our environment in placing ourselves in wilderness. This lack of common familiarity, this strangeness of these conditions may present itself as an alien foreignness. Here one is anything but at home. However, this very foreignness, this lack of common familiarity with things of depth in this place is the special condition which encourages the possibility of coming to be at home with them in an uncommon way. Here things are brought near in their farness that establishes them both as uncommon and dear.

Yet, this homecoming experience may be ephemeral. It is not the way we experience literal wilderness all or even most of the time. In our walks along city sidewalks and driving on freeways it may seem very distant and forgotten, seeming to have taken place in a time before we were born. The technological order pulls us another way. Furthermore, as long as this experience exists merely side by side the technological order and is not somehow integrated with it, the experience does not inform our life, although it may assume a special place in our thoughts. We must do more. Our entire age is adrift in a state of homelessness and this homecoming in a broader sense is needed for the technological society. We take another step in this direction by learning to communicate our concerns with things.

CHAPTER 11

TO SPEAK AGAIN

I've been thinking and dreaming of a new language
One that everyone can understand
Thinking and dreaming of a new language
To cross the sea and light the land

—from *A New Language,* song by Emily Cantrell of *The Cantrells*

The man who states a mathematical formula, even if he does not judge it necessary to go over the proof that has established the formula, is always in a position to do so if he wants to. I have expressed that elsewhere, in a metaphor which perhaps sounds rather frigid in English, by saying that round the cogs and springs of mathematics the golden watchcase of demonstration, a sort of handsome protective covering, is never lacking. And it is the same with all the laws of nature. It is always at least theoretically possible to repeat the experiments from which such laws have been inductively arrived at. But this cannot be the case for us. Existential philosophy is at all times exposed to a very serious danger; that of continuing to speak in the name of various kinds of deep inner experience, which are certainly the points of departure for everything that it affirms, but which cannot be renewed at will. Thus the affirmations of existential philosophy are perpetually in danger of losing their inner substance, of ringing hollow.

—Gabriel Marcel[1]

Why do we need to learn to speak again? We have seen in chapter 2 how the language of quantity has become the 'poetry' of our age. It is easy for people to describe a day's fishing in terms of numbers of fish caught, size of those fish and how long it took us to catch them. It is easy for us to communicate to another the character of a hike in terms of number of miles, altitude climbed, number of lakes or the numerical height of a peak. The importance of a mountain lake or a sculpture might be spelled out in terms of numbers of people who visit it. To be able to quantify quality is to be able to get quality under control—have it available at the tip of our tongue.

In this vein, the timber industry and economists generally call for a rational basis for political decisions. By this they mean that the various features that count in a decision should be literally counted. Whether or not Cottonwood Canyon should be logged ought to be decided in the quantification terms of costs involved, volume of timber, numbers of jobs provided, income, and effect on a quantifiable hunter opportunity index. Given that quality is gotten under control by quantifying it, our society can make the decision, they argue, on the basis of what is really out there and what everyone will really get from it. By doing so, the public will guard itself against, they maintain, the rhetorical and emotional appeals made by well-intentioned but sentimental people who are incapable of seeing the big picture.

Of course, by now, we can see that the big picture which these latter people do not share turns out to be the framework of technology. Given that our society wants to transform reality into devices procuring commodities, then seeing the forest in terms of its raw material to be reshaped and the commodities which its reshaped shape will provide is a reasonable vision of the Cottonwood Canyon, the Crazies, the Gallatin National Forest, the Earth itself and beyond. But, if we find that assumption questionable, find such quantity talk shallow, and find this vision misleading, what are we to do? How can we reply? What language can and should we speak?

The Language of Philosophy

When we turn to philosophy for answers to these questions, we find that contemporary philosophers, too, are seeking alternative modes of discourse. Argumentation or discursive reasoning, once thought to be the essential tool which would deliver anything and everything for philosophy—even the divine—has had serious questions raised concerning its value, scope, and effectiveness. Reviewing analytic philosophy from 1951–1981, Richard Rorty sees the optimism of taking philosophy from speculation to a science, ushered in by the logical positivist founders of the analytic movement, such as Hans Reichenbach, to have been undermined when the central core of the movement, logical analysis, was turned upon itself.[2] He finds that analytic philosophy now is mostly identified, not by its subject matter, but rather, by argumentative skill. The model has become, not the scholar, as earlier, nor the scientist, as the positivist hoped for, but the lawyer. "The ability to construct a good brief, or conduct a devastating cross-examination, or find relevant precedents, is pretty much the ability which analytic philosophers think of as 'distinctively philosophical.'"[3] Rorty sees cleverness here but not wisdom. He credits this movement with enlarging a linguistic and argumentative repertoire, and thus our imaginations. But beyond this achievement, a professional philosopher provides arguments "for whatever our client has decided to do, making the chosen cause appear the better."[4] Hence, argumentation itself fails to provide the kind of guidance which people at least in other times expected to find at the core of philosophy. Alternatively, he encourages philosophers to rejoin the conversation of humankind.

Robert Nozick is even more forthright in his attack upon argumentation. Ideally, arguments are coercive: they have the power to "knock down," "punch," and "force" another to a belief.[5] He thinks that such arguments are not "nice," that is, that they do not respect the dignity and autonomy of others. They are also ineffectual because they do not "most improve" the other, and, ultimately, the conclusions of such arguments can be dodged in various ways, including ones willingness to be labeled irrational. Nozick attests that he has learned more from writings which did not attempt to push him around. He becomes "open to what another has to teach"[6] when he is not forced into an adversarial stance, that is, into a kind of reading that is devoted to shooting down arguments.

In keeping with this criticism, Nozick sees an alternative which is "morally better (and) . . . more in accord with one's philosophical motivation,"[7] i.e., puzzlement, curiosity, a desire to understand, not a desire to produce uniformity of belief. He thinks he has come upon this better alternative with his proposal to offer not arguments but philosophical explanations: hypotheses which show the unproven and typically unprovable formal conditions for the possibility of what we take to be important. Hence, his work is an attempt to explain "how knowledge is possible, how free will is possible, how there can be ethical truths, and how life can have a meaning."[8] Here he is concerned with giving *possible* explanations, not ones that are demonstrably true.

Yet, Nozick's criticism of demonstrable truth is too harsh and misplaced. Truly demonstrable truth can and should be compelling for another. If environmentalists prove that the biological arguments supporting the Cottonwood Ibex timber sale are flawed, the courts can and should force the Forest Service to withdraw the sale. It should not matter how bull-headed or close-minded the supervisor of the Gallatin Forest happens to be. The mistake is to think that whatever is logically or empirically true is also and therefore significant. Most of these truths are simply not worth our attention. I can prove that my pen is on top of my desk, that it lies so many inches from the left edge, that it is black and silver, that it weighs so much, and on and on indefinitely. Without conceding to Nozick that cogency is impersuasive, one can agree with him that a philosophical concern guided—and this is the key—*solely* by the search for cogent truth is bound to be distracting and devoid of informing significance because there is too much of such truth. Cogent truth *alone* is trivially true. Because Nozick directs his criticism against both cogency and truth, he is left with demonstrable possibility as his only alternative.

Against Nozick's alternative, our concern with the Crazy Mountains is not with possibility but with actuality. Wilderness 'as such', an abstract idea, makes sense only as long as we see through it to this particular mountain range. On the other hand, formal preconditions, including necessary ones, remain too abstract and minimal to capture more than the possibility of particulars. As these formal conditions get taken up by philosophy as the really real, a kind of *misplaced reality*, the actual concrete particular things escape and fall into oblivion. So, an account of the conditions for the possibility of things never reaches the things themselves and, in fact, tends to blind us to them. This philosophical approach, what I call metaphysical formalism or apriorism, is either reductive and impoverishing, and, therefore, a mode of technological domination; or, if it respects the complexity of things, it becomes aimless, unenlightening and unhelpful and, thus, lacks significance. We need to find a language which allows particular things their full voice.

Against Rorty's alternative, we need to let *things* have a voice in the conversation of humankind. Thoreau writes:

> Here is this vast, howling, mother of ours, Nature, lying all around, with such beauty, and such affection for her children, as the leopard; and yet we are so early weaned from her breast to society, to that culture which is exclusively an interaction of man on man—a sort of breeding in and in, which produces a merely English nobility, a civilization destined to have a speedy limit.[9]

We need to liberate things, too. Things tie us together. They tie friends, families, and communities together. They make the conversation meaningful.

As with the appropriateness of cogency, so, too, with the quantification of quality. What is apt to come to mind first is how appropriate this move to quantify is. Certainly, the objectivity of scientific investigation depends on qualities being spelled out in quantifiably measurable terms. When we are concerned with precise physical laws, there are no suitable qualitative substitutes for 9.8 meters per sec per sec or $E = mc^2$. Likewise, when I have a high fever, I want to know what my fever is quantitatively. I want to know if the numerical weight of a fly line matches the flex of my flyrod. I want to know the exact length of a wall before building a book-case. "Pretty high," "moderate weight," "rather small," would not do as well as 104, #6, or 9'.

But can the worth of a home be measured in its square footage? Isn't something wrong with my day's fishing when I talk about it only in terms of numbers of fish and how many inches long they were? Roderick Haig-Brown's reflection on catching grayling, we saw earlier in chapter 2, discloses some of the deeper reasons that make fishing attractive to people and shows what it means to have a good day. Along these lines, we can develop an alternative way of speaking about things which is neither reducible to quantitative measurement nor presenting knockdown arguments for our insights. Nor is this way of speaking merely expressing our subjective, psychological states. In accord with correlational coexistence, it teaches the importance of things. It shows us insights into the character of these things and our world. Without using quantity, it teaches us what counts.

The Particularist Nonarbitrary Alternative to Cogency

Particular things are important. A particularist's philosophical approach does not seek universals—answers which are true and adequate once and for all and all time regardless of context. This latter approach is either oppressive and impoverishing when it is significant or unhelpful because it is by itself trivially true. For a particularist, the first question is: What is the specific issue we are addressing? How can we meet this issue in our time and place? Thoreau and Bugbee both counsel us,"Take the case that is." We need to find ways of speaking suitable for addressing this issue.

Locating the Issue

The issue of our age is technology and how we will come to terms with technology. We have looked at the issue of technology from several standpoints. First, from the standpoint of environmental ethics and the environment generally, the issue is one of petty homocentrism. We set upon nature and natural beings, rearranging them regardless of any claims they make on us in their own right. Nature, plants and animals are interpreted and taken up with as mere resources to be developed. If nature and natural beings are going to count for more, we need to be liberated from this way of challenging and being challenged by them.

As we saw with the need for timber from Cottonwood Canyon, we would not take up with natural things in this manner if there were not a deeper reason for our doing so. So, secondly, from the standpoint of our theory of technology, we saw how spellbound we are by the attractive vision of technology. The ways we walk and talk generally show agreement with the basic framework of technology. So, technology appeals to us by way of a promise. In its consequences, however, technology is an ironic good, one which seems good in its immediate appeal, but turns out to be otherwise, becomes ashes in our mouth. Coming to terms with this irony is pivotal for the reform of technology and hence, since it is the fundamental reason for our petty homocentrism, pivotal for establishing a respectful relationship with the natural world.

Thirdly, from the standpoint of one concrete thing, we see in the Crazy Mountains the conflict between things and the technological culture which continually threatens to transform them. We are faced with a choice. Will we remain spellbound by the vision of technology and its life centered around consumption? Or will we see through it and give up our fixation on consumption, thereby allowing many things, such as the Crazy Mountains, to be in their own right? How can we articulate a way to deciding this central issue for our particular time and place? How can we thoughtfully weigh what matters?

Avoiding Foundationalism

Since the thing-to-device pattern is so prevalent in our culture, one instance of the pattern illustrates the general pattern and its consequences and can show their ironic outcome: Devices rupture our bonds of engagement, do not replace these bonds, and, therefore, especially if universalized, cause disengagement. As pointed out earlier, philosophers tend to be attracted to these, if not universal, at least general apriori explanations which cover so many instances. We can carefully analyze commodities and consumption, show the ensuing disengagement that results from them and be done with the philosophical task, once and for all, it seems. So one part of this choice can be weighed using a mode of discourse familiar to philosophy.[10]

How about the other part of the choice, weighing things? Can one use a general method to disclose their importance? Do they exhibit a similar pattern such that once you have seen one thing you have seen them all? To be sure, things do exhibit patterns. We saw that they are material, that they engage us on many levels, and that they illuminate and focus the natural and cultural world. Learning this may be genuinely enlightening. They exhibit other patterns as well, but in an important sense no thing's life was ever defined by any pattern. Authentic things are the *original sources* with regard to how they finally bear a world and how they engage us. That is to say, the ways things mean is discovered in how we have to do with them. Without freshly derived insight (Thoreau calls this "deriving our words"), things may be approached but not touched. We do not come into contact with them, and they do not fire our minds. It took the living response of Thoreau to Walden Pond to disclose its powers that animate him. We need to find a language which exposes the animating nature of wild places and things. Applying the device pattern or any pattern in general will not work in bringing out what is finally significant about a thing.

So, too, a philosophy which highlights formal considerations of things is likely to concentrate on what we can get down in advance about them to the exclusion of other more concrete and contextual considerations. Taking things in this misplaced way, a mode popular in philosophy since Plato, is, in fact, a way of dominating them. Such domination may get things *correct,* a hearth is an instance of a heating system, but it fails to regard the thing and to let oneself be captured by it. Because attention is drawn, diverted to the abstract form, the thing drops out unnoticed. In lifting a minimal characterization from a real thing, a mere aspect of the thing, and offering that characterization as the really real (what the real function of hearth is: to provide warmth) such domination is fully congruent both with the means/ends split of the device and with the rule of technology in general. This misplaced real opens the way to technological subversion. Technology in the modern sense may have even originated with this approach to things.[11] In any case, just as the Forest Service's categories fail to measure the worth of the Crazy Mountains and the impact the planned changes will have on them, so too, our modes of discourse and thought in conventional philosophy fail to be a match for things in their importance. The challenge is to find some way of communicating what is important and engaging about things without becoming merely persuasive regardless of truth and falsehood. How can we avoid apriorism and arbitrariness yet approach things intelligently and intelligibly so as to give an account of them which enlightens, which speaks of what counts in the way that it counts, and which persuades charitable but discerning minds?

Avoiding Arbitrariness

How can cogency be given up without giving up, as Nozick does, the true as well? Without public truth, without an intelligible and noncoercive way of resolving controversial matters, arbitrariness reigns ultimately. Let us first rule out two possibilities in order to focus the task. In a narrow sense, the mystic has private, incommunicable experiences which are credited with being of ultimate importance. The charge can always be leveled against mysticism that these experiences are either mistaken in meaning or do not exist. One does not have to exclude the mystic's testimony simply because it has nothing to show for itself, but mysticism can be avoided when we speak in a correlational way of things which are publicly visible.

So things are tangible and publicly accessible, but the criteria of tangibility and public accessibility are insufficient by themselves to establish nonarbitrariness.[12] After all, empirical truth is also accessible. But if we look to the laws and theories of science to disclose significant truth, we find that all these accessible and tangible facts stand equal to each other. Scientific laws and theories, insofar as they apply to everything, explain nothing in particular. Why should we select one publicly accessible and tangible fact rather than another? Why should the Teals have selected the salt marsh they did rather than another or some other natural place? To this question, the laws by themselves must remain silent. Thus, public accessibility and tangibility, by themselves, offer no guidance.

Likewise, the fanatic, unlike the mystic whose truth is interior and private, has a mission that seems outward and visibly exposed. But like the mystic, the fanatic's project cannot be justified to others—he or she "just knows" what is right. Although incommunicable, knowledge here is claimed with such smugness, possession and control that the fanatic seems to grasp in advance the order of his or her life and know exactly what must be done on behalf of his or her mission. Thus, the fanatic is not moved by the ever gentle power of things, does not respond to the bidding powers of things, is not moved so to move, but rather, takes up a position of *willed resoluteness* toward implementing the decision the fanatic feels he or she must decide.[13] The result that the fanatic seeks to produce is, at bottom, arbitrarily chosen. So here again the event or object may be publicly accessible, but arbitrariness rules. In the midst of this arbitrariness, the fanatic hopes that through sheer will and force the fanatic plan may prevail.

What other possibility is there? What alternative is there to formalism and arbitrariness? What other criterion must be added to tangibility and public accessibility? We can be fans without being fanatics, for things *stand out* for all to see. They are not just an X alongside other indistinguishable X's. They are significant, and, hence, we can point them out. What gets passed over and forgotten with approaches too committed to formal metaphysics are the resolving powers of particulars, of things. The way to avoid the shortcomings of fanaticism, mysticism, and the merely trivially true is through an appeal to things.[14] I attest to the importance of the Crazy Mountains, but I cannot provide a knockdown argument demonstrating their importance.

Unlike thin formalism, things are thick with uncontrollable and unforeknowable meaning. Unlike the mystic's private truth, things are public and can be felt, heard, seen, pointed to. Unlike the fanatic's objectives, things are neither graspable, controllable, mute, nor neutral; they stand out for themselves. They speak for themselves. Others do not have to be forced to see things "my way." Things in their own right have the power to appeal profoundly to ourselves and to others. Unlike willed resoluteness, our response to them is resolutely *for* them. Our decisiveness and our decisions are nonarbitrary because, in contrast to the arbitrariness of having no reason to decide one way or another, we have good reasons, intelligible and justifiable ones, for responding the way we do. Their resolving powers enable us to be authentically resolute.

The Language of Correlational Coexistence

The language of correlational coexistence discloses things in their importance. We have seen how things take into account a rich fourfold context of Earth and sky, mortals and divinities, the depth of the thing correlating to the complexity of the world. Things are rich in their capacity to reciprocate each and every tie to the world. I have called this the considerability of things. Now we need to investigate the characteristics of the language of correlational coexistence that best correspond to this deep considerability of things.

From the standpoint of correlational coexistence, we can account for feelings in two ways—by giving an account of the feeling or by giving an account of what evokes the feeling. Similarly, we can speak of interests, desires and motives or we can speak of what is attractive, appeals to us or moves us. I could have written earlier in terms of motives, interests, and feelings, but such language eclipses what is at issue for us with technology. We cannot *be (or feel) with* devices the same way we can *be (or feel) with* things. The technologically reshaped shape of our surroundings matters most. Since our being depends on our *being with things* I have tried whenever possible to speak in phrases such as "devices calling forth consumption and little else," "the attractive promise of technology," "the appeal of things," "the pull of things," "things call for engagement, make demands on us, claim us," and so on.

Following from this general way of articulating our coexistent relation with our surroundings, I chose the concept, "animating nature," to collect together the ways we are made to feel, think and do by wild things. Animating nature stands for all the ways wild nature engages us. Animating nature, then, is the nature humans—or at least practitioners of hiking in the wilderness—are both beckoned by and come to consummate in their living encounter with wild things. This animating nature is communicated to us best through art. Through these works of art we are brought in touch with the affect things have on people. But all of us, to an extent, use this language of correlational coexistence. What are its characteristics?

The language of correlational coexistence is the language of engagement. Things have powers that engage us. These powers move us, orient us, and are worth being free for, thereby distinguishing things from commodities which are merely glamorous and short-lived. These engaging powers decide us for one thing and not for some other thing or commodity.

The role of embodiment is important here, too. Although some forms of engagement may be mostly cerebral, the metaphor of being "moved" would be bankrupt were it not that we are moved as embodied beings. Consciousness is always consciousness of some thing; but our lives demand that we be with things more than mentally. The fullness of the thing requires the fullness of our bodies for it to be realized.[15] All along we have seen this, especially in chapter 6, "Granting the Thing its Eloquence." The Crazy Mountains move and orient me, involving me in ways ranging from friends and family to fingers and toes. The language of correlational coexistence conjures up these embodiments.

The language of correlational coexistence is the language of testimony. What orients us in this way does not appeal to us anonymously; rather such powers single us out. What engages us engages us personally. Only by being in this personal or existential relation with them do we come to realize the powers that make things significant. We must *be* with things in order to register them in ways that are moving, that move us for them. We can gain an impersonal, objective distance from them only at the expense of losing what is particularly attractive about them. Though this impersonal distance may be a safer position because it allows us not have to disclose anything intimate about ourselves, and though at times this may be the wiser position, still, things realized in their fullness, as seen in chapter 6, are not objects that we "know about" or that can be studied by "looking at" or "reporting on" them.[16] Because of the inescapable requirement of our personal relationship with things, being engaged with what engages, we do not merely *observe*, but we *witness* the felt presence of those claims. In the legal sense, we are in a special position as witnesses to and participants in these events, and, when we speak, we testify to what we have experienced personally. The language of correlational coexistence is, therefore, testimony. It affirms and attests to the presence of those engaging powers of things.

The language of correlational coexistence is the language of acknowledgement. Things single us out and claim us personally. Knowing how often and easily we can be out of touch with things, we understand that things are not under our control. As Marcel points out, however confident we may be in its trustworthiness to show itself sometime, the claim of things is not something we can lay claim to know. Such a claim-to-know rings hollow the very moment it is made.[17] We cannot present it to the teller-machine and cash it in at will, we do not get its number, we cannot take its temperature, rather, we find ourselves having to wait upon its warrant. Its truth is not a truth we can wield or push another person into, for we do not have that kind of control over it. We can only invoke it. At times it seems the most I can do is wave, as it were, to the mountains in the distance. So when we speak of the claim of things most authentically, we speak on the strength of its felt presence. We acknowledged it. To register things in this way, we must be with things and they must cohabit with us. Acknowledging what engages, a language of engagement is the language of acknowledgment.

The language of correlational coexistence is the language of disclosure. The language of acknowledgment points to the presence of what it acknowledges, to the presence of things.[18] So this is a language disclosive of the engaging presence of things, disclosing things as presences not as mere objects. It discloses things in their importance. It is what I call disclosive discourse. As long as the Crazies are pictured from the highway it is difficult to assess what there is. As their potential significance finds articulate expression, we see into the unforeseen and unsuspected wilderness of things.

The language of correlational coexistence is the language of appeal. In pointing to the thing, the language of correlational coexistence discloses the presence of what is acknowledged in a way that appeals. Because it shows the thing to others, such language in turn appeals to others for acknowledgment. When effective, it brings these other people within proximity of the pull of the thing. As Robert Frost writes, "You come too."[19] Disclosive discourse is, thus, a discourse of appeal.

The language of correlational coexistence is informative. Since the language of correlational coexistence not only appeals to others, but discloses to others the way things can engage us in appealing ways, it is informative. Graceful and profound testimony teaches insights into things which we are glad to have learned. We see more deeply into things, what they have meant to us and what they might come to mean. Because correlational language is informative, it can be put to fair tests by charitable but discerning minds. What is said to engage us may ring hollow, seem forced, or seem shallowly considered. That does not mean that its truth is always easily discerned for it is certainly not susceptible to tests we can contrive. We cannot set up a repeatable experiment for the moments that issue into testimony—one may have to be that person in that place at that time. Even so, there are times we can scrutinize testimony, live into its insights, and put it to fair tests. Another's testimony may agree with our own experience or may be believable on the basis of our more profound experiences. Homer, through similes, often gets his readers to credit and understand Odysseus' experiences this way, in turn, encouraging these readers to become more deeply reflective.[20]

In any case, the thing warrants or does not warrant what is spoken about it in disclosive discourse. That is, we can ask whether things are realizable or not in the way attested to. We can ask whether such testimony is a profound disclosure of them. Accordingly, we can ask about what place this experience of things has with respect to other experiences of the same thing and with regard to the greater context of our lives and times as a whole. Some would make a mountain out of a mole hill. Thus, distinguishable here from sophistry, the persuasiveness of disclosive writing ultimately holds up or fails depending upon whether or not things hold up, are capable of such engagement. The disclosive discourse employed by advertisements often fails when we test it in this way.

Philosophically considered, we have here a language which shows, discloses, appeals but does not attempt to force cogently. It points not only to something tangible and publicly accessible, but to things and features that stand out and move a person as well. Though testing is not always under our control, we can check out whether testimony is insightful and reliable or not. A fair test occurs when one discovers what is written with seeming eloquence does not hold up to our personal experience of things. It is a risk.

Reminding

Wilderness reminds. One often admires aspens, cottonwoods, willows, oaks, maples, and other deciduous trees, and one admires conifers as well, but, aside from this experience of them, pines and firs point. Especially in winter, I habitually, and sometimes deliberately, follow these trees. Trails take you on, tracks take you across the landscape, but pines and firs take you upward. Upward they take you to sky and sun and peaks. Wilderness calls on you to become ecstatic—upward and outward. That is not to say you cannot be dark in wilderness, for there is much to carry you down as well, but, on the whole, the mood of the place works against it, and it works without your knowing it.

When approached from the east, Crazy Peak stands much higher than the surrounding peaks. Because it stands in the middle of the range it gathers the rest to a point. Like the Crazies themselves, this peak cannot be ignored. It gathers the range, gathers the landscape, gathers the sky, and gathers the onlooker to it. The weather is overhead. Goats are in the cliffs. Eagles soar in the updrafts of peaks. To see them, you must look up. Seeing them may just carry you away to yet higher ground, to more alpine places. It could happen.

My friend, Victor, and I set up camp at Twin Lakes a couple of years ago. We climbed to the top of the high divide the next day. Because of the steep climb, we were hot and sweaty when we got to the top. At the very top a chilly wind was blowing hard, driving us to take cover on the leeside of the low cliffs jutting from the ridge. Below the canyon wound about, finally spilling out into the plains which disappeared in a distant light haze. We were contemplating this scene when we were startled from not ten feet overhead.

Whoosh! Whoosh!
Two eagles flying down ridge
Now gone.

How fast events come off! How quickly things return to the way they were, only different from now on.

That evening, just as we got back, it began to rain. We cooked in the rain, walked about the lakes for awhile, each on his own, and then turned in. The next day it was socked in so we came out. When we got to the trailhead, a family from a nearby town was cutting firewood. I could see that they were of a school which saw these mountains for logging, grazing, firewood, and hunting. To them, backpacking seemed frivolous and something only outsiders did. So they took special delight in seeing that the rain had seemed to ruin our trip. "Too wet back there, huh!" "Bet you're cold?" The son, about fourteen years old, who was the last in line, began to follow through with something about its not being such a good time, but we were like awakened ones coming out of those mountains. I can see the surprised look on that boy's silent face when his eyes met mine. In and out of eternity we moved as I passed by. Could it be that moment imparted the wonder I had felt when I was four, listening to the stories of my brother and father? How fast events come off! How quickly things settle back to the way they were, only different from now on!

CHAPTER 12

TO BUILD AGAIN

The nature of building is letting dwell.

—Martin Heidegger[1]

Practically speaking, a life that is vowed to simplicity, appropriate bold-
ness, good humor, gratitude, unstinting work and play, and lots of walking brings us close to the actually existing world and its wholeness.

—Gary Snyder[2]

Although for a variety of reasons, many may care about wilderness
and the natural world, most people do not hike in the wilderness. Comparatively few have had one of their favorite trails replaced by a road. Imagine,
too, what would happen to the Crazy Mountains if a great many of us tried
to admire them at close range rather than from a distance. Most of us,
however, sense the need to dwell again.

Having one foot still in the modern period, we are apt to want blue-
prints for any further building. It seems that with a clear and comprehensive idea of the good life, we can draw up a guide book, and undertake a
full-scale reform of technology; get the plan in place and then implementing it will be relatively simple. Yet consider how much remains in the
dark. How does tomorrow, even, call to be shaped differently? How should
we be different in our work and leisure, with others, with friends, with
family? What would the reform of technology mean for agriculture, towns,
and cities? What would it mean for businesses? For travel? For Third
World countries? For symphonies, theaters, restaurants, and television?
For the homeless and for children? Not much has been said about even the
bulk of the year that I spend outside the wilderness. Something more will
be said about these matters, but we need to realize first that expecting a
program is itself a sign of the unreformed, universal and a priori approach
of technology. Ultimately, much that matters most cannot be laid out in

advance or be articulated in isolation from the context of each of our individual lives, communities and regions. We need to respect the indomitable dignities of time and place.

What, then, remains to be done for a turning of technology? Much, and much that will remain unimaginable and unforeseeable until it is accomplished. The reform of technology will not be masterminded; rather it will be the result of communities of people who are able to speak and convey to each other what things matter in the way they matter. It will be the result of people working together and taking a few deliberate steps at a time, as possibilities open up. The true frontier for us is not literal wilderness any longer, nor is it a frontier we can conquer without irony and contradiction. Accepting and insisting on a particularist approach to a wilder future is the first of many steps toward reforming technology, toward learning to build again.

Wilderness and the Crazy Mountains pose a challenge to the culture of technology. We can now see how important a thing the Crazy Mountains are, and we see how the culture of technology threatens to ruin them by logging and by blasting roads up their canyons. If we do not take the necessary steps to protect them, a valuable thing will be lost. Of course, even without the writing of this book, the Crazy Mountains may be protected, for even now congressional aides speak of the "wilderness value" of the mountains and the "threat of development" to that value. These mountains may well be protected and yet do little to challenge the overall trajectory and vision of our present technological culture. In these circumstances, the Crazies would constrain the petty homocentric heedless power of the technological culture in an inconsequentially small manner, posing no greater challenge on a deeper level. Here, although the Crazy Mountains may be protected, most of our genuine concerns with nature and natural things will continue to be subverted by technology. However, the Crazy Mountains as disclosed in these pages do call for a fundamental change. We need *to be* another way.

The Fundamental Choice of Vision

Environmentally or culturally, many choices may not matter much. Within a certain range of choices, which brand of toothpaste, which writing tablet, which bakery I buy bread from, seem a matter of indifference to cultural and environmental concerns, yet many other choices on this level do have environmental and cultural consequences. I may buy Bernice's Bakery bread in part because that bakery cultivates good work. It is better to buy a product from a flyshop that shows more than a token commitment to a clean environment. Conversely, I will boycott Exxon and companies with similar records. These choices are worthy of our deliberation; still, more fundamental decisions need to be made, for, unless we decide to release ourselves from the vision of technology, most of our better concerns with environmental degradation and degradation of the work place will not be met. Accordingly, we should fund research and development for alternative energy sources, and we should utilize smart designs and inventions such as superconductors to save energy. Nevertheless, all this could be and, in fact, is being accomplished from within the vision of technology. The decisive step, then, is to reconsider the relationship between the "goods" supplied by this energy, wherever it comes from and however much of it is saved, and the standing these goods have in a good life. The demand for timber and energy would decrease if we were to interpret the great numbers of large homes as more a sign of blight than of a good life.

What is this new decisive choice we are faced with? How have we been brought to its threshold? Switching from one mode of consumption to another mode of consumption, no matter how much such changes relieve our lives of boredom and fill it with momentary excitement, is not a sufficient response to the challenge technology poses us. It is as if an almost invisible net has been thrown over us and we keep thinking we can escape this way or that way, only to discover we really are trapped and slowly drowning. Having learned this, having seen the net for what it is, we cannot go home again to home deluxe. To lodge we first must be dislodged. I have not argued that we *cannot* go forward in the same way. I have raised the question: Do we want to? Do we choose to continue the technological project? If we do not want to get where we are headed, our lives and living arrangements will have to take on a much different character. We need to inhabit the human condition differently, the Earth differently, the technological setting differently. We need to be more philosophical in our outlook.

How can we emancipate ourselves from this fundamental technological vision? We saw that the events which fetch the world near show Thoreau the pointless character of consumption as a way of life. Only these events refresh and restore the world, releasing Thoreau from the illusory attractions of the technological vision and confirming his choice for things. What about us? How do Thoreau's insights apply to us? How can we make an educated response to our situation so that we challenge technology? Disclosive writings show us this intimacy of things. Discovering the gladness of being there, Henry Bugbee realizes why it makes sense to be in the grey swamp. In this way these writings remind us what we have and can encounter in things. These writings remind us what we can encounter across the threshold in the wilderness of things, for the reality across that paradoxical boundary can easily remain unsuspected. These works provide instructions for encountering things in depth and realizing the reality of the wilderness of things. We received and can again receive the vigor, the tonic of wildness. We awaken from our sleepwalk. For a time, at least, we see, more clearly than ever before how the world hangs to-gether—what is up, what is down, what is what. Seeing this way quickens our flesh as well as our spirits. And it quickens the creatures and creation about us. We have entered into friendly relations with these things.

From these encounters we learn to counter technology. Thoreau ad-monishes us to cherish these waking moments, for they are the landmarks of a reality we are ever falling away from in our daily pursuits of life.[3] If we cherish them, we will not give them up easily, not without a struggle. This determination makes us cautious about the use of technological devices. Devices narrow our experience of things, detaching us from them, and most of the time, these devices damage things, too. Thus, events bringing the world near, events of morning and wildness, of wilderness as reality, of animating nature, come to be eliminated. Why be freed up from smallpox only to fall into another kind of disease? Following the vision of technol-ogy we succumb to technological irony. If we cherish these landmarks, we see we can do better. Thoughtfully considered, technology provides us with many deep choices for arranging our workplace, for example, but under the influence of the ruling framework, we seem to be determined merely to produce and consume more. By inhabiting the possibility space provided by technology in a wiser way—by not universalizing technology—we can make room for things in our lives so that they now and then can come near. We can let go of consumption as a way of life, and release ourselves from the technological framework that bars us from experiencing things. No longer does this "rational" framework seem so reasonable. Technology's promise of happiness is given the lie and loses its appeal. Yet one is not merely saying no to the technological framework, the universalization of technology. One is allowing seemingly crazy things and events to have a say, to talk us out of consumption and into imagining better ways to in-habit our planet and better ways to inhabit the technological setting.[4]

Countering the technological framework one is not only voicing an objection; beyond that, one invokes, as Odysseus with the suitors, the far side, the wilder side, of the paradox of things which *shocks* the nearside into exposing its weightless irony. As Colin Fletcher writes,

> Naturally not everyone understands . . . A smooth and hypersatisfied young man once boasted to me that he had just completed a round-the-world sightseeing tour in seventy-nine days. In one jet-streamed breath he scuttled from St. Peter's, Rome, via the Pyramids, to a Cambodian

jungle temple. "That's the way to travel," he said. "You see everything important . . . " When I suggested that the way to see important things was to walk, he almost dropped his martini.[5]

For a moment at least, the other person catches sight of what has been ignored, lost sight of, forgotten, and the underlying troubling nature of technology is exposed. The prickly pear of the plains defend beautiful flowers.[6]

Finally, through encountering and countering we find a counterbalance to devices. All along I have maintained that technology, if appropriate, is good. Here I do not mean by this that technology is helping to develop new things. Hang gliders and wind surfers show new features in the landscape and wind currents of this region. Downhill skis disclose the mountains, ridges, and cirques in ways unavailable in the past. Bicycles, like these other things, open up the world rather than close it off as devices do. So do other nondevice instruments, such as my eyeglasses. Jesse Tatum shows that the people in the "home power" movement often have integrated some of the most advanced technologies with the kind of engagement things elicit.[7] Certainly, these are directions of technology I embrace and wish to see explored and developed.

But here I am maintaining, aside from these other good possibilities for technology, that *devices as devices* are good. The danger of technology is neither the presence of devices nor this or that device. It is an unquestionable good to be relieved of genuine burdens, and we can be thankful for a variety of recent devices. We can be consciously grateful *if* we preserve a reality with which to counterbalance them. The danger of devices—and the virtual reality they procure—is that they eclipse the reality of things, eliminating all counterbalancing reality. We need to plant our feet firmly on the Earth if we are not to float off to overblown fantasy worlds. Although it will not make or break the quality of my life, the Internet can be useful *if* it is counterbalanced with important things, *if* it is counterbalanced with contact with real things and real people, with real substance. When the Internet becomes a substitute for these, one's activity is no different from any other mode of consumption. Devices as subordinates, yes; as substitutes, no. Counterbalancing technology, we become watchful of time and reality. What percentage of our time is spent staring at screens? What percentage is spent merely consuming? What could we be doing otherwise? How much of our lives is devoted to what?

The wilder and crazier response to the culture of technology, the work of placing ourselves in the world again, entails encountering, countering, and counterbalancing.[8] The hills of the plains, however numerous, are small compared to the Crazy Mountains. We would do well to bear that in mind. Encountering discloses to us our landmarks, new standards to live by. Countering brings into relief and into question the irony of technological domination. Counterbalancing shows an appropriate, watchful acceptance of devices.

Correlational Coexistence Building

Turning technology requires building a lasting response on our part. Can we bring technology into a peaceful relationship with our lives and with the Earth? Homelessness is the plight of our age, and so our entire age needs to come home. What may heal us, that is, restore our bonds of engagement with the world, exacts unusual measures not found in any other age.

Building plays an active role in our ability to dwell. Ideally, good building ought to encourage and nurture dwelling, but if our building is without insight into dwelling and is not guided by dwelling, the nature of our building and our "buildings" will not let us dwell. All around us we hear calls for building. Build Billings. Build Long Island. A company may claim to be building America. Today these calls are usually issued in economic terms since a developed economy is assumed to mean more commodities and more commodities, a better life. Interpreted philosophically, building here means expanding the framework of technology—the vision that is the guiding blueprint for our building. That was the old challenge. Now the challenge is not to stop building but to build differently, for the building we have undertaken is preventing us from dwelling. It unsettles us. Transcending this kind of building and finding one in harmony with dwelling is the *new challenge* for us.

So both dwelling and good building require each other and are required by each other. How is building guided by dwelling? How is dwelling cultivated by building? The quality of our lives corresponds to things so that the flourishing of our lives is bound together with the flourishing of things. In these terms, our new challenge is to emancipate ourselves from the vision of the petty homocentric, monocentric building of the culture of technology and become free for a new vision of symmetrical and coexistent building. What does correlational coexistence building entail?

Wilderness can guide us to a sense of what it means to dwell. Wilderness is a place where we can come to be at home in the world again. Homecoming for the Greeks is a place where motion and striving come to rest, an ideal the fulfillment of which leaves nothing to be desired.[9] Homecoming in the wilderness often does make us pause and linger. We find ourselves a part of nature in a hidden harmony with our surroundings.

Nothing, especially no amount of distracting consumption, can substitute for wilderness.

There is nothing to bring us home, nothing to come home to, without literal wilderness, or, more generally, without the centering things that devices are replacing. So, for correlational coexistence we need these things, and so too, will the new technological setting, if it allows us to inhabit the Earth harmoniously.

Given the presence of these things, we can ask what ought to be our correlational relationship with them. Our relationship to things could be one of indifference toward them, one where we set upon them, one where we reluctantly give them up in favor of consumption, or one where we respect, care for and nurture them. The current vision of technology prescribes dominating them. Once we reconsider things from a standpoint of correlational coexistence, however, we find that *things prescribe* ways for us to be with them, informing our conscience. We need to make room for them. The Crazy Mountains prescribe protection from logging and roads and even from littering. So building correlational coexistence prescribes at times that we do not build, or at least do not rebuild things into devices because a valuable thing prescribes steps to protect it. Understanding the significance of de facto wilderness for genuine dwelling and seeing that its capacity to bring us home is threatened prescribes for us steps to guard it; by legally designating this place as wilderness, we shelter dwelling.[10]

More generally, other things demand that we protect them against harm by designating them "wilderness." The challenge of protecting the vitality of the Greater Yellowstone Ecosystem exacts far more comprehensive measures than we are now taking. We need to let the Yellowstone Ecosystem have more than a muted say in what "developments" go on around it. If, even here, we do not let nature have more of a say in what we do, where on Earth will we? The Yellowstone River ought not to be ruined by damming it or by polluting its headwaters. It ought to be protected for its entire length by receiving the legal status of a Wild and Scenic River. A family farm ought not to be turned upside down by a coal company. A city park ought to be protected with zoning laws. A potluck supper may lose its flavor if it is turned over to the food service industry. These imperatives to protect as "wilderness areas" these particular valuable things emerge out of considering injury from the standpoint of the thing; we can also consider from the other pole, our experience of the thing. Inappropriate devices insulate us from wilderness.

To build also means to cultivate. Things prescribe that we build our relationships with them and with each other. To keep ones engagement with things meaningful and alive, one must *cultivate wildness*. Cultivating demands special efforts. One should give thought to things, nurture openness, mend breaks, and maintain commitments to them. The tonic of wildness is not technologically available, not producible on demand. We can, however, reach out to it through cultivating focal practices. Yet cultivation—practices and habits—can degrade to dead and deadening ritual. Wildness is not in opposition to domestic life; tameness is. Wildness informs the health of domestic life. Wildness keeps cultivation alive and cultivation of correlational coexistence keeps things bringing the world home to us.[11]

Cultivating means in part listening. Science, storytelling, reading, music and art sensitize one to things. The more I learn about the Crazy Mountains and the sky above them from ecology, biology, geology, and physics, the richer my experience tends to be. Scientific insight provides a difference that makes a difference to my life. I do not set upon geology to find out where the gold is. Instead I wander around with people who are geologists, botanists or wildlife biologists. They teach me in the same way the Teals teach us about salt marshes. If these sciences disclosed unique landforms, species or ecosystem types, this information would provide additional reasons to protect the Crazies. Besides sciences there are other ways to disclose importance of the Crazies as well. I will never forget Burton Pretty On Top's narrative of his vision quest in the Crazies. The Crow stories and practices he has shared with me have improved my practices. Dean Bear Claw has helped me to see the traditional significance of the Crazies for the Crows. I also learn to see differently from Russell Chatham's artwork of the Crazies. The Crazies sing through Janet Haarvig's cello songs.

Literal wilderness, a given thing, alone is *not* sufficient to reform the culture of technology. Cultivating wildness must be much more widespread in a culture built around things. Just as there are a plurality of ways of revealing the splendor of the Crazy Mountains, so too are there other things akin to the Crazies—crazy things. Most of these are artifacts—built things—as indicated by the following lines from Rilke's "Sonnet to Orpheus 24," which also conveys a similar fate for these things and for us:

> We have removed our banquets, our baths, afar,
> and their messengers, long since too slow for us,
> we always overtake. Lonelier now, wholly dependent
> on one another, without knowing one another,
> we no longer lay out the paths as lovely meanders,
> but straight. Only in boilers now do the former
> fires still burn, heaving the hammers that grow
> always bigger. But we, we diminish in strength, like swimmers.[12]

Technology not only dominates nature; it equally dominates culture. So this sonnet shows how these other crazy things are endangered and are being lost as animating centers of our lives. Nor are they being replaced by new things. Only displacement occurs. To choose things, we need to rescue them from danger. Built things, too, need wilderness protection. All these crazy things enable us to pass beyond the glamorous advertisements to the more hidden and profound wilderness in which things make sense. A sane culture would cultivate stories of the animating powers of things, including cultural things. As Gabriel Marcel writes:

> Coming home the other evening from an excellent Bach concert, I thought to myself, "Here is something that restores one to a feeling that one might have thought lost, or perhaps more than a feeling, an assurance: the assurance that it is an honor to be a human being."[13]

The animating powers of crazy things—both wild and cultural—prescribe consistency in human beings. Only consistency will undo the painted veil vision of technology. Consistency enables the seed-like powers of things to take root and develop fully. Acting consistently with things, we build world. We may live *for* wilderness but no one lives *in* wilderness. None of us spend more than a proportionately small amount of time in actual wilderness. This implies, first, that what we do outside of wilderness calls for being consistent with what wilderness has come to mean for us. Legal protection alone meets the problem only part way. The styles of life technological citizens align with everyday illustrate the danger technology poses to wilderness. You can support the protection of grizzlies and own a second home in their habitat, but you can not do this consistently. Not wasting wood but using it tastefully and sparingly would be consistent with wilderness. So, too, to avoid buying gold. It would be consistent to minimize the use of oil and minerals through maintaining the least environmentally damaging transportation. It would be consistent to support public transportation proposals, strict air pollution laws and recycling programs.

However, simply following "don'ts" outside of wilderness will not suffice to heal the means/ends split which is at the root of our homelessness in the first place. If we merely followed the "don'ts," all our time outside of wilderness would seem like "mere-means" time. Consistent with the practice of hiking, and necessary as well, would be to have other practices which one can enter more regularly. Music, study, writing, teaching, walking, biking, running, skiing, cooking, fishing are some of mine. These other practices are good in their own right and good for keeping wilderness in mind outside of literal wilderness. Metaphorically, one needs wilderness areas, that is, sacred places and times, in ones life where one can renew oneself on a daily basis. What does one say yes to before saying any no's regarding inappropriate technology? If consistent, a practitioner of hiking will *want* to relinquish the goal of consumption in order for there to be wilderness and in order to be with wilderness. When this "yes" occurs, modern technology, although accepted and used appropriately (in the service of things and practices, not consumption), is no longer the ruling vision of that individual person's life.

But beyond this individual level, what roles do other people play in the building of a culture of correlational coexistence? The day of the Lone Ranger is over. While meeting the expectations of things may be the fundamental way in which we are claimed, we should not overlook the deep, complex and enabling human relationships that are fostered by things. Things gather people. Building our relationships with things helps build ties to others. Having things in common keeps vitality in friendship and community. Similarly, building our relationships with others strengthens our ties to the things we share. Moreover, just how things speak and what they demand is often first recognized by us in conversation with each other. As Socrates was fond of saying, when two go together, one sees before the other. Then too, other people hold us to a fidelity and consistency with things that enable us to mend and to continue to build when otherwise we would have knuckled under and gone with the flow of our time. Being inconsistent is easy for us as individuals.

Whether or not the Crazies are protected is a collective not an individual choice. So, too, with many other fundamental choices. Rilke, in a letter to an aspiring poet writes:

> This above all—ask yourself in the stillest hour of your night: *must* I write? Delve into yourself for a deep answer. And if this should be affirmative, if you may meet this earnest question with a strong and simple "*I must*," then build your life according to this necessity.[14]

There is much wisdom for building here, yet many of us, not of Rilke's stature, are not free to do our heart's desire. A person may be every inch a poet, a musician or a farmer and be forced, unless fortunate, to resort to some other occupation in order to earn a living. Far too little public support goes toward arts and crafts or symphonies. Farmland needs to be made available for those who would be dedicated to it. Fascinated by goods, we eliminate good opportunities for us to be human beings. We cripple ourselves and each other.

To speak of the largest issue, individual and even collective efforts to challenge and reform technology will fail unless sufficient numbers of us who join together grasp that building correlational coexistence requires a cultural transformation. Living a life of voluntary simplicity is essential and will certainly help foster this change, for it must first be and must remain a revolution of hearts and minds, yet nothing short of an effort on the part of the national community will bring such a development to pass. How can we initiate a national conversation about these coexistent things and our culture? How can a counterculture be actually consequential and not be subverted, co-opted and marginalized? How can we build a culture of correlational coexistence?

To be consistent, one must see technology on a social level, for, no matter how little I may consume, if our society surges forward with consumption, wilderness is doomed. Until the goal of consumption is given up by society, the vision of technology rules. What are the various cooperative ways to counter technology effectively? How can we learn to cultivate an entire culture and refrain from building where building is not called for? Legally protecting a wild place, such as the Crazy Mountains, does not mean one is then at home in the world. If wilderness and things akin to it fail to challenge and turn the larger technological society, we could protect all the wild land now remaining and still not make much more of a difference than do the reservations to Brave New World. Pivotal here is that the technological society give over its goal of consumption on behalf of things, including wilderness. Then things, not technology, order the world. To build a culture of correlational coexistence, things, both *given* and *built* things, must take the central place. The powers of things enable us as a culture to say no to consumption without this "no" being felt as a sacrifice. When this occurs, technology no longer is the ruling vision of our age, the plight of our homelessness is seen for what it is, and we begin the journey home.

Last time I hiked into the little lake up Cottonwood Creek my hiking companion and I had been musing about the relationship between cirque, circle, circus, circus rings, Ringling Brothers, the nearby town of Ringling, the Big Top, and the Big Sky. At the lake we laid our packs down, and since Ed had not seen one before, we looked carefully for mountain goats. However, I knew the population had been troubled in recent years by disease. Not seeing any goats and not really expecting to, we decided to have a look at the lake and walked through the trees to the other end. It was then I noticed in the far distance, a goat running down through the cliffs. I was sure that we had spooked it but we hid among the rocks and shrubs anyway. So when it got to the snowfields below the cliffs, we were prepared for it to turn away and run for the lower ridge, as previous goats had done, dodging out of sight. Instead it turned our way, running then bucking and turning cartwheels in the snow, around and around, stopping and waiting now and then as if dizzy, then resuming, repeating the same clowning pattern, again and again. A crazy dizzy dancing goat. It came all the way around the snowfield rim at the bottom of the cliffs, paused a long time, then came straight toward the water, toward us, halting forty feet away to blink its black eyes in wonder before wheeling around and fleeing for the base of the cliffs again, following the same direction. Finding a dike in the cliffs, in a flash it zigzagged its way up to the sky, pausing there broadside on the horizon, just for a minute, before it lowered its head, turned and disappeared.

NOTES

Chapter 1

1. T.S. Eliot, "Little Gidding," *Collected Poems* (New York: Harcourt, Brace, and World, 1970), 208.

2. According to John Montagne, Department of Geology, Montana State University, Bozeman. He also maintains that this is one of several hypotheses about the formation of the Crazies. For example, Plate Tectonics, active in this region about the time of their formation, may well be responsible for the downward bending of what geologists call the Crazy Mountain Basin.

3. What surveys we do have record these other species and communities of special concern, listed with the Montana Natural Heritage Program: Idaho Fescue Association, Park Milk-Vetch, Colville's Rush, Cascade Willow, Fan-Leafed Daisy, Great Grey Owl, Yellowstone Cutthroat Trout, and Heart-Leaved Buttercups.

4. Stone tools were found from the Clovis period at the Anzick site a few miles from the peaks of the Crazies near Wilsall. See Thomas Y. Canby, "The Search For the First Americans," *National Geographic* 156 (September 1979): 341, 348–49.

5. According to Dean Bear Claw, Sore Belly fasted and received his vision in the Crazies. See Tom Yellowtail, Burton Pretty On Top, Eleanor Pretty On Top, John Pretty On Top, Dean Bear Claw and David Small, *Appeal of the Gallatin National Forest Plan.* Available from Gallatin National Forest Headquarters, Bozeman, MT.

6. Washington Irving, "The Adventures of Captain Bonneville," *The Works of Washington Irving,* Vol. II (New York: Co-operative Publication Society, n.d.), 161–2.

7. Burton Pretty On Top, *Appeal of the Gallatin National Forest Plan.* According to C. Adrian Heidenreich, Native American Studies, Montana State University—Billings, there is not general agreement on this matter, differences depending in part on the time period considered. Here and elsewhere my account is indebted to Heidenreich.

8. Ibid., B. Pretty On Top.

9. Ibid., Exhibit 1: Letter of C. Adrian Heidenreich.

10. Ibid., B. Pretty On Top.

11. Peter Nabokov, *Two Leggings: The Making of a Crow Warrior* (Lincoln: University of Nebraska Press, 1967), 58–9.

12. Dean Bear Claw, *Appeal of the Gallatin National Forest Plan*.

13. Frank E. Linderman, *Plenty-Coups: Chief of the Crows* (Lincoln: University of Nebraska Press, 1962), 57–76.

14. The Crows claim that changes to the wild character of the Crazies will "drive the spirits away." Today, the Crow traditionalists still find the Crazies to be a difficult challenge, but some have come away inspired and speak with eloquence of them. See Affidavits of Tom Yellowtail, Burton Pretty On Top, and Dean Bear Claw, *Appeal of the Gallatin National Forest Plan*.

15. According to Jim Garry, a western folklore specialist, this story is one of several versions. The crazy woman story, he maintains, originated in northeastern Wyoming.

16. Spike Van Cleve, *Forty Years Gatherin's* (Kansas City, MO: Lowell Press, 1978), xv.

17. Ibid., 83.

18. Ibid., xiii.

19. Ibid., 174–5.

20. Ibid., 252.

21. See Henry Bugbee, "Wilderness in America," *Journal of the American Academy of Religion* 42 (1974): 614–15.

22. When the Northern Pacific Railroad, a land-grant railroad, was built up the Yellowstone Valley in 1883, every other section of land was given to it for twenty-five miles on each side of the tracks to provide economic incentive for its construction. The Crow Reservation at that time extended along the southern side of the Yellowstone as it flowed past the Crazies, causing the government to double-up to fifty miles its land granting to the north side of the river where the Crazies are. Hence, the Crazies were "checkerboarded" with public and railroad holdings every other section. Today the Burlington Northern Railroad, the company the Northern Pacific became part of, no longer owns any of these sections. Many have been returned to public ownership. Some are owned by the Nature Conservancy. Many remain in private hands. A current wilderness bill (1994, sponsored by Rep. Pat Williams, D-Montana) would, if passed, protect the consolidated land with legal wilderness status and direct the Forest Service to study the feasibility of consolidating as public lands the other de facto wilderness lands of the Crazies with the view to wilderness designation. In other words, the Forest Service would be directed to the bargaining table with willing landowners. I believe this measure is a reasonable

step forward toward a solution of a knotty problem I will not be addressing in the coming pages.

23. The Rationalist philosopher, Rene Descartes, usually thought to be the initiator of modern philosophy and the modern period, is one of these visionaries of the coming age of the culture of technology. A contemporary of Galileo and a physicist himself, Descartes writes of his scientific studies: ". . . they have satisfied me that it is possible to reach knowledge that will be of much utility in this life; and instead of the speculative philosophy now taught in the schools we can find a practical one, by which, knowing the nature and behavior of fire, water, air, stars, the heavens, and all the other bodies which surround us, as well as we now understand the different skills of our workers, we can employ these entities for all the purposes for which they are suited, and so make ourselves masters and possessors of nature." *Discourse on Method,* trans. Laurence J. Lafleur (Indianapolis, 1956), 40.

24. Vandana Shiva, "Environmental Values in Traditional Societies" (address before the Mansfield Conference at the University of Montana, Missoula, 19 May 1992).

25. William Rees and Mathis Wackernagel, "Ecological Footprints and Appropriated Carrying Capacity: Measuring the Natural Capital Requirements of the Human Economy," in A-M Jannson, M. Hammer, C. Folke, R. Costanza, eds., *Investing in Natural Capital: The Ecological Economics Approach to Sustainability* (Washington, DC: Island Press, 1994), 363–390.

Chapter 2

1. Cited in *The 1994 Edward Abbey Wilderness Calender,* Ken Sanders, ed. (Richmond, CA: Golden Turtle Press, 1993).

2. Henry G. Bugbee, Jr., *The Inward Morning* (New York: Harper and Row, 1976), 137–38.

3. Dennis Havig and Bill Queen, *Summary of Analysis for Ibex Cottonwood Compartment Analysis Area,* USDA Forest Service, Gallatin National Forest, Livingston Ranger District, Livingston, MT (1984), 1. (Emphasis added.)

4. "Approximately forty percent of the suitable timber production lands have stands which are in high need of treatment due to the presence of or susceptibility to spruce budworm, mountain pine beetle, the age of the stands and/or the growth characteristics of the stand." Ibid., 2.

5. For a sensitive and careful account of such projects, see Robert H. Socolow, "Failures of Discourse," in Lawrence H. Tribe, C.S. Schelling and John Voss, eds., *When Values Conflict* (Cambridge: Ballinger, 1976), 1–34.

6. This is a ballpark figure based on the expected receipts from the timber

sale, the cost of the road system to and in a roadless area, sale preparation and so on. This data is available from the Gallatin National Forest Headquarters, Bozeman, MT. In general, because of the roadbuilding expenses, the most costly sales are those in de facto wilderness. Road-cost alone for the Ibex-Cottonwood Sale was estimated by the Forest Service in 1986 to be $444,000.

7. This figure is what the Forest Service annually loses on its timber program in Montana.

8. According to Mike Shaw, Forest Economist for the Gallatin National Forest in the 1980s, these figures are correct for the years prior to 1988. Since that time the Forest Service has publicly disclosed its own losses in annual reports called Timber Sale Program Inventory Reporting System (TSPIRS) reports. Wilderness Society figures, based on these reports, show the following losses for the Gallatin: 1.8 million in 1988, 1.8 million in 1989, 2.3 million in 1990, 3.2 million in 1991, 1.9 million in 1992, 1.9 million in 1993.

9. The Forest Service plans several more timber sales in this same area in the next one hundred years, eventually cutting over the entire area.

10. This is a dubious proposition at best, considering most of timber is small diameter lodgepole pine. The other justification for these sales has been "community stability," maintaining a timber supply to the local mills even if it means a loss for the Forest Service. For further discussion of these points, see chapter 3.

11. As evidenced by many letters from millworkers and loggers commenting on the Proposed Gallatin National Forest Plan. These letters are available at the Bozeman headquarters.

12. "Study Additions Needed: Crazy Mountain Timberlands Should Be Added to the Wilderness Bill," editorial, *Bozeman Daily Chronicle,* Bozeman, MT (May 13, 1988): 4.

13. According to a Brand-S brochure in 1987.

14. Erica Abeel, "Magnificent Obsession: A House in the Country," *New York Times Magazine* (April 19, 1987): 20.

15. Ibid., 24.

16. Ibid., 26.

17. Ibid., 23.

18. Ibid., 20.

19. Ibid., 26.

20. Ibid.

21. Ibid., 23.

22. Ibid., 30.

23. Ibid.

24. This was done in 1984. Regulations have changed. See note 33.

25. Even a finding of "significant impact" may not stop a sale. The Environmental Policy Act only requires disclosure of such impacts. To halt a sale, a significant impact would also have to violate other federal laws, e.g., the Endangered Species Act, or not meet objectives and standards established by the Gallatin Forest Plan.

26. Recreational opportunity is supposed to be evaluated from a number of different perspectives by the initial *Resource Area Analysis* [RAA]. It sets forth three conflicting objectives to meet for Cottonwood canyon:

> A)Provide a variety of dispersed recreation opportunities, and parking facilities as measured by number of acres in each recreation opportunity spectrum class,
>
> B) Maintain the area's undeveloped nature and associated dispersed recreation opportunities, and
>
> C) Maintain the integrity of the RARE II [roadless] study area in the southwest portion of the Crazy Mountains.
> (Dennis Havig and Bill Queen, *Summary of Analysis for Ibex Cottonwood Compartment Analysis Area,* 5.)

The RAA did not study an alternative which met the third (C) objective which would be to leave Cottonwood Canyon as de facto wilderness. Aside from stating that it does not meet this objective, the RAA does not indicate the significance of this failure, as we will do later. Rather, this objective and the timber management objectives are seen as incompatible and a choice had already been made. Similarly, the second objective, maintain the undeveloped nature of the area, is incompatible with timber development. Thus, the alternative selected meets only partly this second objective for recreation. Again, no attempt is made to disclose the significance of this choice for recreation. About four miles of trail will be replaced by high-impact logging roads. Eight square miles of wild land either will be clearcut now or planned to be clearcut at some time in the next one hundred year timber rotation cycle. The selected alternative action, logging, is said to meet only objective A, providing diversified recreation.

27. Ibid., last page (unnumbered).

28. According to Montana Fish and Wildlife elk biologist Terry N. Lonner on the basis of *Coordinating Elk and Timber Management: Final Report of the Cooperative Elk-Logging Study, 1970–1985,* Montana Department of Fish, Wildlife and Parks (1985).

29. Ibid.

30. Ibid.

31. Ibid.

32. William Queen and John Decker, *Decision Notice Environmental Assessment and Finding of No Significant Impact: Ibex Timber Sale,* Livingston Ranger District, Livingston, MT, 5.

33. Ibid., 4.

34. Something else is wrong with the relationship between the amount of old growth, wildlife habitat effectiveness, and the rotation cycle used which illegally, I think, had to stretch to 120 years from the standard normally used of one hundred years in order to make the figures come out right. See Havig, *Summary of Analysis for Ibex Cottonwood Compartment Analysis Area,* 12 and unnumbered Sec. V., Wildlife.

The Forest Service assures me that this timber sale is no longer under active consideration. The Ibex Sale was appealed. While awaiting a decision, it got delayed further because parts of Sale needed to be adjusted to conform to the recent Final Forest Plan. Finally, the Forest Service Chief, forced by a court decision, ordered that all timber sales in roadless areas require a more comprehensive Environmental Impact Statement; the earlier Environmental Assessment could not serve as a substitute. So the Sale was withdrawn, and, although I expect this to change anytime, there are no current plans for a Cottonwood-Ibex Timber Sale.

35. The management at Brand-S, for instance, often shows in terms of acreage what a disproportionate amount of Gallatin Forest is wilderness compared to what is managed for timber. What they neglect to tell their audience is that most of the Gallatin Forest is unsuitable for timber harvest, i.e., alpine regions. They then argue that the decision should be made 'rationally', using numbers, and not emotionally or politically.

36. Dan Heines in a talk before the Greater Yellowstone Coalition Annual Meeting in June of 1988.

37. David Perry, *Forest Ecosystems* (Baltimore: Johns Hopkins University Press, forthcoming).

38. Dr. David Perry, Forest Sciences, Oregon State University in a talk before the Greater Yellowstone Coalition Annual Meeting in June 1988. According to him, since WWII about eighty percent of the forest serving as habitat for neotropical migrants has been cut.

39. Robert Pirsig, *Zen and the Art of Motorcycle Maintenance* (New York: Bantam, 1974), 4.

40. What is likely to come to mind first are all the ways this procedure has been good for human existence. A vaccine insulates us from parts of the environment we would not want to come into contact with. But Pirsig and others are not really speaking about the ways technology can appropriately be used to deal with

genuinely harsh features of the human condition. They are concerned, here, about the ways technology has reduced and impoverished the experience of our more benign surroundings. So, too, the Crazy Mountains are not a burden on the back of humankind; they are not a plague which warrants our concern.

41. See chapter 10 for development of this point.

42. From air and water pollution to species extinction, no ecosystem on Earth now escapes interference to some degree from the human order.

43. Roderick Haig-Brown, *Fisherman's Summer* (New York: Morrow, 1959), 128.

44. Quoted from John Varley, head biologist for Yellowstone Park. "The Benefits of Wildfire," *Bozeman Daily Chronicle* (July 31, 1988): 21.

45. An argument often forwarded by the timber industry and the Forest Service.

46. Literally, things move us because we are moving beings, and we are moving beings because we are bodily beings. Wilderness to be worthy of the name requires the possibility of our bodily presence. What goes on in a drop of swamp water may be just as wild as it was ten thousand years ago, but we cannot apprehend it as wilderness. While deserts are certainly wild, Mars' surface is not. We are always and already Earthbound beings requiring Earth even in outer space. Up close, we can experience Mars' surface only from Earth, whether through cameras or Earth-enclosing spacesuits. We are not free to lie naked against its surface, literally. Like outer space in general, Mars scape, while certainly a curiosity to investigate, finally holds no wilderness appeal; it is unmoved unmoving. Through photographs it is experienced as absolutely sterile. It is a withering scape, devoid of all meaning. Nothing calls mind up and out, and, hence, here a mind might go flat. It is not sufficient for humans; one cannot find one's bearings on its surface without a return in mind to Earth and the fundamental projects there. Perhaps even the monotonous ice cap regions of Earth are not wilderness. As one explorer attests after a two-month dog sled trip across Greenland's icecap, "After a while it was kind of like a jail term."

47. To the contrary, increasing numbers of studies show that roads are detrimental to wildlife. For instance, see Henjum, M.G., J.R. Karr, D.L. Bottom, D.A. Perry, J.C. Bednarz, S.G. Wright, S.A. Beckwitt, and E. Beckwitt, 1994. "Interim Protection for Late Successional Forests, Fisheries, and Watersheds: National Forests East of the Cascade Crest, Oregon and Washington." The Wildlife Society, Bethesda, MD.

48. Subsequently, the inholding was sold. The new property owners were granted not just a special use permit as with the previous owners but a right of way and allowed to grade and double the road in width. Ordinarily, this development in a 'roadless area' of Forest Land would have required at least an Environmental Impact Statement in which alternatives would have been evaluated. However, the

Gallatin Forest granted a "categorical exclusion" from this review process. This exclusion was granted even though Congressman Pat Williams' wilderness bill protecting this area had passed the U.S. House a few months before and the Senate had failed to act on it before adjourning. After one year, the land, not serving the purposes the owners believed it would—they thought they could live there year around—has again been resold. Had the Gallatin Forest followed the normal procedures and undertaken an EIS, this new damage to the Crazies, I believe, would never have occurred.

On the issue of the "checkerboard" landownership see chapter 1, note 21.

49. Advertisement in the *Bozeman Daily Chronicle* (June 14, 1988): 12.

50. The amendment was introduced by former Democratic Senator John Melcher of Montana.

51. That the place had the still-standing shack and old home on it is important. When a home burns to the ground, a rearrangement of matter has taken place but not a simple rearrangement by any means. All that has made itself known and dear to one is gone. All that supports and remains steady and continuous, and reminds and calls forth the same is gone. The deep material things of the familiar historical world of a family went up in smoke. Even if hardened, one cannot feel unstirred by such rearrangement. For an interesting comparison between the presence of a dwelling and the presence of wild nature, see Erazim Kohák, *The Embers and the Stars: A Philosophical Inquiry Into the Moral Sense of Nature* (Chicago: University of Chicago Press, 1984), 189–90. For a discussion of the relationship between belongings and belonging to a place, see chapter 12, note 11.

Chapter 3

1. Aldo Leopold, "The Land Ethic," *A Sand County Almanac and Sketches Here and There* (New York: Oxford University Press, 1968), 224.

2. Berry is discussing his rich sense of health. Wendell Berry, *The Unsettling of America: Culture and Agriculture* (San Francisco: Sierra Club Books, 1978), 112.

3. Holmes Rolston, III, *Environmental Ethics* (Philadelphia: Temple University Press, 1988), xiii.

4. Leopold, vii.

5. My entire discussion of Leopold is indebted to J. Baird Callicott's "The Land Aesthetic" and "The Conceptual Foundation of the Land Ethic" in Callicott, ed., *A Companion to A Sand County Almanac* (Madison: University of Wisconsin Press, 1987).

6. Leopold, 96.

7. Ibid., 204.

8. Rolston, 232.

9. Ibid., 173.

10. Ibid., 230.

11. Ibid., 244.

12. To be fair, Rolston does discuss and classify human values found in nature. Developing an account of environmental altruism is much more important to his environmental ethic, however.

13. Mark Sagoff, "Fact and Value in Ecological Science," *Environmental Ethics* 7 (1985): 99–116.

14. Ibid., 106–107, 109–110.

15. Ibid., 102–103.

16. Ibid., 116.

17. Ibid., 105.

18. See Albert Borgmann, *Technology and the Character of Contemporary Life: A Philosophical Inquiry* (Chicago: University of Chicago Press, 1984), 17.

19. To be precise, ecology lacks the predictive power of the harder sciences such as chemistry and physics. Hence, it uses general rules rather than laws in the strict sense. See K.S. Shrader-Frechette and E.D. McCoy, *Method in Ecology: Strategies For Conservation* (Cambridge: Cambridge University Press, 1993).

20. John and Mildred Teal, *Life and Death of a Salt Marsh* (New York: Audubon/Ballantine, 1969).

21. Ibid., 7–52.

22. Ibid., 39.

23. Ibid., 93.

24. Ibid., 1–3.

25. This apriori approach is inimical to the way things must assemble the world, not vice versa. Acting from the guidance of principles of Self-realization, biocentrism and even ecology puts the cart before the horse. Principles, guidelines, tests (a list of "where are you questions?") of a sense of place are too contrived, too canned to be authentic. Part of acknowledging things in their own right is seeing in a listening way what they uniquely show and evoke. We need to learn to trust that we can bring to living speech, as Henry Bugbee has taught, the unforeseen importance of things found only in our living encounter with them. *Coming at* things, we are not as open to *being with* them as we can and need to be.

26. Leopold shows wild things and their relationship to his start in ecology in this light in, "Red Legs Kicking." See Leopold, *Sand County*, 120–22.

27. Ibid., 126.

28. Rolston, xii–xii.

29. Rolston tries to separate and keep separate nature and culture, interhuman ethics and environmental ethics. For instance: "Marriage, truth-telling, promise-keeping, justice, charity—these are not events at all in spontaneous nature. They are person to person events. By contrast, eating is omnipresent in spontaneous nature; humans eat because they are in nature, not because they are in culture. Eating animals is not an event between persons but a human-to-animal event, and the rules for it come from the ecosystem in which humans evolved and which they have no duty to remake" (p. 80). But, as we can see from the above, such a sharp division cannot really be maintained. Eating a meal is not only a natural event; it is a cultural event. The rules which govern the practice of the culture of the table do not come from the ecosystem. Meals can provide a third thing that keeps our *being with* others alive. The practice of preparing and sitting down to a meal involves fidelity, promise-keeping, charity, and the virtues of justice and truth-telling may find some of their primordial grounding there. Alternatively, the kind of eating that is only ruled by ecological reasons may, for instance, show vices, as with the suitors in *The Odyssey*.

30. Rolston, 85.

31. Ibid., 88.

32. Ibid., 85.

33. Ibid., 259ff.

34. Ibid. 286.

35. According to Ed Madej of Desktop GIS, Helena, MT 59401.

36. Rep. Carolyn Maloney (D-NY) is characterized by the Montana Congressional Delegation and Montana newspapers this way. She is the sponsor of a five state wilderness bill: HR 2638, the "Northern Rockies Ecosystem Protection Act of 1993," proposing 16.3 million acres of wilderness in Washington, Oregon, Idaho, Montana and Wyoming.

37. Even though this is the most significant gain for the environment, what I will later call correlational coexistence will not equal all our concerns for natural things and the natural world. Environmental altruism, in the way Rolston develops it, advances beyond the quality of human life issue. However, when the technological society callously disregards the poor in this country and those abroad, it can hardly be expected to honor the claims of environmental altruism which call for going out of our way for nature if not for genuine sacrifice. Living more simply, we may be more open to altruism.

38. For instance, George Wuerthner of Livingston argues this point.

39. This figure according to Mike Scott, Director of The Wilderness Society,

Regional Office, at Bozeman, Montana. Because only a fraction of the 6.9 million acre of de facto wilderness would ever be protected in their bill, the Montana Congressional Delegation since 1980 has demanded that environmental groups design their own wilderness proposal—including only those roadless areas of National Forest most suitable for legal Wilderness designation. This proposal, named "Alternative W," called for protection of roughly half the de facto wilderness. Recently, the groups have dropped this compromise proposal because many of them desired more land than it included ("why not all of it?"), because it became a political liability where too much comprising had already occurred, and because many more scientific studies are showing the importance of roadless areas for wildlife and unique plant communities—log trucks, for instance, spread foreign weeds.

40. I initiated this argument.

41. For instance, Bob Decker, in 1987, of the Montana Wildland Coalition in Helena, Montana.

42. I argue this.

43. *Greater Yellowstone Ecosystem Report,* printed for the use of the U.S. House of Representatives Committee on Interior and Insular Affairs by Congressional Research Service. 99th Cong., 2nd Sess., (1987), 69.

44. George Wuerthner, for instance.

45. Rundars Rudzitis and Harley E. Johansen, "How Important is Wilderness? Results from a U.S. Survey," *Environmental Management,* Vol. 2, No. 2 (1991): 227–233.

46. For instance, after a Congressional hearing on wilderness, the first sentence of a front page news story read: "The economics of wilderness dominated the debate Wednesday in Livingston during Senate hearings on the Montana wilderness issue." Robert Ekey, "Wilderness Issue Leads to Sharp Exchanges," *The Billings Gazette,* July 6, 1989, 1.

47. However, it should be noted that very few environmentalists argue entirely or even mostly from an economic point of view. Thanks to such people as a forward-looking economist of the state, Thomas Power, most will argue that the quality of life that wilderness makes for is an economic benefit the typically higher standards of living in other places cannot purchase. But mainstream environmentalists have not followed up this point by calling for full-scale economic reforms, making the economy as hospitable as possible to wilderness and the quality of the environment. See Thomas M. Power, *The Economic Pursuit of Quality* (Armond, NY: Sharpe, 1988).

48. Fortunately, for their sake, the intense heat from the intrusion that formed the Crazies seems to have driven any oil away from them out into the plains.

Chapter 4

1. Robert Frost, "The Oven Bird" in Louis Untermeyer, ed., *Robert Frost's Poems* (New York: Pocket Books, 1971), 196.

2. William Carlos Williams, "A Sort of Song," *Selected Poems* (New York: New Directions Books, 1968), 109.

3. Aldo Leopold, *A Sand County Almanac and Sketches Here and There* (New York: Oxford University Press, 1968), 225.

4. The following recent remarks and polls are reasons to be optimistic.

James R. Lyons, Assistant Secretary of Natural Resources in the Department of Agriculture, told the Northwest Wilderness and Parks Conference (Seattle, Oct. 8, 1994) of new plans the Administration has for the Forest Service concerning Roadless Areas (de facto wilderness). "Our intent is to proceed cautiously in these areas so as to preserve future options. For this reason, extractive activities like timber production and oil and gas leasing are being redirected to roaded areas." If this redirection is actually carried out, it may save places like Cottonwood Canyon.

According to a poll done under contact with the Forest Service in Montana and Idaho: 1) Depending on the location, 83–99% of the people "using" the Forest in these states are apt to be driving and enjoying the scenery, or watching wildlife and birds. Most people using the forest camp and fish. 2) A strong majority are opposed to more motorized recreation. 3) Between 61–86% of those polled think the Forest Service should be more concerned with fish and wildlife. 4) The most frequently mentioned problem was too much logging and clearcutting. In eleven out of thirteen Montana and Idaho National Forests (the Gallatin being one of the eleven), 59–78% of the people do not want more timber to be harvested. 5) Most people residing around twelve of these thirteen National Forests (such as the Gallatin at 65%) agree with the idea that the Forest should be managed more for wilderness values. E.B. Eiselein, *Northern Region Communications Planning Summary* (Kalispell, MT: A&A Research, 1993).

According to a poll by Lee Newspapers of Montana, 32% of Montanans favor Rep. Carolyn Maloney's (D-NY) five state wilderness bill for protection of 16.3 million acres. Three other wilderness bills protecting much, much less and sponsored by members of the Montana Congressional Delegation were each favored by only 14–16% of Montanans. "Five-State Wilds Bill Has Support," *The Billings Gazette* (June 1, 1994), 1A, 9A. See chapter 3 for more on these bills.

5. Important wildlife habitat surrounding the Greater Yellowstone Ecosystem is rapidly being subdivided for summer homes, for instance.

6. Henry David Thoreau, "Walden" in *The Portable Thoreau*, Carl Bode, ed. (New York: Penguin, 1975), 337.

7. Ibid., 415.

8. Ibid.

9. Ibid., 415 and 444.

10. Wendell Berry, *The Unsettling of America: Culture and Agriculture* (San Francisco: Sierra Club Books, 1978).

11. Martin Heidegger, "The Question Concerning Technology," *The Question Concerning Technology and Other Essays,* trans. William Lovitt (New York: Harper & Row, 1977), 3–35.

12. Rainer Marie Rilke, "Letter to Hulewicz: Appendix 4," *Duino Elegies,* trans. J. B. Leishman and Stephen Spender (New York: W.W. Norton, 1939), 129.

13. Heidegger, "The Question Concerning Technology," 16.

14. Heidegger, *Poetry, Language, Thought,* trans. Albert Hofstadter (New York: Harper & Row, 1971), 152.

15. Ibid.

16. Ibid., 177.

17. Albert Borgmann, *Technology and the Character of Contemporary Life* (Chicago: University of Chicago Press, 1984), 80.

18. In his lectures on religions of the Plains Indians at the University of Montana, Missoula. John C. Ewers documents eighty-seven uses that the Blackfoot Indians made of the bison. See his *The Horse in Blackfoot Culture* (Washington, D.C.: Government Printing Office, 1955).

19. Ibid.

20. Aristotle attempts to derive the function (in Aristotle's rich sense) of humans from what humans have the unique capacities for. See *Nicomachean Ethics,* Book I, Chapter 7.

21. T.S. Eliot, "Hamlet and his Problems" in Cyrus Hoy, ed., *Hamlet* (New York: Norton, 1963), 179. Critics, of course, were quick to point out that this idea as a view of all works of art is too limited. However, it is relevant for many works of art and the significance of the insight is especially relevant for understanding the way technology has changed the "objective correlative" to human existence.

22. Kenneth Goodpaster, "On Being Morally Considerable," *The Journal of Philosophy* LXXV (1978): 309.

23. See especially Peter Singer's remark, "If a being is not capable of suffering, or of experiencing enjoyment or happiness, there is nothing to be taken into account." Ibid., 316.

24. Ibid., 311–12.

25. Ibid., 310.

Chapter 5

1. *The Ethics of Authenticity* (Cambridge: Harvard University Press, 1991), 100–01.

2. Marx Weber's term.

3. See Taylor, "The Iron Cage," *The Ethics of Authencity*, 93–108.

4. Albert Borgmann, *Technology and the Character of Contemporary Life: A Philosophical Inquiry* (Chicago: University of Chicago Press, 1984), 41ff.

5. Ibid., 36.

6. David Ehrenfeld, *The Arrogance of Humanism* (New York: Oxford University Press, 1981).

7. Borgmann, *Technology*, 42.

8. Ibid., 196.

9. Ibid., 196–210.

10. Ibid., 42.

11. Witold Rybczynski, *Home: The Short History of an Idea* (New York: Penguin, 1986), 219–20.

12. Borgmann, *Technology*, 47.

13. Don Ihde, *Technics and Praxis* (Boston: D. Reidel, 1979), 21.

14. Borgmann, *Technology*, 53.

15. Ibid., 140–41.

16. Robert Kubey and Mihaly Csikszentmihalyi, *Television and the Quality of Life: How Viewing Shapes Everyday Experience* (Hillsdale, NJ: Lawrence Erlbaum Associates, 1990), ix.

17. Ibid., 173–74.

18. Ibid., 102–03.

19. Ibid., 108–17, 173.

20. Ibid., 189.

21. Ibid., 173–74.

22. Ibid. 79.

23. Ibid., 171–74.

24. Ibid. 208–09, 213.

25. Ibid., 183.

26. Ibid., 101, 119–27, 173.

27. Ibid., 83.

28. Ibid., 172.

29. Ibid., 108–17, 172.

30. Ibid., 127–29, 172–73.

31. Ibid., 133–35, 172–73.

32. Ibid., 101.

33. Ibid., 185–90.

34. Ibid., 181–216.

35. Ibid., 157–69, 172.

36. Ibid., 117.

37. Ibid., 168, 173, 184ff.

38. Ibid., 157–169, 172–73.

39. Ibid., 204.

40. Ibid., 190.

41. Ibid., 145.

42. Ibid., 147.

43. Ibid., 100–01 (emphasis mine), see also, 196.

44. Ibid., 207.

45. Ibid., 215–16.

46. Nancy Debevoise, "Hiking with Llamas in Montana," *New York Times* (April 20, 1986), Sec. 20, 10.

47. Ibid.

48. Ibid.

49. In his most recent work Borgmann sees virtual reality or hyperreality vs. focal realism as pivotal. Accordingly, he has modified the terms of his criticism, e.g., disposability and discontinuity vs. commanding presence and continuity. See his *Crossing the Postmodern Divide* (Chicago: University of Chicago Press, 1992).

50. Borgmann, *Technology,* 53.

51. Ibid., 223.

52. Ibid., 123.

53. Ibid., 52.

54. Ibid., 105.

55. Ibid.

56. Ibid., 107.

57. Aldo Leopold, "The Land Ethic," in *A Sand County Almanac and Sketches Here and There* (New York: Oxford University Press, 1968), 224.

58. Borgmann, *Technology,* 112.

59. Ibid., 127.

60. Ibid., 126.

61. Ibid., 127–29.

62. Ibid., 148. Yet, even if technology succeeds by its own standards, it exacts a price. "If that technological totalitarianism comes to pass, life will take on an essentially secure, trite, and predictable cast," 144.

Chapter 6

1. Vincent van Gogh, *Dear Theo,* Irving Stone, ed. (New York: Doubleday, 1957), 173.

2. Leslie Marmon Silko, *Ceremony* (New York: Penguin, 1986), 117.

3. *The Phaedrus* in *The Symposium and The Phaedrus: Plato's Erotic Dialogues,* trans. William S. Cobb (Albany: State University of New York Press, 1993), 103.

Chapter 7

1. James Welch, *Winter in the Blood* (New York: Perennial Library, 1981), 172.

2. For example, see Aldo Leopold's remarks about *The Odyssey* and *The Bible* in "The Land Ethic," *A Sand County Almanac and Sketches Here and There* (New York: Oxford University Press, 1968), 201–5.

3. William Aiken, "Ethical Issues in Agriculture," in Tom Regan, ed., *Earthbound* (New York: Random House, 1984), 255–6.

4. Viewing other people and things as mere instruments is considered a vice

in many cultures, as we will see with *The Odyssey*. Strictly speaking, viewing people and things in the extremely self-conscious and shallow way of devices is unique to our time. Close inspection usually reveals that even here, with traditional instrumental view of people and things, the means/ends split is not nearly as radical and self-conscious as it is in the technological age.

5. Wendell Berry, "Horses," *Collected Poems* (San Francisco: North Point Press, 1985), 225.

6. Ibid., 227.

7. Matt. 6: 26.

8. For my reading of *Job,* I am indebted to Henry Bugbee and John Lawry at the University of Montana. I am also indebted to Simon Weil, "The Love of God and Affliction," *Waiting for God* (New York: Capricorn Books, 1959), 117–136.

9. Job 42: 3.

10. Job 38: 25–6.

11. Job 38: 41.

12. Job 38: 37–8.

13. Job 39: 13–16.

14. Job 38: 41.

15. Welch, 172.

16. Job 42: 3.

17. Job 39: 26–27.

18. Marie Sandoz, *Old Jules* (New York: Hastings House, 1955), 19.

19. Ibid., 22.

20. Ibid., 43.

21. Ibid., 57.

22. Ibid., 61.

23. Ibid., 406.

24. Ibid., 388.

25. Ibid., 388.

26. Heraclitus, fragment #25 in Philip Wheelwright, ed., *The Presocratics* (Indianapolis: Bobbs-Merrill, 1981), 71.

27. Homer, *The Odyssey,* trans. Robert Fitzgerald (New York: Anchor, 1963), 1.

28. Aristotle, *Nicomachean Ethics,* Bk. III, Ch. 6–9.

29. Homer, 151.

30. Hence, Edward Abbey's intuition that wilderness needs no defense only defenders follows from a similar understanding of the thing. So, too, were the prescriptions derived in chapter 2. Retrieving things requires us to go beyond this unarticulated assumption of the significance of things, however. The defense that can be provided will not be one that can *push* people into its conclusion, rather its force will be that of *appeal* to others.

31. Homer, 161.

32. George Sturt, *The Wheelwright's Shop* (Cambridge: Cambridge University Press, 1976), 45.

33. Homer, 160.

34. Ibid., 157.

35. Sturt, 45.

36. Ibid., 202.

37. Joseph Epes Brown, "Inipi: The Rite of Purification," *The Sacred Pipe* (Middlesex, England: Penguin, 1971), 31–43.

38. Max Horkheimer and Theodor W. Adorno, *The Dialectics of Enlightenment,* trans. John Cummings (New York: Continuum, 1969), 58–59.

39. Homer, 85.

40. Aristotle, *Nicomachean Ethics,* Bk. III, Ch. 4.

41. Immanual Kant, *Critique of Judgement,* trans. J. H. Bernard (New York: Haphner, 1951), 105.

42. Homer, 497–503.

43. Ibid., 433.

44. Ibid., 409.

45. Ibid., 410 (emphasis mine).

46. I am aware of the difficulties surrounding the literal meanings of the words in the passages in the original Greek text. However, I trust that Fitzgerald's splendid poetic translation is truer to the spirit of the text. At least this translation is true to the things that bring me home.

47. Homer, 436.

48. Ibid.

49. Ibid., 437.

Chapter 8

1. Henry David Thoreau, "Walden" in *The Portable Thoreau*, ed. Carl Bode (New York: Penguin, 1975), 441.

2. Martin Heidegger, "The Question Concerning Technology," *The Question Concerning Technology and Other Essays*, trans. William Lovitt (New York: Harper & Row, 1977), 16.

3. Erazim Kohák has followed out this alternative in his *The Embers and the Stars* (Chicago: University of Chicago Press, 1984). He distinguishes between "artifacts," which are made and owned by humans, and "nature," which is God's. In contrast to the impersonal and alien universe brought about both by our nearly complete immersion in human artifacts, e.g., lighting systems that abolish the night and detach us from any nonhuman otherness, and by our scientific and other theories or "constructs," e.g., nature as matter in motion and ourselves as biomechanisms, Kohák develops a philosophy of personalism. Aware of and in touch with the nonhuman otherness of nature, we discover at bottom a deeper harmony and "person-al" intimacy with the world, that is, we discover not the absurdity of existence but the sense of life. Personalism finds affinity with the inward gatheredness of people, porcupines, trees, boulders and all things. Kohák, I believe, emphasizes more than I do the person side of correlational coexistence. Because of my concern for the transformation of things, whether natural or artifactual, into devices, my emphasis has been somewhat different. I claim that the very shape of devices brings about our disengagement in an unfamiliar or impersonal universe. Thus I have tried to use a language that maintains our focus on this problem. Rather than personalism, I speak of things bringing near a familiar world, making us intimate with that world.

4. Thoreau, "Walden," 422.

5. Of course Thoreau is speaking metaphorically here. If everyone went to Walden pond to bathe it would be destroyed. The same is true of wilderness in today's world. His more general point is that when we procure things with devices we miss the experience of the thing.

6. Thoreau, "Walden," 424.

7. Ibid., 339.

8. Heraclitus, Fragment #17 in Philip Wheelwright, ed., *The Presocratics* (Indianapolis: Bobbs-Merrill, 1960), 70.

9. Thoreau, "Walden," 349.

10. Ibid., 432.

11. Ibid.

12. Ibid., 539.

13. Ibid., 435.

14. Ibid., 426.

15. Ibid., 437.

16. Ibid., 539.

17. Albert Camus, "Return to Tipasa," *The Myth of Sisyphus* (New York: Vintage Books, 1955), 144.

18. Thoreau, "Walden," 493.

19. Ibid., 567.

20. Ibid., 435.

21. Ibid.

22. Ibid., 484.

23. Ibid., 341.

24. Ibid., 426.

25. Ibid., 364. For an especially vivid account of this, see his contemplation of Walden Pond on a September afternoon in "The Ponds," 435–437.

26. Ibid., 363.

27. Ibid., 297.

28. Ibid.

29. Ibid., 429.

30. Ibid., 433.

31. Ibid.

32. Ibid.

33. Ibid., 525–6.

34. Ibid., 428.

35. Ibid., 439.

36. Ibid., 428.

37. Ibid., 440.

38. Ibid., 441.

39. Ibid., 442.

Chapter 9

1. Rainer Maria Rilke, *Letters to a Young Poet*, trans. M. D. Herter Norton (New York: Norton, 1962), 68–9.

2. Herman Melville, *Moby Dick* (New York: Signet, 1963), 431.

3. Aldous Huxley, *Brave New World* (New York: Harper & Row, 1969).

4. See Martin Heidegger, "The Question Concerning Technology," *The Question Concerning Technology and Other Essays*, trans. William Lovitt (New York: Harper & Row, 1977), 26–28.

5. Heidegger, "The Thing," *Poetry, Language, Thought*, trans. Albert Hofstader (New York: Harper & Row, 1975), 165.

6. Immanuel Kant, *Critique of Judgment*, trans. J. H. Bernard (New York: Haphner, 1951), 101.

7. Ibid., 105.

8. Eugen Herrigel, *Zen and the Art of Archery* (New York: Random House, 1971).

9. William Faulkner, *Go Down Moses* (New York: Random House, 1973), 163.

10. Ibid., 166.

11. Ibid., 181.

12. Ibid., 187.

13. David Harms, "A Guide's Guide to Technology," *Alternatives* 14 (May/June 1987): 71.

14. Ecclesiastes, 9: 10.

15. Ecclesiastes, 11: 7.

16. Henry David Thoreau, "Walden" in *The Portable Thoreau*, Carl Bode, ed. (New York: Penguin, 1975), 344.

17. Thoreau, "Walking" in *The Portable Thoreau*, 616.

18. Thoreau, "Walden," 341.

19. Ibid., 338.

20. Ibid., 342.

21. Ibid., 338.

22. Ibid., 342.

23. Ibid., 343.

24. Ibid.

25. Ibid., 572.

26. Ibid., 350.

27. Ibid., 343.

28. This account, as it moves from concrete literalness to transcendental everywhereness, comes up against problems which make it unacceptable in its present, unqualified form. See chapter 10.

29. Thoreau, "Walden," 557.

30. Ibid., 457.

31. Thoreau, "Walking," 613.

32. Thoreau, "Walden," 515.

33. Ibid., 526–7.

34. Ibid., "Walking," 627.

Chapter 10

1. Mary Oliver, from "Wild Geese," *Dream Work* (New York: The Atlantic Monthly Press, 1986), 14.

2. Henry G. Bugbee, Jr., *The Inward Morning* (New York: Harper & Row, 1976), 128–29.

3. Gabriel Marcel, Introduction in Henry G. Bugbee, Jr., *The Inward Morning* (New York: Harper & Row, 1976), 24.

4. Bugbee, "Swamping," 42–3; "Building a Dam," 44–5; "Rowing," 45–51; fishing, 86–7; boating, 82–3; birds, 193–4; bells, 229–30; music, 112, 231; at sea, 176–193.

5. Ibid., 71–2.

6. Ibid., 106.

7. Ibid., 43.

8. Ibid., 94.

9. Ibid., 92.

10. Dante, *The Inferno*, trans. John Ciardi (New York: Mentor, 1954), 76.

11. *The Embers and the Stars: A Philosophical Inquiry Into the Moral Sense of Nature* (Chicago: University of Chicago Press, 1984).

12. Henry David Thoreau, "Walden," *The Portable Thoreau*, Carl Bode, ed. (New York: Penguin, 1975), 454–5.

13. Colin Fletcher, *The Complete Walker III* (New York: Knopf, 1984), 5.

14. John Dewey, "Having an Experience," *Art As Experience* (New York: Putnam, 1980), 35–57.

15. Bugbee, 40.

16. Ibid., 182–4.

17. D. T. Suzuki, Introduction for Eugen Herrigel's *Zen and the Art of Archery* (New York: Random House, 1971), viii.

18. This Promethean climbing is a traditional instance of the will to dominate; technological domination is uniquely different. To technological dominate a mountaintop would be to secure it with a device and make it technologically available, e.g., mountaintops secured with highways, trams, or helicopters.

19. Fletcher, 428.

20. Thoreau, 380.

Chapter 11

1. Gabriel Marcel, *Mystery of Being, Vol. I* (South Bend: Gateway Editions, 1950), 213.

2. Richard Rorty, "Philosophy in America Today," *Consequences of Pragmatism* (Minneapolis: University of Minnesota Press, 1982), 216.

3. Ibid., 221.

4. Ibid., 222.

5. Robert Nozick, *Philosophical Explanations* (Cambridge: Harvard University Press, 1982), 4.

6. Ibid., 6.

7. Ibid., 13.

8. Ibid., 21.

9. Henry David Thoreau, "Walking," *The Portable Thoreau*, Carl Bode, ed. (New York: Penguin, 1975), 621.

10. For clarity, I am oversimplifying the argument here. It is Borgmann's achievement to see devices as unique to our time and place; the means-ends split is not true of all technology (tool things, for instance) in all times and places. Hence his theory is not universal to that extent. Secondly, other paradigmatic theories of

technology are possible. Why should one choose Borgmann's rather than another? One is guided to select this theory over another only if, on a deeper level, one cares already about our engagement with things. So even the theory itself remains tethered to particular things. In this way it avoids foundationalism. See Albert Borgmann, *Technology and the Character of Contemporary Life: A Philosophical Inquiry,* (Chicago: University of Chicago Press, 1984), 73–77.

11. John Dewey, for instance, sees the means and ends separation occurring in the metaphysics of Plato and Aristotle. See his "Experience, Nature and Art," *Experience and Nature* (LaSalle, IL: Open Court, 1971), 287–318.

12. See Borgmann, 169–181.

13. This seems to have been early Heidegger's view of resoluteness in *Being and Time,* trans. John Macquarrie and Edward Robinson (New York: Harper & Row, 1962), 352 ff.

14. Heidegger seems to have learned this need for things in his later works. See, "The Thing," in *Poetry, Language, Thought,* trans. Albert Hofstadter (New York: Harper & Row, 1971), 181.

15. One can view what is happening with the exchange of things for devices, and the kind of detachment that leads to, as an increasing disembodiment of ourselves. The machinery of the device, if its accessible at all, is merely cerebrally accessible. Moreover, the slim aspects of what once were things do not require the body. Nature through the windshield is no longer nature warming the top of the head, nor nature against the face, in the ears and nose, nor nature taken in through the legs and lungs. I have emphasized and will continue to maintain that things gather and focus at the most primary level, so that, the absence of things is the troubling problem. However, the body, as a counterpoint to things, gathers and focuses the felt claims of things. As we saw with hikers, through embodiment and only through embodiment do we experience the felt presence of things in depth.

16. See Henry G. Bugbee, Jr. *The Inward Morning* (New York: Harper & Row, 1976).

17. See passage from Gabriel Marcel and Bugbee's commentary on it, *The Inward Morning,* 124–126.

18. Presence as opposed to a mere object. The distinction is worked out at length in Marcel's and Bugbee's works. See Gabriel Marcel, "On the Ontological Mystery," *The Philosophy of Existentialism* (Secaucus, NJ: Citadel Press, 1956), 9–46.

19. Robert Frost, "The Pasture" in Louis Untermeyer, ed., *Robert Frost's Poems* (New York: Pocket Books, 1971), 15.

20. For instance, in Book V: "What a welcome thing life seems to children whose father, in the extremity, recovers after some weakening and malignant ill-

ness: his pangs are gone, the gods have delivered him. So dear and welcome to Odysseus the sight of land, of woodland, on that morning."

Chapter 12

1. Martin Heidegger, *Poetry, Language, Thought,* trans. by Albert Hofstadter (New York: Harper & Row, 1971), 160.

2. Gary Snyder, "The Etiquette of Freedom," *The Practice of The Wild* (San Francisco: North Point Press, 1990), 23.

3. "The greatest gain and values are farthest from being appreciated. We easily come to doubt that they exist. We soon forget them. They are the highest reality." "Walden," *The Portable Thoreau,* Carl Bode, ed. (New York: Penguin, 1975), 463. He would have us sew our lives to these events so that we momently expect the dawn and listen always for the cock's crow. Recognizing the importance of these events, we are more likely to give ourselves over to them and to what is demanded of us by them.

4. Experiencing the tonic of things and having a well-articulated understanding of their importance, one can counter the tendency of technology to bring everything under control, within the technological framework. For instance, such experience gives one firm grounds to stand on in challenging and examining Vern's remarks in chapter 9 about high-tech equipment making "a hell of a lot better fishing." Having derived one's standards from the wilderness of things, one finds it would not be better to make fishing more technologically available, for this makes fishing all too tame. It is no longer wild or crazy enough. Experiencing the wild allows us to see the seemingly terrible in an altogether favorable light.

5. Colin Fletcher, *The Complete Walker III* (New York: Knopf, 1984), 8.

6. Finally, countering and challenging technology can be accomplished through a more direct appeal to things. While the writer of *Ecclesiastes* points out mostly what is not the human portion, Thoreau and I try to appeal to others to turn from the vision of the framework by our positive encounters with Walden pond and the Crazy Mountains. Releasing the full unmuted appeal of things is a fundamental task for reforming technology.

7. Jesse S. Tatum, "Technology and Values: Getting Beyond the Device Paradigm Impasse," *Science, Technology, & Human Values* 19 (1994), 70–87.

8. We can speak of this choice and vision in another way. To turn homeward, we need to *place* ourselves in the *world* again. Now we are *situated* in the technological *universe.* This universe is composed of entities having familiar surfaces and unfamiliar backgrounds, the resources from which they are developed, and a general orientation toward disburdened novelty. Because these entities are quickly consumed, there cannot be a focal commodity to which we would be committed for

long, but rather we have a general understanding of the pattern of life and its requirements; we wax poetic about the commodities in our advertisements and become tough-minded about managing our resources. The most striking feature of this techno-universe, which sets it apart from a world, is the separation of means and ends. Unlike the continuous familiarity of a world, this division creates the injurious discontinuities of technological life. Placing ourselves in the world again is carried out against a history of having already been in place and having stepped out of place. We take this step when we fish not with simple, thingly tools, traditional fishing rods, but with machinery-commodity devices, stripping the practice of fishing of its worldly continuity and insulating us from any exposure to the wilderness of things. The things are what they are because they are conjoined to a continuously familiar world. This is why they cannot be taken in any other way and still be encountered. When we mix ourselves with things, they come to own us by bestowing on us their blessings almost unnoticeably, like light snow fall. Occasionally, we trigger them, and, like avalanches, they gather the world and sweep it clean, carrying us out of our minds.

9. See Plato, *Symposium*, Diotima's speech, 210e–212a. Aristotle *Nichomachean Ethics*, Bk. 1, Chapter 7. Homer, *The Odyssey*, Book 23.

10. Ironically, then, leaving the wilderness unbuilt will enable it to house our lives.

11. Tilling our experience of things over and over, we become more deeply reflective, not just critical thinkers. For instance, things teach us the difference between possessing and belonging, for things too, not just commodities, fall prey to the illusion that possession can bring fulfillment. As Erazim Kohák writes,

> Whatever I come to possess, to dominate, be it a tool, an animal, or a fellow human being, can no longer be a companion. It becomes alien . . . The possessed world becomes a dead world in our hands, lifeless and meaningless.
>
> —Erazim Kohák, *The Embers and the Stars: A Philosophical Inquiry Into the Moral Sense of Nature* (Chicago: University of Chicago Press, 1984), 104.

Our first reaction to this kind of disillusionment with things is apt to be to turn away from things altogether, but, since human beings have a body, our relationship between being and having cannot be so simple. From a wiser standpoint, having a body and belongings actually enable us to belong, belong here. "What I would claim to possess can never belong to me—and whatever belongs to me I can never treat as a possession. It was the land that taught me the difference." Ibid., 106. From walking, sitting, working, singing, listening, pondering, and from building his house, Kohák learns, "I came to belong to the land—and the land came to belong to me in turn." Ibid. To take possession of the land would be to violate this mutual belonging, degrading and depersonalizing the land. Instead of rejecting things, we need to cultivate carefully our relationship with them, repersonalizing the world. *"Things need to be loved,* used, and cared for." Ibid., 108. Things need this for their fulfillment, too. *The Embers and the Stars* evokes a sense of how "humans can raise the world of nature to eternity." Ibid. However, without this personal involvement with them, even a world of things remains impersonal. And so, "it is precisely in investing life, love, and labor that we constitute the world as personal, as a place of intimate dwelling." Ibid., 213.

12. From Rainer Marie Rilke, "Sonnet 24, Part I" *Sonnets to Orpheus,* trans. by H.D. Herter Norton (New York: W.W. Norton, 1970), 63.

13. Gabriel Marcel, *Man Against Mass Society* (Lanham, MD: Gateway, 1962), 249.

14. Rilke, *Letters to a Young Poet,* trans. by H.D. Herter Norton (New York: W.W. Norton, 1962), 19.

INDEX

245

ADD-2716   3/4/96

T
14.5
S8
1995